# MANAGING RESTAURANT AND BAR BUSINESS

**Dr. B.K. CHAKRAVARTI**
*Department of Catering Technology*
*Birla Institute of Technoloy*
(Deemed University)
*Mesra, Ranchi*

***Director***
*Hotel International Tower, Kolkata*

(*Formerly Director, Bihar State Tourism Development Corp. and Principal, IHM, Patna*)

**AMAN PUBLICATIONS**
NEW DELHI

*Published by*
Rajiv Jain for Aman Publications
LG-4A, Ganpati Bhawan,
4675-B/21, Ansari Road,
Darya Ganj, Delhi - 110002
PH: 23255012, 23282127
E-mail: sshjbs@yahoo.com



1st edition 2008

ISBN-978-81-8204-044-1


SOLE DISTRIBUTOR
**JINDAL BOOK SERVICES**
LG-4A, Ganpati Bhawan,
4675-B/21, Ansari Road,
Darya Ganj, Delhi - 110002

*Laser Typesetting by:*
M.S. Graphics
New Delhi

*Printed by:*
Indus Press, Delhi, India

# PREFACE

Restaurant and Bar Operation are ever growing activities and are part of civilisation and the society.

In modern days, with the growth of tourism and economic development and with the change of life style – the growth of restaurant and bar business took place beyond any estimate in India as well as throughout the world. Because of travelling population, there had been tremendous interaction among customers who visit restaurants and bars for food, beverages and entertainment.

Global menus, cocktails, food festivals, guest entertainment etc. have now became a part of daily life. Growing kids are getting accustomed to the ambience, menus and indoor decor and environment of these places.

The restaurant and bar business attracted many celebrities to open signature restaurants namely Saurav's at Kolkata, Tendulkar's at Mumbai to name a few.

Big multinational chains also started their business in India such as KFC, Mcdonald, Wimpy, Dixy Brostar, Pizza Hut etc. In America, Australia, Canada, Japan, everywhere one finds Indians engaged in restaurant and bar business in big way and having enviable goodwill. But, sadly, they have not yet explored the Indian market fully to its potential.

No doubt, there are some books on the subject selected. While writing this particular volume, I have selected the contents of the volume for business entrepreneurs and for teachers and students of professional and vocational institutes imparting education in the field.

It is hoped, that the readers and users of the book will be benefited in their objectives.

**Dr. B.K. Chakravarti**

# ACKNOWLEDGEMENTS

I tender my thanks and gratitude to my numerous students and colleagues all over India and abroad who constantly extend encouragement for my works.

I particularly thank Prof. S.K. Mukherjee, VC, BIT Mesra, Ranchi for his constant support and academic encouragement. My thanks to Shri Suborno Bose, MD, Hotel International Tower, Kolkata.

I thank Shri Rajiv Jain of M/s. Aman Publications, Ansari Road, New Delhi, India for publishing the present volume with interest and expertise and thanks to Shri Kashi Nath Dutta, for typing work for the manuscript.

**Dr. B.K. Chakravarti**

# CONTENTS

## CHAPTER 1

# INTRODUCTION: HISTORY AND DEVELOPMENT OF RESTAURANT

The word restaurant comes from French word "*restaurer*" which means "to repair". It is said, the earliest inscription over its doorway is, "*venite ad me qui, stomacho laboratis et ego restaurabo vos*" come to me all whose stomachs, cry out in anguish and I shall restore you. In fact, Restaurant is a non-residential catering establishment, which supply food for consumption in the premises. The main characteristic of restaurants is that they supply food to the general public and they do not provide sleeping accommodation. According to their mode of operation they may be divided into service and self-service establishments. In the former, food is served at tables, in the later category, the customer collects his own food and sitting accommodation is either provided at tables or the food is consumed at the counter. In any case, the nature of service, type of food, the price and décor etc., depend upon the size and type of the establishments. Though this type of catering has enormously increased in different countries but at the same time large typical restaurants have become rare mainly because of economic reasons. The principal pattern of food services in restaurants range from at the most formal a la carte or tablé d'hóte service. By the "a-la-carte" service, it is understood that the customer would choose his food from a set of items. On the contrary the "tablé d'hote" service indicates fixed items for a fixed price. In most of the Indian restaurants the a-la-carte service is common. Apart from snacks these types of catering can provide light meals and even lunch and dinner. In some places, drinks and entertainments are also provided along with the usual catering services.

A restaurant is a commercial establishment committed to the sale of food and beverage. A restaurant may be a licensed part of a hotel operation, whereby the sales of the restaurant contribute to the sales performance of the hotel as a whole. Restaurant may also be independent business entities under individual ownership and management. Basically restaurants provide tables and chairs for people to sit and eat food prepared by an attached kitchen. They are equipped with crockery, cutlery and linen which may vary in quality according to the standard of the restaurant which is determined by its décor, independent bar, entertainment facilities and above all the quality of service.

## RESTAURANT: A HISTORICAL REVIEW

During the period of Roman Empire the eating delight reached its speak, because Rome as a victorious nation, received supplies of food and wine from subjects of all parts of the known world. Romans used to eat large quantities of meat, eggs, poultry, shell-fish etc. From the Roman times till early $18^{th}$ century many changes were noted mainly in European eating habit which is the sources of modern catering.

The ordinary restaurant as is known today, is described from Tavern. Eating houses with separate table for dinners were opened first in France in 1780 and the idea soon spread to England. During the early years of $19^{th}$ century after the decline of coach inns, the restaurants were most popular kind of eating houses. By 1820 many good and elegant restaurants were established in London but such restaurants were not available in smaller town and cities. The public club for entertainments and food etc., were established in large number by 1875. After the revaluation and the arrival of number of French, Australian and Italian immigrants, the restaurant business spread to a great extent particularly in the Soho district of London. It was only in 1870 the taking of women in the restaurant to dine become acceptable in the society. Meals in the train were first introduced in England in 1879. The first school meals were introduced in and around 1906 and it was not in present style but often operated from outside the schools. In the Second World War, the Government started industrial canteen system.

Up to the first half of the 20th century food and beverage services were considered as minor importance by many hotel operators. But the whole concept was changed by 1950. Food and beverage services were reviewed with new look.

The beginning of modern restaurants as we know now, cannot be traced back to ancient civilization in India because offering of food and drinks were considered as natural hospitality to the people. The gradual change from that to the present are due to many factors and socio-cultural evaluation for centuries. However, from ancient literature it is evident that considerable attention was paid for drinking and eating and choosing food in those time. It is also evident from the ancient literatures that our ancestors knew the use of so-called sophisticated foods such as rice, meat of various animals, games, sweetening agents, spices, honey, milk, animal fat etc.

From the archeological evidence located at Harappa and Mohen-jodero, we find the existence of organized food storage facilities, kitchens used by earlier Indians. Utensils made of metals, stone that were obtained, indicate better living style and advanced culinary abilities.

Historical evidence state that the travellers of earlier days usually had to take long walk but the rest and food were obtained free of cost in temples. The temples at Puri used to feed more than ten thousand people per day and were known to have the big kitchen of the world. During the Islamic period, India was exposed to the culture of the outer world which enriched culinary arts of Indians without much change in the eating habits. Later on because of colonial rules by French, Portuguese and English, the western influence took root in Indian dieting, particularly in urban areas. The terms, Babarchi, Khansama etc., are incorporated in our language have been contributed by the external culture. The main three streams of culinary art i.e., French, Persian, and Mogal with many modifications found appreciation in India since a long time. The regional talents, skills and methods were also exported in other parts of the world.

The concept of our modern restaurant was established by the British rulers during the 17th century in their colonial towns and in fact the first hotel in Asia was established in Culcutta under their patronage. Gradually, western types of hotels were established in other metropolitan cities such as Bombay and Madra. In 1840 British hotel was established in Mumbai and in 1871 the Esplanade Hotel was established.

After independence, the British style of operation has been retained though there were growth of other establishments dealing with food and beverage for growing number of population in our cities in particular. But catering outlets are still largely distributed in cities and big towns leaving many other areas particularly void of any reasonable sanitary food service arrangements in India.

With the realization of the economic importance of tourism industry, catering has actually taken a firm footing in our present-day society and attention are being paid to give it a real organized shape, without much conflict with our age old eating, drinking and living characteristic.

It is also evident that wherever man lives some form of catering exists. Depending upon the society, cultural and economic viability and objectives of the operators the nature, place and type of catering varies. Lastly, the catering involves the health and comfort of the consumers of the industry and profits of the operators and such objectives can be achieved only by sound management principles.

## CONCLUSION

Restaurant in some form or another have a very long history and there is no doubt that they will continue to serve food and drink for many years. Despite the growth of fast food outlets and take away restaurants, people enjoy dining out and restaurant satisfies this demand whether they are unique or part of large chains.

This sector, perhaps more than any other, offers the opportunity to individuals to fulfil his ambition. A restaurant requires less investment than a hotel, it is smaller in scale than many other type of operations and has greater status attached to it, then public houses or outside catering. In many respects it fulfils the criteria of business suitable for many budding entrepreneurs. However, at the same time it must be recognized that a restaurant is a risky business venture.

Although there are examples of successful restaurateurs, there are equally many unsuccessful restaurateurs. The main reason for this is that apart from being proficient and expert catrers/restaruers must also understand the market in which they operate. The restaruers sells non-essential product and luxury item and must compete with other products for the customers' hard earned disposable income.

## TYPES OF RESTAURANTS

As we know a restaurant is a commercial establishment committed to sale of food and beverage. Basically, restaurants provide tables and chairs for people to sit and eat food prepared by an attached kitchen. They are equipped with crockery, cutlery and linen which may vary in quality according to the standard of restaurant which is determined by its décor, independent bar, entertainment facilities and above all the quality and type of service.

There are different types of restaurants which are as follows:

### 1. Coffee Shop

The concept of coffee shop is borrowed form the United States. Coffee shops may be found in many of the large hotels. They provide the opportunity for the guest to be provided with a quick meal, snack or beverage at reasonable prices in pleasant surroundings and in a minimum amount of time. The menu here is generally a form of a la carte menu with all food items individually priced. The coffee shop is open almost 24 hours of the day, providing a plate service usually by team of waitresses who work on a shift basis. Many coffee shops are decorated to follow particular theme and this assists in promoting atmosphere.

**1. Organisation Chart of a Coffee Shop of Elite and Classic Category**

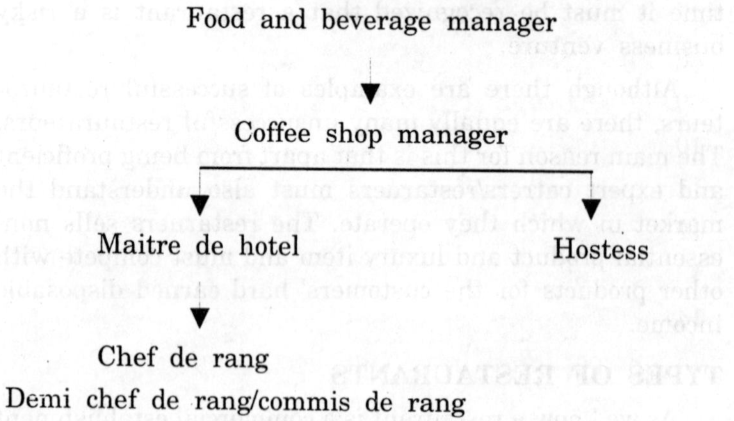

**2. Organisation chart of a coffee shop of comfort category**

Manager (Hotel operations/F & B Manager

▼

Maitre Dé Hotel/Chef Dé rang

▼

Commis dé rang

**Some important tasks in the coffee shop**

1. Opening windows
2. Cleaning of furniture, fixtures, tables and chairs
3. Arranging tables and chairs (including dusting and checking)
4. Changing linen
5. Cleaning all ashtrays
6. Polishing cutlery
7. Filling of cruets sets
8. Collecting stores
9. Adjustment of tables and covers after briefing
10. Taking inventory-cutlery and crockery
11. Cleaning and refilling sauce bottles
12. Preparing side boards
13. Laying of covers
14. Filling of water jugs
15. Preparing of fresh mustard, pickles and chutney
16. Preparing butter dishes
17. Checking of mis-en-place
18. Maintenance reports

## GENERAL SERVICE STANDARDS

| Sl. No. | Items | Served in | Presentation | Cover | Accompaniment |
|---|---|---|---|---|---|
| 1. | Juice | Juice glass (50z) | — | — | — |
| 2. | Tomato juice | -do- | on a quarter plate with doiley paper and a lemon wedge | Tea spoon | Worster shire sauce and cruet set |
| 3. | Fresh fruits | Half plate | — | All purpose | Finger bowl with cold water on a quarter plate and doiley paper. |
| 4. | Cereal | Soup cups | On a soup saucer | A.P. Spoon | Castor sugar in a sugar bowl with a tea spoon |
| 5. | Eggs (boiled) | Egg cups | On a quarter plate | Tea spoon | Cruet set |
| 6. | Eggs to order other than boiled. | Hot half plate | - | A.P. Knife and fork | Cruet set acompani-fying saucer. |
| 7. | Mini meals | Full plate | - | A.P. Knife and fork | Cruet set |
| 8. | Rolls & Roast | Bread basket | Toasts wrapped in a paper nakin | - | Butter & preserves. Butter in a butter dish on a quarter plate with a side knife. |
| 9. | Beverage Hot: Tea/coffee | Respective cups | On a salver with milk pot, Pot holder, strainer for tea | Tea/cup/sauce with a tea spoon and sugar pot | Hot water in coffee (with not holder) |
| | Cold coffee | | - | | |
| | Milk shake | High ball cups (100 z) | On a quarter plate | - | Sugar syrup in a milk pot when asked for. |
| | Lessi and fresh lime | High ball glass (100 z) | with doiley straws | | |

| | | | | | |
|---|---|---|---|---|---|
| | Juice cold coffee with ice cream | | On a quarter plate with a doiley straws in a straw doiley straws in a straw holder and parfait spoon | | |
| 10. | Hors'd Oeuvre | Cold half plate | - | A.P. Knife & Fork | Cruet set. |
| 11. | Prawn/shrim/ florida lobster/ fruit cocktail | Ice cream cup | On a quarter plate with a doiley | Tea spoon | - |
| 12. | Soup | Soup cup on a soup saucer | - | A.P. Spoon | Bread and butter propieratory sauces. |
| 13. | Fish | Hot full plate | - | A.P. Knife & fork | Tomato sauce/tartare sauce in a sauce bowls on a quarter plate with a doiley paper and tea spoon. |
| 14. | Pasta | Hot full plate | - | A.P. Knife and fork | Sauce bowl doiley paper. |
| 15. | Sandwiches | Cold half plate | - | A.P. Knife/fork | Appropriate sauces (Tomato chilli, mustard) |
| 16. | Salads | Cold half plate | - | A.P. Knife/fork | salad dressing in sauce bowl on quarter plate and doiley paper. |
| 17. | Cold cuts | Cold half plate | - | A.P. Knife/fork | Mustered |
| 18. | Masala dosa/idli | Full plate hot | - | A.P. Knife/fork | Finger bowl in a quarter plate Sambhar in a soup cups on soup saucers with A.P. spoons chutney in a bowl. |

| Sl. No. | Items | Served in | Presentation | Cover | Accompaniment |
|---|---|---|---|---|---|
| 19. | General Indian snacks | Hot half plate | - | A.P. Knife/fork | Chutney in jam pots on a quarter plate and tea spoon |
| 20. | Cream/fruit salad | Ice cream cup | Quarter plate and doiley paper and tea spoon | - | - |
| 21. | Common desserts | Cold half plate | - | A.P. Spoon & fork | - |
| 22. | Pastry | Half plate | - | A.P. fork/ Pastry fork | - |
| 23. | Gateaux | Half plate | - | A.P. fork/knife | - |

19. Cleaning all dirties from sideboard
20. Removing dirty linen
21. Receiving guest
22. Seating the guest
23. Service of water
24. Taking order for food and beverage
25. Presenting the menu
26. Placing order in kitchen
27. Cover adjustment
28. Pick-up of food and beverage
29. Service of soup
30. Main course
31. Service of desert
32. Placing tea/coffee/tea
33. Service of coffee/tea
34. Presentation of bill
35. Collecting cash/returning change

**2. Continental restaurant**

In this type of restaurant, the atmosphere is more sophisticated. The accent is on good continental food and elaborate service. The restaurants offer a la carte and table d hote menu. They use the triplicate checking system and have a full brigade of waiters/waitresses.

**3. Speciality restaurant**

Speciality restaurants are particularly tend to be owned and operated either by individuals, families or as partnership. In this type of restaurant the entire atmosphere and décor geared to a particular type of food or theme. In other words the restaurant which offers Chinese, Japanese, Indian and polynesian cuisine, would be termed as speciality restaurant. The service is based more or less on the style of the country from which the particular originates.

The growth of speciality restaurant is influenced by the following factors:

(a) *Individualism*: Restaurers are strongly motivated by the desire to work for themselves, running one's own restaurant satisfies needs for freedom of action, personal rewards for hard work and contact with customers.

(b) *Ethnic origins*: For many reasons people from different countries have go to alive in other country. Many of them have a catering background and so they are willing to set up their own catering establishment.

(c) *Eating habits*: Ethnic restaurants are encouraged by the changing eating habits of the people.

(d) *Industrial training*: During the Second World War, firms took it upon themselves to begin catering for their employees. Many [people, who had only rarely eaten out, begin to do so regularly at work. With the gradual rise in living standards, more and more people were willing to spend money on this.

**4. Grill room (Rotisserie)**

Various meat cuts are grilled or roasted here. Normally, a grill room has a glass partition between the restaurant and the kitchen so that the guest can choose his meat cut and see the actual preparation.

**5. Dining room**

Dining room is found in smaller hotels, motels or inns who find it uneconomical to have more then one eating place. The dining room is basically meant for the residents of the hotel but may be open to non-residents also.

**6. Snack bar, café, milk bar**

This type of restaurant is informal in nature and the service is quick. The snack bar may have a counter for self service and specializes in snacks, soda fountain specialties, ice-creams etc. the décor is relatively inexpensive.

**7. Discotheque**

A restaurant which is principally meant for dancing to recorded music. A live band may also perform. An essential part of a discotheque is a bar while the food offered consists mainly of snacks.

**8. Night Club**

Night club is principally open at night for dinner, dance and cabaret. A dispensing bar is always provided. Décor is lavish while service is elaborated. A live band is important to the set up.

## REQUIREMENTS OF LICENCE AND OTHER LEGAL PAPERS FOR SETTING UP A RESTAURANT

Like any other business or industry, restaurants are within the licensing act. Restaurant licence can be granted by the liquor licensing magistrates for premises which are structurally built or adapted and intended to be used for the habitual provisions of the main mid-day and/or the main evening meal.

The licence will authorise the sale or supply of intoxicants in the premises to the people who take table meals there, but such liquor must be as an ancillary to the meal. In other words, customers must not came this establishment merely to drink, they must take a meal.

For this purpose, the meal must be a table meal. This means it must be eaten by a person seated at a table or a counter or at some other structures which serves the purpose of table. Such counters must not be used for the service of food to people who are not seated for table meals. Another aspect is that drinks other than intoxicants must be available to the dinners, if they required them.

## TYPES OF LICENCE

There are two main type of licences:

**1. On-licence**

This authoris s the sale of intoxicating liquor for consumption either on or off the premises. It prescribed the sale of liquor of all descriptions or may restrict sale to wine, cider and beer only.

**2. Off-licence**

This authorizes sale for consumption off the premisses only.

The magistrate can revoke or refuse to grant licenses for the following reasons:

(a) If the licensee or the applicant is not considered a proper person, or

(b) If they feel that the premises are not used or intended to be used for the purpose stipulated in the licence, or

(c) If the premises are unsuitable due to the risk of fire, or

(d) If the customary main meals are not being served, or

(e) If the premises are being used mainly by unaccompanied persons who are under eighteen years of age.

## LICENSED RESTAURANT

Such establishments are allowed an extra half an hour, at the end of the normal permitted hours, for the consumption of alcoholic liquor with a meal. This liquor must, however, be ordered before the end of the normal permitted hours. No ordering of liquor, but only the consumption of liquor, may take place during the extra half an hour. For example if the end of the normal permitted hours is 3 pm then consumption may be until 3-30 pm. At 3.30 pm it would be the wine waiters responsibility to ensure that all the glasses and bottles are removed from the table.

## THE RESIDENT

A resident in licensed premises is allowed to consume alcoholic liquor at any time. The resident guests may also consume drink outside of the normal permitted house provided the resident orders and pays or signs the bill and guest does not.

## PERMITTED HOURS

This is the time during which alcoholic liquor may be served and consumed in the premises. These are occasions in certain areas where the licensing authorities may grant earlier opening hours or an extension of the normal permitted hours e.g., 'Market day, New years' eve, Air show etc.

There are a number of variations which may apply to the basic permitted hours. This would depend whether the establishment had been granted one of the following types of licence/certificate.

### 1. Special order of exemption

This is an extension of the normal permitted hour of on licensed premises for any special occasion. Normally, special occasions, do not continue for more than a few days. The duration of the extension is determined by the licensing authority and can be determined by reference to the order itself.

### 2. Occasional licence

This allows a licence already holding an on-licence to sell similar liquor in premises other than his own. This licence would be granted for social functions held on unlicensed premises and allow the sale of alcoholic liquor in such premises e.g., dance engagement parties, birthday parties etc. Any occasional licence cannot be granted for a period in excess of three weeks. The actual hours during which the sale be fixed by the local magistrate upon granting the licence and will be stated on the face of licence. The magistrate has complete discretion as to whether or not to grant an occasional licence, and may refuse for any reason. When granted the occasional licence, is free from any restrictions which may have been imposed on the licensee's full on licence.

**3. General order of exemption**

This allows a licence to be exempted from the normal permitted hours during a certain day or for a certain time. Such a notice must be displayed outside the premises for all to see. The effect of a general order of exemption is to extend the licensing hours to whatever time the licensing authority sees fit, either on one particular day or several days, or generally throughout the week. Therefore, the general order of exemption is for the benefit of people who for example might attend a local market at times during which licensed premises would normally be closed, or for those following a particular trade. The hours of general order of exemption may vary from one establishment to another and can only be ascertained by reference to the order itself.

**4. Super hour certificate**

This is a grant by the licensing authorities. When they are satisfied that the premises are suitable then an additional hour is permitted for the sale and consumption of alcoholic liquor with a table meal. This certificate allows any other bars and dispensing bars to remain open for the additional hour often the end of the permitted hours. A supper hour certificate may be withdrawn if the premises at any time cease to qualify within the laid down conditions, but otherwise, if continues in force without need for renewal.

**5. Special hour certificate**

This certificate is applicable only to that part of premises which fulfils the following conditions:

1. The establishment itself is a licensee.
2. A music and dancing license has been obtained.

3. All or any part of the premises structurally adapted and intended be used for the purpose of providing live music and dancing and substantial refreshment, to both of which the sale of liquor is ancillary.

Therefore, special hours certificate will not be granted for any isolated special occasion or for any area in which a music and dancing licence is not required.

A special hours certificate may be removed at any time if it appears that:

(a) the premises no longer possess music and dancing licence.

(b) the certificate has not been used.

(c) the certificate is being used for the wrong purpose.

(d) the premises have been conducted in a disorderly or unlawful manner.

**6. Extended hour certificate**

This extension is for the benefit of premises which qualify for a supper hour certificate and which also provide regular musical or other entertainment, together with the table meal. Here the sale of liquor is ancillary to both the table meal and the entertainment. The refreshment and entertainment must be provided in a part of the premises normally set aside for the purpose.

The licensing authorities have complete discretion as to whether or not they grant this certificate and it may be revoked at any time if it appears that the premises no longer qualify or that the use of such a certificate has led to noisy and disorderly conduct.

**Application for such licence or certificate**

Application for the extension to the normal permitted hours to obtain one or other of the above-mentioned licence or certificate would normally be made either by the local magistrate, the local licensing authorities or by the appropriate authority.

Depending on the exact nature of the licence or certificate required, there are certain conditions to be fulfilled and procedure to follow. These procedures must be strictly adhered otherwise the application will fall.

## LEGAL ASPECTS FOR SETTING UP A RESTAURANT

Within restaurant operations there are a number of situations which are the subject of legal regulations.

There are mainly three areas which are related to laws and regulations. These areas are:

1. The premises.
2. The product.
3. The people.

Restaurants are regulated by basically the following laws and regulations:

1. Agricultural Produce (Grading and Marketing) Act, 1937 (Act 1 of 1937).

   Directorate of Marketing and Inspection, Ministry of Agriculture.
2. Fruit Products Order, 1995.

   Deptt. of Food, Ministry of Food and Civil Supplies.
3. Sugar (Central) Order, 1966.

   Directorate of Sugar, Ministry of Agriculture and Irrigation.
4. (a) Vegetable Oil Product (Control) Order, 1947.

   Directorate of Vanaspati, Ministry of Civil Supplies and Cooperation.

   (b) The Solvent Extracted Oil, Deoiled Meal and Edible Flour Control Order, 1975.

   Directorate of Vanaspati, Min. Of Civil Supplies and Cooperation.

   (c) Vanaspati Control Order 1975.

Directorate of Vanaspati, Min. of Civil Supplies and Cooperation.

5. Technical Standardization Committee (TSC), 1944.

   Army Purchase Organization, Deptt. of Food.

6. Export (Quality Control and Inspection) Act, 1963 and Rules, 1964.

   Export Inspection Council of India, Ministry of Commerce.

7. Bureau of Indian Standards.

   BIS, Deptt. of Industrial Dev., Ministry of Food and Civil Supply.

8. Meat Food Products Order, 1975.

   Directorate of Marketing and Inspection, Ministry of Food and Civil Supply.

9. Prevention of Food Adulteration Act, 1954 and Rules 1955.

   Directorate General of Health Services, Ministry of Health and Family Welfare.

10. The Standard of Weight and Measure Act, 1976.

    Deptt. of Civil Supplies and Cooperation, Ministry of Commerce.

11. Consumer Protection Act.

A restaurant requires a licence for manufacture, sale, stock or distribution of certain food articles. Though all food articles have to be manufactured, stocked, sold or distributed in conformity with the provisions of the Prevention of Food Adulteration Act and Rules, these required to be sold under a license and according to the conditions of licence. Thus, if food articles of which a valid licence is essential are manufactured, stocked, distributed and sold without a valid licence or in violation of rules or conditions of licence then it would be an offence under the various acts.

Rules framed by the Government of India and state governments stipulate the conditions of a licence and specify conditions of a licence which a licensee has to comply.

For sake of convenience, it will be helpful to know some of the terms defined under the Maharashtra Prevention of Food Adulteration Rules, 1962.

(i) *Manufacturer*: Means a person engaged in manufacturing any article of food for the purpose of sale.

(ii) *Wholesale*: Means a person engaged in the business of sale of any article of food in bulk to another trader for the purpose of resale. If such wholesales dealer sells to other retailer 500 g of food article, even then it shall be sale by the wholesale.

(iii) *Retail dealer*: Means a dealer in any article of food, other than a wholesale dealer. It means that he does not sell any article of food for resale to another trader. Having got knowledge as to who is a manufacturer, wholesale dealer, or retailer.

Let us have a look at the rules regarding grant of a licence and condition of licence for manufacturer sale, distribution or stocking for sale of food articles.

It is necessary for a restaurant to obtain a licence for the following food articles under the Prevention of Food Adulteration Rules, 1955 made by the Central Government, now amended:

(a) Milk of all classes and designations.

(b) Milk products, such as cream, *malai*, curd, skimmed milk cheese, processed cheese, ice-cream, condensed milk, sweetened and unsweetened, condensed skimmed milk, milk powder, skimmed milk powder, partly skimmed milk powder, *khoa*, infant milk food, table butter and *deshi* butter.

(c) Edible animal body fats, such as beef fat, mutton fat, goat fat and lard.

(d) Edible vegetable oil.

(e) Edible fats including margarine.

(f) Pulses gram, nuts starches, sago, *suji* such as *maida*, *besan* and articles made out of flour including bakery products.

(g) Non-alcoholic beverages such as carbonated water, tea, coffee, cocoa and chicory.

(h) Spices and condiments, whole or ground including saffron, curry powder, mustard seeds as asafoetida and compounded asafoetida.

(i) Sweetening agents such as sugars, honey, *gur* or jaggery.

(j) Flavouring agents, antioxidants, emulsifying and stabilizing agents and preservatives permitted for use in food container wrappers.

(k) Artificial sweeterners.

(l) Confectionery sweetmeats and savoury.

(m) Ice candies

(n) Edible gelatin

(o) Molasses

(p) *Copra*

(q) Meat and meat products, fish and fish products.

(r) Silver leaf for human consumption.

(s) Sweetened ice threads candies and similar products.

(t) Sugar cane juice - fresh fruit juice and sorbates.

(u) Prepared foods and ready to serve food.

## CHAPTER 2

# DESCRIPTION OF RESTAURANT AREA AND RESTAURANT PLANNING

A restaurant is a commercial establishment committed to the sale of food and beverage. It depends largely on certain service areas for effective functioning. So, the planning of restaurant is most important to ensure an even flow of work by the various members of staff. The planning itself may vary with different types of restaurants according to their needs.

The service area is usually between the kitchen and food service areas. It is an important unit in the make up of a restaurant establishment acting as the link between kitchen or food preparation unit and the restaurant or food service units. It is a meeting point for staff of various departments as they carry out their duties and therefore there must be close liaison between these various members of staff and the deptt. under whose jurisdiction they come. The service area itself is one of the busiest units of a catering establishment especially over the service periods. Because of this is most important that department heads ensure that all staff know exactly what their duties are and how to carry them out efficiently and quickly. A price in the job and doing it well means that the staff will cooperate with one another to give a complete and efficient service to the customer.

The service area is made up of five sections as follows:

1. Still-room
2. Silver or plate-room
3. Wash up
4. Hotplates
5. Spare linen store

These above areas fall into two categories, those for guest and staff usage and for staff usage only. Staff and guest usage areas included consumption area such as dining areas, service areas like cafeteria bars and the associated services. Staff areas include the still-room, wash up storage and cellar areas.

## 1. THE STILL-ROOM

The main function of still-room is to provide items of food and equipment required for the service of a meal and not catered for by the other major departments in a hotel such as kitchen larder and pantry.

The duty performed in a still-room will vary according to the type of meals offered and the size of the establishment concerned.

### Staff of the still-room

In a large restaurant a head still-room man or maid is in charge of the still-room. Depending on the size and the duties to be performed he or she may have a number of staff under their control. The person in-charge would be responsible for the completion of work rotos for all the still-room staff. A further responsibility of the head still-room man would be the ordering of supplies from the main dry goods store and the effective control of these when issued to various departments.

All requirements is written out on a requisition sheet in duplicate sheet while ordering goods from the main dry goods store. The top copy goes to the store to be retained by the storekeeper after issuing the goods and the duplicate remains in the requisition book as a means of checking the receipt of goods from the store by a member of the still-room staff. Because of the number of hours that the still-room has to remain open and running efficiently the staff will normally work on a straight shift basis doing an early shift one week and a late shift the next.

### Equipment of the still-room

Due to the same requirement of the most still-rooms their equipment is of a similar nature. To ensure the correct, storage preparation and presentation of wide range of food items, a considerable amount of equipment is used in still-room. Some of the essential equipments are following:

(a) *Refrigerator:* This is used for storage of milk, cream, butter, fruit juice etc.

(b) *Butter machine*: It is used for portion control purposes.

(c) *A coffee machine*: Depending on the type of establishment and its requirements the type of machine used here may be of the following type: Cafe coffee machine, Cona coffee machine, Automatic coffee machine.

(d) *Large double sink and draining boards*: For using up purposes and a washing up machine of a size suitable to a particular still-room.

(e) *Tea dispenser:* for portion control purposes.

(f) *Salamander*: for the preparation of breakfast or melba toast.

(g) *Bread slicing machine.*

(h) *Hot cupboards*, for plates and cups etc.

(i) Working top table and cutting board.

(j) The necessary storage space for all the small equipments such as china glassware and silverware that is in every day use.

(k) A storage cupboard for all goods held in stock.

(l) A double gas range for preparation of porridge and boiled eggs.

(m) Coffee grinding machine.

**Provisions of the still-room**

Normally, a still-room dispensed following food items:

(a) All beverages such as: coffee, tea, chocolate and other food drinks.

(b) Assorted fruit juices: orange, pineapple, tomato, grapefruit.

(c) Milk and cream.

(d) Sugars: loaf, pre-wrapped portions, brown coffee crystals.

(e) Preserves: marmalade, cherry, plum, raspberry, strawberry, honey.

(f) Butter either passed through a butter pat machine, curled or pre-wrapped portions, once prepared it is best kept in bowls of ice water.

(g) Sliced and buttered brown, white and malt bread.

(h) Rolls, brioche, croissant may be issued from here.

(i) Melba toast: it is prepared by toasting a slice of bread on both sides. It is generally offered to the guest in place of rolls or gristicks at the beginning of the meal, either lunch or dinner.

(j) Breakfast toast.

(k) Starch reduced rolls.

(l) Dry cracker, water and digestive biscuits for service with the cheese board. Sweet biscuits for service with early morning/afternoon tea.

(m) Assorted breakfast cereals: Cornflakes, wheatabix, shredded wheat, rice crispies etc.

(n) Toasted scone and tea cakes: prepared to order and generally served with afternoon tea.

**Control of the still-room**

It is necessary to keep control on everything issued from the still-room. There are mainly two ways of controlling for goods to be sued namely:

(i) By receiving items in bulk on receipt of a requisition received from a food service area. The requisition must be signed by someone in authority. This would include such food items as butter, preserves, sugar etc.

(ii) By issuing tea, coffee or any other beverage required in the necessary portions on receipt of waiters check.

## 2. SILVER OR PLATE ROOM

Generally the silver room or plate room is a separate unit in the most of the larger luxurious restaurants, in the smaller restaurants it is more often combined with the pantry and wash-up.

The silver room should hold the complete stock of silver required for the services of all meals together with a slight surplus stock in case of emergency, it will often be found that the silver for banquet eating service is of a different design and kept specifically for the purpose. The store of silver is most important, the large silver such as flats, salvers, soup, tureens, etc., will be stored on shelves with all the flats of one size together and so on. All shelves would be labelled in showing where each different items will go. This makes it easier for control purposes and for stacking. It should be remembered when stacking silver that the heavier items should go on the shelves lower down and the smaller items of silver such as ash-trays, cruets, butter dishes, special equipment, table numbers, menu holders etc., are best stored in drawers lines with green baize. This help to prevent noise and stops the various items sliding about the drawer when it is opened and closed and becoming scratched. Items should be cleaned by a head plate man to ensure that this is carried out and that all silver is cleaned regularly. Obviously those items in constant use will require more attention. He will also put on one side any articles of silver broken or that require buffing up or replating so that they may be sent to the manufacturers for any faults to be corrected. The cleanliness of all service silver is most important. There are various methods of silver cleaning and the method used generally depends on the size of the restaurants. The larger restaurants use a burnishing machine which would be constant use all through the day whereas the smaller establishment which possibly could not afford a burnishing machine would use 'silver dip' which is a much speedier method.

## 3. THE WASH-UP

The wash-up is a most important part of the service area, and must be sited correctly so that the brigade can work speedily and efficiently when passing from the food areas to the kitchens. The waiter should stack trays of the dirties correctly at the sideboard, which all the correct sized plates together and tableware stacked on one of the plates with the blades of the knives. All glassware should be stacked on a separate tray and taken to a separate wash-up point. On entering the service area the waiter should immediately meet the wash-up where he will deposit all his dirty plates, stacking them correctly and placing all the tableware in the special wire basket container in readiness for washing. The waiter must place any debris in to the bin or bowl provided. All used serviettes, doilies or kitchen paper will be placed in a separate bin. The china itself may be washed by one of the two main methods.

### (a) Tank method

The dirty china will be placed into a tank of hot water containing a soap detergent. After washing the plates placed them into wire racks and deeped into a second sterilization tank containing clean hot water at a temperature of approximately 75°C. The racks would be left for two minutes and then lifted out and the china left to drain. If sterilized in water at this temperature the china will dry by itself without the use of drying up clothes. This is, therefore, more hygienic. After drying, the china is stacked into piles of the correct size and placed into shelves until required for further use.

### (b) Machine method

Many of the larger restaurants have washing up machine. These are necessary because of the high turnover rate of china, the instruction for use of a washing-up machine are generally supplied by the manufacturer together with details of detergent to be used and in what quantity. These directions should be strictly adhered to, the china itself has nay debris removed and is then placed into either wooden or wire racks. The racks are then passed through the machine. The china being washed rinsed and then sterilized in turn. Having passed through the machine the china is left to drain for 2-3 minutes and it is then stacked and placed on shelves until required for further use. As with the tank method, the plates do not require drying with tea cloths.

## 4. THE HOT-PLATE

The hot-plate may be regarded as the meeting point between the food service staff and the food preparation staff. It is most essential that there is active co-operation and good relationship between the staff of these two service areas. This helps a great deal to ensure that the customer receive an efficient and quick service of the meal from polite courteous waiter who has not been rough because of bad service at the hotplates. This co-operation will also ensure that all the dishes served are well and attractively presented. At the same time all orders written by the waiter must be legible to the aboyeur so that there is no delay in calling up a particular dish. Also the food service staff should queue at the hot plate and not cause confusion by jumping the queue.

The aboyeur is in charge and controls the hot-plate over the service period. As an aid to the food service staff the aboyeur would control the off board which tells the waiter immediately any dish is off. It should be sited in a prominent position for all to see. The hot-plate itself should be stocked up with all the china necessary for the service of a meal.

This would include some for all of the following items; soup plates, fish plates, joint plates, sweet plates, consumme cups, platters soup cups and demitasse. The silver required for service is often placed on the top of the hot-plate and used as required. The hot-plate is usually gas or electrically operated and should be lit well in advance of the service to ensure all the necessary china and silver is sufficiently heated. The aboyeur who controls the hot-plate over the service period will initially receive the food check from the waiter. He or she checks that it is legible and that none of the dishes ordered are off the menu. Then the order from the various corner of the kitchen is called up as each particular dish is required. It is important that if a dish required to be prepared and cooked to order. That the aboyeur orders this is to be done before the waiter, comes to the hotplates to collect it. Then there will be no major delay by the waiter who is going to serve the dish for the customer who is waiting for the next course to be served. When a food check is finished it is placed into a control box. The box is kept locked and can only be opened by a staff member from the control department, who for control purposes marries up the copy of the food check from the kitchen with the copy of cashier and the duplicate copy of the bill.

To ensure there is no delay in any food dish reaching the hot-plate, the aboyeur should call them up allowing time for preparation, cooking and presentation, there are some special kitchen terms which are used to warm the food preparation staff working in various corners to get ready the dishes. These terms are as follows:

(i) General warming to kitchen that the service is about to commence 'la service va commencer'.

(ii) An indication to the kitchen of the number of covers ca marche trois couverts.

(iii) Inform the parties concerned of the order, 'poissoner faites marche trois sole veronique'.

(iv) When the order is required at the hot-plate by the waiter the aboyeur calls it up from the appropriate parties, poissoner, envoyer, los trios sale veronique.

(v) Each 'chef de parties' must reply to the order called out by the aboyeur. The reply being 'oui'.

(vi) Where an extra special order is required the term called out by the aboyeur before the actual order is 'bien soigne.'

(vii) To hurry up an order use the words "Depechez vous".

## 5. SPARE LINEN STORE

Generally, a spare linen cupboard is found within the service area. This is normally the responsibility of a senior member of the food service staff. It is kept locked for control purpose, this spare linen stock is held near the food service area in case of emergency, the linen changes when necessary on a basis of one clean for one dirty.

### The size and shape of the area

The customers enjoyment of the meal is not affected only by the size and shape if the room but also by the location of the tables in table service areas.

Some issues to consider are:

* The location of tables in a food service area

especially taking into account the single dinner and couples.

* Access for those with disabilities.
* Ease of work flow.
* Evenness of temperature and ventilation.
* Access to exit and toilets.

**Restaurant planning**

Probably every restaurant has employed experts to design the layout, restaurateurs who may become involved in the planning rarely have completely free hand in the choice of equipment, fittings and furniture. To a great extent they are limited by what is available from manufacturers and suppliers. Nonetheless, one can imagine many situations where the restaurateurs is asked to participate in this process, particularly where changes in consumer trends or operating policy necessiate altering an existing operation.

**Layout and seating arrangements**

As we have seen the different sectors of the industry much of the difference between styles of service depends upon the alternative configurations of the service area and seating within the unit. But irrespective of the style of service, there is a minimum area that a customer needs in order to consume a meal when seated: about 0.8 square metres. This does not mean that 0.8 square meters is the desirable amount of seating space that should be provided in all operations.

Consideration must also give to spacing between tables. The minimum distance between adjacent seated customers is recommended 0.25 m, while for service to take place 0.9 m, self-service requires little space between customers seated by side whereas silver service requires a gap to enable the waiter to serve and gueriden service requires a large amount of space to enable the passage of service trolleys.

**RESTAURANT SEATING**

Sizes of table to seat various numbers.

| Number of covers | Shape of table | | |
|---|---|---|---|
| 2 | Round (diameter) | Square | Rectangular |
| 2 | 0.8m | 0.75m × 0.75m | 0.6m × 0.7m |
| 3 | 0.9m | - | 1.0m × 0.75m |
| 4 | 1.0m | 1.0m × 1.0m | 1.2m × 0.75m |
| 6 | 1.2 | not advisable | 1.5m × 0.75m |
| 8 | 1.5m | not advisable | 2.4m × 0.75m |

The above table indicates the sizes of tables needed to seat between 2 and 8 customers. This is based on the requirement that a person needs a minimum of 0.6m to avoid touching people on either side and table will need to be 0.7m deep to avoid two people's knees touching when seated opposite each other. Although for four customers the round table appears to require less space than the square, both take up the same amount of floor space, whereas, the rectangular effectively takes up slightly less but can be arranged in combination with other tables more effectively than either the square or the round table.

There is also the need for flexibility in the lay-out to accommodate larger parties which round table cannot provide and for which square tables tend to take up more space and be less comfortable.

Using square table, only 14 covers can be sited in the same amount of space and the distance between tables is not really wide enough for service staff to pass through with comfort. Lastly, if round tables are employed it is impossible to locate them as square tables so that the number of covers possible is reduced to no more than 12. Quite obviously the restaurateur must weigh up very carefully the use of round tables with the practicabilities of rectangular ones. In addition, a flow pattern must be established within the unit.

Planning the seating in a restaurant must also take into account the type of customer using the unit. Research has shown that customers prefer a certain amount of selection when eating out and choose tables near walls or in booths or near windows, if these are not on view to passes-by. Partition screens and other form of divider may, therefore, be needed to break up the space, particularly in large restaurants. Restaurants should be placed emphasis on providing for the needs of the disables. Facilities should be made available for accommodating wheelchairs.

### Cafeteria seating

Cafeteria service requires less space per customer than restaurants operating with waiter services. It is usual to assume that 25 to 30 per cent of an establishment's total workforce will use the catering facilities on average and dining rooms are planned accordingly. Once the seating capacity had determined the restaurateur must ensure that the speed of service is fast enough to achieve the required seat turnover. Thus, if the cafeteria become more popular, the variable factors affecting the availability of seats is the speed of the service, the length of the dining period and the time customer stake over their meals. For example, if six customers per minute are served, then for every minute of the service six seats must be made available.

Where a large number of customers are expected and only a short time available in which to serve them, the service speed must be kept high end the average meal time for each customer must be kept short. Many establishments provide coffee lounges or similar to encourage quick vacating of tables in the main dining area.

## FUNCTION SEATING

For functions seating arrangements may be formal or informal. The type of function will determine the particular style adopted.

## Side Board and Trolleys

Restaurateurs have to consider also about the position of service points in waiter service restaurants and position of cleaning trolleys in self-service units.

(a) *Sitting of service points*: It is preferable to place sideboard on island sites, particularly if there are columns in the room. This has the advantage that staff must take greater care to maintain the sideboards in a clean and orderly manner since they are not in a seclude position.

(b) *Siting of clearing trolleys*: These trolleys should be situated away from the service counter, near to the exit to avoid congestion between customers about to eat these about to leave.

## Establishing Stations

In those restaurants where staff works from a sideboard, care must be taken to ensure that the allocation of covers per station is equitable so that all staff serves approximately the same number of covers. This is desirable since they will be paid more or less the same wage. It should be remembered that by allocating the same number of tables to each station that restaurant manager cannot be sure that each station waiter will serve the same number of customers.

## Furniture Planning

The restaurant should select table and chairs according to their appropriateness for the type of operation, cost, east of cleaning and maintenance, durability and appearance, the restaurateur may select two basic modes of seating, free standing or fixed.

(a) *Free standing*: This means tables and individual chairs. The advantages of this kinf of furniture are freedom of movement, ease of replacement and easier cleaning.

(b) *Fixed*: The restaurateur may select this style of furniture because less floor space is needed per cover, well designs units minimize obstruction which makes cleaning quicker.

Generally an up market unit will select furniture that is comfortable, for example, chair with arms, upholstered and so on and aesthetically pleasing, a self serve operation however, will consider functional design durability and ease of cleaning the more important criteria. But whatever the unit tables and chairs, should comply with the following recommendations:

1. The foot of the chair or table should be fairly broad to spare the lead, so avoiding damage to the floor surface.
2. Tables and chairs should offer minimum resistance when moved on carpet but at the same time be slip-proof on most type of floor surface.
3. Upholstered chairs should be made of easy to clean materials and where possible upholstered chairs should be easily removed for cleaning and repairs.
4. Upholstered chairs should have a gap between the seat and the back.
5. Chairs with arms should have the arms low enough to allow the chairs to be pulled up to the table.
6. Table legs should have no sharp edges or protruding fixtures to avoid damaging shoes and stockings.
7. Table tops should be non-slip where table cloths are used.
8. Tables with removable legs to facilitate movement and storage should be easily dismantled and parts should be fully interchangeable.

## KEY COMMENTS OF SUCCESSFUL RESTAURANT OPERATION

There are three essential components of successful restaurant operations, people, food and service. The presentation dwells primarily on service and to an extent, on people. To be able to get close to zero error service, there must be an effective services strategy and service design. The service strategy must be developed keeping in mind the target segment, the product and its positioning. All these must blend with each other.

The service strategy should be build on a service design which in turn should work around the cycle of service. The service design must incorporate a blue print to ensure compatibility of individual elements (the target clientele the ambience, the menu) attempt to identify and satisfy the needs and wants of the target segment, include external as well as internal service guarantees, balance the procedural and convivial sides of service, avoid industrialization of service in hi-tech areas and have a built-in failure mechanism.

The cycle of service must recreate the entire operation in the restaurant, in terms of what a customers goes through - is greeted, seated, presented the menu, order is taken, food served table cleared, cheques cleared. All these must be identified in terms of moments of truth- the moments when the hotel experience is indirect confirmation with the guest.

These moment must be identified in terms of criticals and satisfiers. The criticals must be closely looked in to avoid dissatisfaction and achieve zero error. The satisfaction must be exceeded guest expectations surprised to induct a 'wow' factor so that this experience is not a natural one. The idea is to make your presence fell and focus on smoothing genuine, which gives more value and emerges as a high satisfier. There should be a method of communication built into the cycle of service so that the gaps are a bare minimum.

Once the cycle of service is got in order a service design must be build. There can be three structural alternatives in a service design. A regular process, a lower complexity process which is divergent and a higher complexity which again is a divergent. The second would be built around a no reservation, self seating, menu on blackboard, no frill environment where the customer possibly fills out an order form, the menu is extremely limited and the payment is made when leaving. The higher complexity process would involves specific table selection where the service station holder recites the menu, describe entrees and specials, an assortment of hot breads and hors d oueuveres are served; the order is specially taken by the maitre d', menu is extremely elaborated, there are between the course services; there is choice of payment and so forth, the structural alternatives would be governed by the kind of clientele location and the restaurant product at large. In other words the prices, the facilities, and the value addition should be realistic to operation in line with customer requirements and comprehensible to the customer.

To be able to induct a 'delight' factor, there must be comprehensive understand of the needs and wants of the guest. The need includes the basics which must be had; wants is an unexpressed internal urge. By understanding wants one can exceed customer expectations.

Simultaneously, this is a zone of tolerance which must be understood elaborately. If the guest perceptions fall below the adequate level, you are at competitive disadvantage even though the customer is relatively satisfied. If perceptions fall in the tolerance zone you have a relatively competitive advantage and a fairly satisfied guest, however, if the perceptions exceed the desired level, you achieve customer delight which should be the aim and which gives you a definite competitive advantage. Basically, how close you can get to the want of the customer and move faster than the competition mark is the cutting edge.

Of course, needs and wants vary from person to person, but the very nature of the service industry calls for personalization and recognition of individuals needs. The restaurant must be pro-active to the customer needs, the service design must be accordingly flexible to accommodate individual needs.

The ability to understand is the most complete of all functions - everything else flows from here. There are normally three attitudes towards this, Attitudes No. one, is reactive - where complaints go unsolicited or are catered to only when pointed out. Attitude No. two, is approach - where there is an apparent redressel system, perhaps service desks, sales, data, customer reponse. However, they are all inert systems. Attitude No. three is pro-active - where the restaurant makes effort to find its faults whether through personal interviews, designed surveys, mystery, dinner, or internal bench making and appraisals.

A service design should also include external as well as internal service guarantees. The external guarantees should be unconditional, easy to understand, meaningful, easy to invoke and easy to collect. The internal service guarantee should consist of time limits for all services including tea, beverages, courses, cigarettes, bill presentation, bill clearance, laying fresh covers etc. The internal service guarantee must be monitored consistently by supervisors.

A service guarantee in fact is a very good tool or staff to focus on customer. Set clear standards, generate feedback, understand failure and built market presence. The whole approach is proactive so that that guy down the line can understand why he is failing.

There are two sides of services and two distinct components, procedure and conviviality, the procedural aspects are based on systems. They should not be overlooked and at the same time not overdone. Conviviality or personalization embodies attitudes, behaviour, verbal kills and so forth, as with procedures, this aspect must be given only as much attention as required. In other words do not regimentalise and do not over personalize.

The level of guest complaints must also be handled discreetly. Minimum technology should be deployed in direct guest complaint areas. Technology should be put to use behind the scenes to enhance efficiency and industrialise operations.

There must be a built in failure mechanism in all operations assuming that you are aiming at zero defect but the very nature of the service industry does not allow you zero defect. Statistics suggest that if a guest goes back home dissatisfied not only will you lose him but he will also tell eleven others about his experience. However, a satisfied guest will only talk to six people about his experience. What follows from this is complaints are inevitable but a dissatisfied guest is not.

A critical aspect of service strategy is its documentation even before the doors of the restaurant have been opened to public, you cannot assume that you will draw out a strategy as things evolve. But on the other hand the strategy must be flexible enough to incorporate changes as they evolve.

Documentation also involves customer event diagrams - possibly

Little symbols for each bread event which are understand by all staff when bills orders etc., are exchanged. It is, however, important that the symbols are not complete and not too many. The importance of these should perhaps be display on boards in each concerned department, also the strategy should be drawn keeping in mind the perspective of the customer.

Next come training. The clinching line is do not sell training, market, learning so that your employees understands it is for his development. Training must involves developing models of all possible operations all activity undertaken by staff, be it setting the guest, pouring the water must be converted into lesson plane and broken down for better comprehension and adequate action by the staff. This would influence their behaviour in the right director, enhance knowledge skill and attitude.

The basic quality service standards that must be understood include anticipation, time lines communication and selling skills.

The supervisors must also be trained regularly so that their skills in terms of headship, training others, managing change and so forth can be improved continuously.

Feedback mechanism is the final attributes of service strategy, this could flow around self-periodic audit, professionals agency and the customer directly through comment forms and verbal communication. From this could be drawn the guest satisfaction index and whether the failure is due to departmental team, or due to human error, process error, product error and equipment error etc.

The feedback mechanism would enable quality enhancement by bridging gaps between promise and performance. This in turn could be achieved by identifying improvement opportunities, strategic quality planning and estimating the cost of poor quality. The feed back mechanism also allows one to be pro-active and pre-emptive to remain contemporary maintain a competitive produce, progress further improve market shares and bottom lines and professional a healthy image.

People are the second important component of successful operations in a restaurant, or for that matter, anywhere. People skills are in fact more complex than technical skills. There are psychological, social and anthropological factors that rule a persons' behaviour all these must be taken into account and accordingly behaviour modifiers reinforcements and extinguishers devised and implemented.

In conclusion the service strategy must have a customer focus and generate value. Standards must be set which are consistent. However, the staff must be empowered to be flexible to a situation, there must be a built in failure mechanism towards service recovery, you must keep thinking in terms of emerging needs and wants to improve quality.

The people aspect must be carefully looked into in terms of recruitment, training, retraining and empowerment.

CHAPTER 3

# DEPARTMENTAL ORGANISATION AND STAFFING

## ORGANISATION OF A RESTAURANT

In general the organization of a restaurant is of the following patterns:

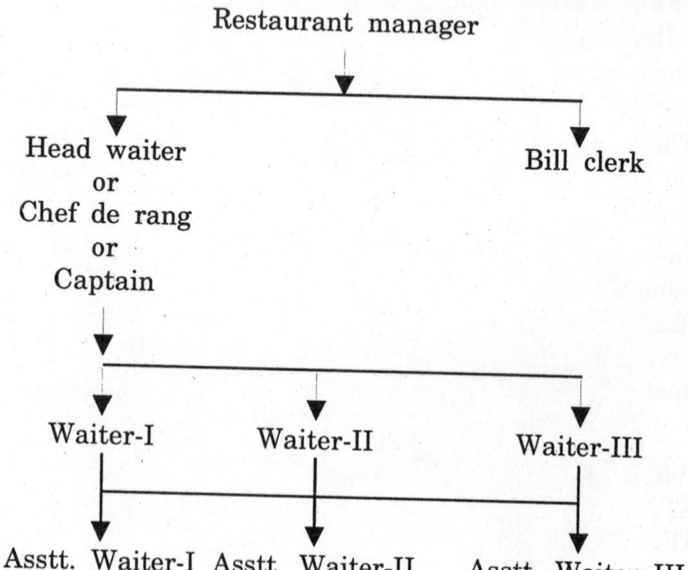

In a large restaurant, whether belonging to a hotels, a non-residential establishments, or within industrial catering, there must be one person in charge. Under him some principal assistance in charge came and under each of the assistants come the general assistant.

A traditionally organized restaurant or dining room is controlled either by a maitre d' hotel, a head waiter/ waitress or a restaurant manager/manageress who is directly responsible to management for the running of his department.

In the restaurant, the room is divided into section called rang or cares. Each rang consists of five tables averaging four customers each, thus serving about twenty customers. The number of rangs or sections will be determined by the size of the room. The waiter in-charge of such a section or rang is called *a chef de rang*. Two rang may be grouped to form a station under the control of a head waiter. In large establishments with elaborate service styles, chefs de ranges are assisted by junior waiters. In most establishments the Maitre d' hotel or head waiter is responsible for showing guests to their tables and should have a personal table plan readily available.

The head waiter is responsible for the smooth working of the stations and if necessary, should be prepared to help others in need.

In small restaurants a head waiter often acts as a wine butler, dealing exclusively with wines and drink order and has his own small team. One or more wine waiters are available according to the size of the restaurant. A sommelier in a traditional operation was expected to look after eight to ten tables.

## PRINCIPAL STAFF OF VARIOUS TYPES OF RESTAURANT AND THEIR JOB DESCRIPTION, STAFF MANAGEMENT

The question that appears to be most urgent and recurring headache for the restaurant management is that of staff management despite the fact that in comparison to many occupations, waiting at table is only a semi-skilled job, the industry has for many years found it difficult to recruit its waiting staff.

Generally, restaurant staff are organized in the style of French restaurant system as a restaurant brigade.

This organization is likely today to be reduced or simplified but a classification of possible staff is as follows:

(a) F. & B. manager

(b) Cutlet manager

(c) Maitre de' Hotel

(d) Hostess

(e) Chef de' rang

(f) Commis de' rang

## JOB DESCRIPTION OF VARIOUS TYPES OF STAFF

JOB TITLE: **Food and Beverage Manager**

RESPONSIBLE TO: General manger/Resident manager.

SCOPE AND PURPOSES: To achieve marketing, sales, profitability and quality service goals for the food and beverage department by developing and executing marketing strategies, preparing and executing the budget, providing quality service to the guests and employing leadership and managerial skills effectively.

### Duties and responsibilities

A. He is responsible for attaining food and beverage sales goals and targets by executing marketing strategies and controlling costs. For this he:

1. prepares market plan by developing strategies to increase market shares. He analyses sales reviews competitive surveys and develops new plan.

2. executives market plan by implementing agreed upon strategies, evaluates results and adjust strategies as required.
3. ensure that menu engineering supports marketing goals by selecting menu items and recommending prices based an competition and market trends.
4. maintains marketing and merchandising standards of operation by following the laid down service standards.

B. He is responsible for achieving profitably goals for entire department while providing the guest with quality service. For this he:

1. develops the food and beverages budget by reviewing the outlet head's recommendations and trends, prepares a budget package and presenting the complete budget to the general manager for approval.
2. implements the approved budget. Monitors revenues and costs on a daily basis and takes corrective action where necessary.
3. controls cost be adhering to standards of operation for forecasting budgeting, scheduling overtime control and other cost control measures.
4. ensures that each department is run in accordance with the food and beverage standards of operation.
5. maintains control of food and beverage supply costs and inventory by adhering to standards for purchasing and inventory control.
6. assists chef in setting up specifications and standards on food materials and beverage items for the purchasing manager.
7. does surprise checking of raw materials to confirm to standards and specifications as stipulated.

C. He is responsible for maximizing employee productivity and satisfaction. For this he:

1. helps in selection of qualifies employees and provide orientation and training.
2. conducts employee meetings and counselling sessions in order to maximize employee morals and productivity.
3. determines and communicate standards of performance to employee. Evaluates employees performance on a regular basis.
4. develops employees to maximize potential and prepare them for future promotional opportunities through career development schemes.

D. He is responsible for ensuring that departmental training goals are executed on an ongoing basis. For this purpose he:

1. ensures that all new employees receive departmental orientation and go through on the job training programmes.
2. ensures that management employees utilize 'Train the trainers' skill and while conducting training programmes.

E. He is responsible for achieving banqueting goals by ensuring that marketing and sales strategies are executed in order to maximize sales and that guest service standards are adhered to. For this purpose he:

1. maximize banquet sales by ensuring that banquet sales personnel utilize sales promotion guidelines like direct selling, verbal merchandising and upselling techniques.

JOB TITLE: **Outlet Manager**

RESPONSIBLE TO: Food and Beverage manager

PURPOSE and SCOPE: Planning, organizing, directing, co-ordinating, controlling, budgeting, providing quality food and beverage service to maximize guest satisfaction and profitability in the restaurant.

**Duties and responsibilities**

1. To ensure that high quality of service and product, standards as specified are implemented.
2. To ensure all staff under his control are properly deployed and utilized.
3. To ensure strict control over his KOT and billing for proper revenue accounting.
4. To ensure that all budgeted/targeted sales and expenditures are achieved to maximize profitability and to assist in annual budget targets for restaurant.
5. To ensure that all forms and registers as specified in formats are maintained.
6. To ensure that inventory of stocks is maintained as per standards.
7. To ensure that all laws of the land, applicable to catering establishments such as Municipal bye-laws shop and establishment act, prohibition and service rules etc. are strictly adhered to.
8. To ensure over all administration with regard to conduct and work performance.
9. To maximize sales by monitoring industry trends and competitors, marketing strategies. To organize sales gimmicks to maintain competitive status.
10. To ensure that all VIP's are personally received and seen off.

JOB TITLE: **Maitre d' hotel**

RESPONSIBILITY TO: Outlet manager

PURPOSE AND SCOPE: To ensure quality service as per standards to ensure smooth operations of his area.

**Duties and responsibilities**

1. To ensure upkeep, maintenance and cleanliness of the entire restaurant.
2. To ensure that all registers forms to be filled in are maintained in the specified manner.
3. Handling all guest complaints with regard to quality of service and staff discipline.
4. To ensure that all records of the outlet are maintained.
5. To implement control measures.
6. To ensure staff discipline and grooming.
7. Maintaining liaison and cordial relations with other departments.
8. To accord personalized attention, service to all VIPs/ CIPs.
9. To maintain good and cordial relations with guests.
10. Briefing to be taken daily with the service staff.
11. To assist the manager in his work and to look after his jobs in his absence.
12. To presence thorough knowledge of the menu/bar card, style and standards of service and all operational procedures and policies.
13. To assist in the planning and executing of special events.

JOB TITLE: **Chef de Rang**

RESPONSIBLE TO: Maitre d' hotel

PURPOSE and SCOPE: To provide quality service, preparation of restaurant.

**Duties and responsibilities**

1. To perform, organize and check mise en place and mise en scene.
2. Attending to the guest, once the hostess/maitre d' hotel has seated them.

3. Presenting menu, taking order and executing them as per the standards specified.
4. Presenting the bill as per bill presentation standards and completing transactions.
5. Receiving/escorting the guest in and escorting the guest out.
6. All housekeeping and maintenance needs to be informed to MDH.
7. Maintaining good and cordial relations with the guest.
8. Maintaining inventory and stock taking.
9. Reporting any uptoward incidents to maitre d' hotel/ manager.
10. Co-ordinating with commis de rang and doing actual food service clearance to ensure prompt/ timely and efficient service to each guest.
11. To assist maitre d' hotel in preparation of special dishes.

Apart from these principal staff there are some other staff also which are as follows:

(a) Receptionist head waiter
(b) Station head waiter
(c) Demi chef
(d) Commis waiters
(e) Bar-boys
(f) Runners
(g) Cleaning assistant waiter
(h) Wine butler
(i) Carver
(j) The floor waiter
(k) Assistant floor waiter
(l) The lounge waiter

(m) Restaurant cashier.

(a) ***Receptionist head waiter (maitre de reception)***: In some large restaurants one senior head waiter is responsible for the reception and seating of guests which is otherwise taken by the maitre d' hotel.

(b) ***Station head waiter (maitre d' hotel de carre)***. He is responsible for a section of the restaurant carrying out similar functions in his own area to those of the maitre d' hotel. He helps in seating, taking order and if necessary with service.

(c) ***Demi-chef***: He has similar duties to a station waiter but normally works a smaller station and often without the aid of assistants or commis.

(d) ***Commis waiters***: There are several kinds of junior assistants known as commis for example:

(i) ***Commis de rang or commis de suite***

(ii) ***Commis de wagen (trolley assistants)***: He is a commis, an assistant waiter, assigned to a trolley usually of hors de œuvres or patisserie.

(e) ***Busboy***: A busboy is smaller to a commis de suitee on a French brigade.

Busboy clear away soiled dishes and replace used table cloths. They may offer bread and rolls, even pour coffee at a meal service. They can assist be replenishing trolleys and buffet tables. They can help in setting up the dining room in advance, in laying covers and in clearing tables when meal is over.

(f) ***Clearing assistant waiter (commis de barasseur)***: He is the most junior assistant, mainly clearing away used plates and dishes and simply fetching and carrying under instruction. He holds this post only during a short period of early training.

(g) ***Wine butler (chef de vin)***: He takes orders for wines, spirits, beers and soft drinks and serves them to guests.

## SOURCES OF STAFF

Restaurant staff can be recruited from four separate labour markets. These are the following:

1. Unqualified and inexperienced.
2. Qualified and inexperienced
3. Unqualified and experienced
4. Qualified and experienced

The advantage of employing unqualified and inexperienced staff are as follows:

1. Their wage cost is likely to be lower than for qualified or experienced staff.
2. They can be trained to meet the specific requirements and standards of the operation.
3. They may be selected for their fresh enthusiastic attitude towards restaurant operations.

On the other hand there are advantages in employing trained and qualified staff. These advantages are as follows:

1. Their qualifications indicate their level of skill and amount of knowledge.
2. Their previous experience means that they may require less on the job training, thereby reducing training costs.

There are a variety of ways to recruit staff, such as:

1. Through recommendations of staff working for you.
2. Through the media.
3. Through professional bodies.
4. Through the department of employment exchange.
5. From other employment agencies.
6. Through colleges by circulating details of job opportunities to the hotel and catering departments.

**Basic etiquettes for restaurant staff**

The restaurant business is an admixtures of showmanship, diplomacy and sociability, the etiquette that a waiter exhibits in a restaurant should comprise the following:

1. Attend to guests as soon as they enter the restaurant.
2. Assists guests to remove warm, they costs in winter and help to put them on when they leave.
3. Wish guests and welcome then to the restaurants.
4. Preferable address them by their name.
5. Be polite to guests.
6. Help to seat ladies.
7. Provide extra cushions or special chairs for children.
8. When speaking to a guest do not interrupt him if he is speaking to another guest.
9. Do not overhear conversation.
10. Avoid bad mannerism such touching hair or nose picking etc.
11. Stand erect at all times. A gentle bow at the time of service is permissible.
12. Remember a guest's special dish and remind him that you know it. Ascertain whether he would like to order it again.
13. Be attentive to guest calls.
14. Talk softly.
15. Strike a match to enable a guest to light his cigarette.
16. Avoid arguing with service staff and guest in the restaurant.
17. Carry pencils in the pockets and not behind ears or clipped in front of the jacket.
18. Desist from chewing gum or nut etc.

19. Present the bill/check to the host discreetly in order to avoid embarrassing him.
20. Avoid soliciting for tips.
21. Remove tips after the guest has left.
22. Enter and leave the restaurant through the service door only.

## ATTRIBUTES OF A GOOD WAITER

To follow up the above-mentioned etiquettes a waiter should have following attributes:

**1. Clear speech:** A waiter's voice should be clear low in pitch and natural. He should be able to pronounce words properly and to express his ideas. He should acquire a good knowledge of English and be able to converse easily.

A knowledge of second language is a help, particularly to waiters who seek service in large restaurants where there are foreign visitors. For them the knowledge of French language is useful because menus often written in French and it is the language used in cookery books.

**2. Handwriting:** A waiter does not need great skill in writing but he will have to write out orders. Such orders must be legible to the kitchen and billing staff. Therefore, clear handwriting is an asset to a waiter.

**3. Courtesy:** It is the hallmark of a good waiter to be courteous on all occasions. Indeed a waiter must often go out of his way to be considerable or forbearing to a critical or ill-tempered person. He will certainly be courteous to customers, but should also carry these good manners through to the service room and the locker room. His manners should not be just a part of the techniques of the restaurant, but inherent in his nature and a sign of well-bred desire to please those with whom he comes into contact. The aim is to be friendly without being familiar.

**4. Memory:** Cultivation of memory is essential if customer's likes and dislikes are to be noted and remembered. Sensitive awareness of what a customer wants should also be sought.

If a waiter studies his customers, preferences, complaints he will find that they will be delighted, when they realize that their wishes are known and anticipated.

**5. Honesty:** A waiter must be honest in all his dealings with guest, colleagues and management. He should take the greatest care of all equipment belonging to an establishment and never think he can deal with it wastefully or carelessly because it is not his own.

**6. Co-operation and reliability:** Since an establishments success depends on effective co-ordinating co-ordination of all staff a waiter should aim to help his fellow workers. He should not be jealous if another waiter has customers who pay higher tips taking his proper turn in the servery queue, learning and keeping to rules of the house in spirit as well as to the latter.

A co-operative waiter cultivates his ability to get on well with customers and colleagues alike and to further the policies of management.

**7. Receiving gratitudes:** A waiter should never indulge in preferential treatment of customers according to tips he may receive from them. Indeed, every customer, irrespective of his financial condition, should be treated alike. Tips should be acknowledged graciously; if placed on the table they should not be removed until the customer has left and never counted in front of a guest.

A waiter must never lean against the wall or sideboard, tables or other furniture, he must especially never lean on a chair back when speaking with a guest.

**8. Conversing:** A waiter must not converse with other staff members and never argue with guests, he should not interrupt a guests conversation with an enquiry, if a customer enters into conversation with a waiter, he must answer politely and as briefly as possible.

A waiter must disciplined himself, not to listen to guests conversation, whether it is carried out loudly enough for him to hear or not. If he has any complaints to make to the head waiter or to colleagues, he must wait until service is over. Waiters should not of course talk among themselves or neglect guests by so doing.

**9. Mistakes and complaints:** If a mistake is made by the head waiter or by one of his assistants a waiter should never demonstrate with or criticize him in the restaurant. Any explanation that may be necessary to prevent and error recurring, or to apportion the blame for it should be made outside the restaurants, preferably at the end of service.

**10. Technical skill:** In addition to cultivating social qualities and modes of conduct to support his sales function a waiter uses technical skills. He must be hungry for

**Fig. 1. A well-groomed waiter**

knowledge and be eager to learn service methods. The skills and knowledge that a waiter needs are following:

1. Knowledge of the catering trade.
2. Knowledge of food that he will serve.
3. Layout of restaurant or dining room and its preparation for the service.
4. Actual method of serving.
5. Services of tobacco, cigarettes and cigars.
6. Service of liquor.
7. A good ground work, general education and attitude, ability to speak a foreign language or understanding French terms used in catering.

Regard this cloth as a tool and part of your dress. Use it only for its intended purpose-carrying dishes, polishing silver, etc., never inappropriately nor unhygienically, for example as a duster or for hand drying, carry the cloth neatly folded over the left arm when not in use.

**Conduct in the restaurant**

When not serving a waiter should stand by his station sideboard, his service cloth folded on to his left forearm. He should not pass in front of a customer, and at all times give right of way to a guest.

A waiter should never run in a restaurant nor in the service. Apart form the undesirable impression created, running is a potential hazard. Waiters should adopt a way of walking which is brisk without appearing hurried, taking care to avoid knocking against guests' seats. Above all he should move quietly. Good service comprises many things but it is always quiet service.

## CHAPTE 4

# RESTAURANT EQUIPMENT

As a restaurant is a revenue generation area so its design and its equipment both are important. Equipping a restaurant is a task for management and has to be consistent with the total concept for the operation and related to the consumer.

The equipment needs of a restaurant are the same throughout the industry, the basic equipment can be best described as (i) equipment for the transporting food-trays, plates, glasses, cartoons, (ii) utensils for eating food-knives, forks, spoons and so on, and (iii) materials for protecting against spillage table cloths and napkins.

Restaurant equipment reflects the standard and style of the restaurant. Several factors are considered when they are chosen:

1. Standard of the restaurant
2. Types of service
3. Décor and theme of the restaurant
4. Type of clientele
5. Durability of equipment
6. Ease of maintenance
7. Availability after stocks run out
8. Storage

9. Flexibility factors
10. Price factors
11. Standardization.

## Sources of Supply

Equipment is an expensive item, of high capital cost so that it is essential to obtain the equipment in the most effective way. There are basically three sources of supply.

1. **Manufacturer:** The advantage of dealing directly with the manufacturer of equipment is that the cost of items should be at their lowest. However, this may be affected by the manufacturers vested interest in supplying the equipment.
2. **Catering supplier or wholesaler:** Wholesalers have no vested interest in supplying one particular brand. They can advise the caterer as to the most suitable type of equipment for the particular operation.
3. **Leasing company:** Nearly all catering equipment need not be purchased at all. As practically every item may be hired from a leasing company. The main advantage of the leasing is that investment costs are reduced and equipment becomes an overhead.

## Equipment Stocks

The caterer must hold the stock level that will ensure a smooth running and efficient operation with the minimum of capital investment. Minimizing the total amount of equipment and also the variety of different items helps to reduce the amount of storage space required and reduced the time needed to take stock.

There will also be difference in the loss and breakage rates of items. Among cutlery items teaspoons are usually high on the list while tea cups are also vulnerable. In the old days and even today large hotels employe someone on a full-time basis to search through all the swill bins to look for items of equipment and the cost of the equipment recovered in this way more than paid for the person's wages.

Restaurant equipment can be divided into chinaware, glassware and tableware.

(a) **Tableware**: Tableware is a term which includes:

(i) *Flatware*: All form of spoon and fork.

(ii) *Cutlery*: Knives and other cutting implements.

(iii) *Hollow-ware*: Any item made from silver apart from flatware and cutlery e.g., teaspoon, milk jugs, sugar basins, oval flats.

Table services consists of the following items:

**Flatware/Cutlery**

When to use the following items:

(a) Soup spoon: Soup served in plates.

(b) Fish knives and forks: Fish/hors d' œuvres.

(c) Large knives and forks: Entrée/main course.

(d) Dessert spoons: All sweet served in plates/oeuf sur le plat.

(e) Desert spoons: soup served on cups/cereals.

(f) Small fruit knives and forks: Fresh fruit.

(g) Coffee spoons; coffee

(h) Teaspoons: tea/fruit cocktail/ice-cream served as "coupes"/grapefruit. Oeuf on cocote.

(i) Service spoons and forks: for service.

(j) Steak knife: steaks.

(k) Grapefruit knife: grapefruit

(l) Egg spoon: eggs

(m) Cheese knife: cheese.

**Hollow-ware**

(a) Soup tureens

(b) Individual soup bowls
(c) Trays
(d) Oval flat with lids
(e) Oval or round vegetable dishes with lids
(f) Oval or round under dish for vegetable
(g) Souffle cases
(h) Oval or round entrée dishes
(i) Oval or round dishes for entrée
(j) Round flats with covers
(k) Asparagus dish
(l) Water jugs
(m) Muffin dish
(n) Cocktail juice container.

**Silver for serving drinks**

(a) Salver for serving
(b) Salver for cleaning
(c) Ice tongs
(d) Ice buckets
(e) Champagne bucket with stand

**Still room silver**

(a) coffee pots
(b) hot milk jug (creamer)
(c) tea pots
(d) hot water jugs
(e) cream jugs (creamer)
(f) toast racks.

**Special tableware**

(a) sugar tongs
(b) asparagus tongs

(c) oyster forks
(d) finger bowls set of cruets
(e) ice cream scoops
(f) Sauce ladles
(g) Soup ladles
(h) Butter dishes
(i) Snail tong
(j) Snail fork
(k) Fondue fork
(l) Cavior knife
(m) Sundy spoon
(n) Ice cream spoon
(o) Pastry fork cum knife
(p) Corn or cop holder
(q) Lobster pick
(r) Butter knife
(s) Cheese knife
(t) Grape fruit spoon
(u) Nut cracker
(v) Gateaux slice
(w) Steak knife.

The majority of restaurant tables ware either plated silverware or stainless steel. Silverware often quoted as 20-25, or 30 year plate. This denotes the length of life of silverware. The length of life of silver also depends upon the weight of silver deposited. There are three standard grades of silver plate full standard plate triple plate and quadruple plate.

The minimum thickness of silver plating quoted should give a life of at least 20 years, depending on usage.

Plane cutlery and flat wares are more popular than patterned because they are cheaper and easier to keep clean.

Stainless steel flatware and cutlery are available in a variety of grades. The higher priced designs usually have incorporated in them allows of chromium and nickel. Stainless steel is finished by different degrees of polishing.

## B. Glassware

Glassware contributes to the appearance of the table and the overall attraction of the room. There are main two types of glassware lead crystal and soda lime. Lead crystal is the best quality and has a brilliant finish that enables it to be engraved or cut and polished. It is more expensive so that most glassware used in the restaurant is soda lime glass. The advantage of soda glass is that it is easily mass produced and the better quality soda glass is hard wearing and relatively resistant to impact and thermal shock.

When purchasing glassware following points should be considered: (i) there is a wide variety of different types and sizes of glassware and a strong tradition that certain types of alcoholic drinks should be served in specific type of glass, (ii) fitness for purpose is probably the most important criterion for glassware, and (iii) apart from these design features it is more a matter of aesthetic taste that determines what type of glass should be used. For instance, spirits with a mixer may be used in a Paris goblet, a tumbler or old fashioned glass.

| Glass | Sizes |
|---|---|
| Wine goblets | 14.20, 18.93, 22.72 cl (5, 6 2/3, 8 fl oz) |
| German/Alsace | 18, 23 cl (6, 8, fl oz) |
| Flute | 18, 23 cl (6, 8, fl oz) |
| Saucer champagne | 18, 23 cl (6, 8, fl oz) |
| Cocktail glasses | 4, 7 cl (2, 3, fl oz) |
| Sherry, port | 4.735 cl |
| High ball | 23, 28 cl (9, 10, fl oz) |
| Worthington | 28, 34 cl (10, 12 fl oz) |

| | |
|---|---|
| Larger glass | 28, 34 cl (10, 12, fl oz) |
| Brandy balloon | 23, 28 cl (9, 10 fl oz) |
| Liquor glass | 2.367 |
| Tumbler | |
| Beer | 25, 50 cl (1/2 1 pint) |

There are many standard patterns available to the caterer. Most manufacturers now supply hotel glassware in standard sizes for convenience of ordering, availability and quick delivery.

## Some tips on glassware

1. Glasses should be stored inverted in single rows with a paper on the shelf to avoid slippage.
2. Racks with individual compartments of reach glass is a better method for storage and transported. These racks should be plastic or rubber lined.
3. In a restaurant glasses must be transported on trays with a tray cloth to avoid slippage.
4. Glasses with a stem must be inverted and held by the stem.
5. Service glasses must be cleaned and hold against a light before use.

In many respects the quality of the glassware can best be judged by its price. A good quality glass should be hard wearing and perfectly clear without any air bubbles trapped in the glass and feel relatively heavy. It should have a steam for holding the wine glass so that the heat of one's hand does not affect the wine on tasting; there should be slight incurring lip to hold the aroma and it should be large enough to hold the particular wine being tasted.

## 3. CHINAWARE

The term china is used for crockery whether it is bone china, earthenware or vitrified-ware.

It is made of silica, soda ash and china clay, glazed to give a fine finish. It should be opaque and free from air bubbles. Chinaware can be found in different colours and designs which are always coated with glaze.

This is an important aspect in the presentation of the table. The china must blend in with the rest of the items on the table and also with the general décor of the establishment.

Today's more and more people are eating out and they like to see china which is cheerful in design and patterns similar to that used in their own homes.

Very few restaurants can afford to buy high quality china for normal days to day-to-day use, because of the high initial capital layout and replacement costs. The restaurateur, therefore, has to turn to what is termed earthenware. This has been vastly improved over the past few years both in appearance and durability.

When purchasing china following points should be considered:

1. Every item of earthenware should have a complete cover of glass to ensure a reasonable length of life.
2. China should have a rolled edge which gives added reinforcement at the edge.
3. The pattern should be under rather than on top of the glaze.

However, this demands additional glaze and finishing. Patterns on the top of the glaze will wear and discolour very quickly, therefore china with the pattern under the glaze is more expensive but is life will be longer.

Some manufacturers stamp the date, month and year on the base of the item. From this the life of china can be determined more accurately. Very often earthenware produced for catering purpose is given a trade name by the manufacturer to indicate its strength. Some examples of these are:

(a) Vitreous

(b) Vitrock

(c) Vitrex

(d) Vitresso

(e) Ironstone

(f) Vitrified

Among these vitrified ware is recognized to be the strongest, but this does not mean that every caterer buys vitrified hotelware as other factors apart from strength and economy are often taken into account.

There are various classifications of catering china. These are as follows:

**(a) Bone China**

This is a very fine and hard china and is very expensive. The decorations are to be found under the glaze only. The price of bone china puts it out of reach of the majority of everyday restaureurs, only a few of the top class hotels and restaurants would use it. The range of design, pattern and colour is very wide, and there is something to suit all the occasions and situations.

**(b) Stoneware**

This is a natural ceramic material, traditionally made in the United Kingdom. It is fired at a very high temperature about 122°C. It is shaped by traditional hand crafting techniques so there is a wide variety of shapes and finish available, it is extremely durable with high thermal and shock resistance. The price is slightly higher than earthenware due to long life guarantee.

**(c) Earthenware**

It is the cheapest and latest durable hotelware. Earthenware is particularly economical where it is in continuous use. 24 hours a day has heavy handling with a high turnover and where hygiene is particularly important of example motor way restaurant.

A domestic weight earthenware is also available, but this is lighter and thinner than the hotel earthenware. Because of its short life, lack of strength and possible high breakage rate it is not suitable for the average caterer, except the seaside restaurants.

### (d) Porcelain

Porcelain has a completely different composition with a semi-translucent body and has high resistance to chipping.

### Sizes

There are wide range of china items and their exact sizes vary according to the manufacturer and the design produced. As a guide the sizes are as follows:

| | |
|---|---|
| Side plate | 15 cm (6 in) diameter |
| Sweet plate | 18 cm (7 in) diameter |
| Fish plate | 20 cm (8 in) diameter |
| Soup plate | 20 cm (8 in) diameter |
| Joint plate | 25 cm (10 in) diameter |
| Cereal/sweet plate | 13 cm (5 in) diameter |
| Breakfast cup and saucer | 23-28 cl (6 2/3 fl oz) |
| | 18.93 cl (2 1/3 fl oz) |
| Tea cup and saucer | 9.47 cl (3 1/3 fl oz) |
| Coffee cup and saucer | 28.4 cl (1/2 pt) 56.8 cl (2 pt) |
| Tea pot | 85.2 cl 911/2 pt) 113.6 cl (2 pt) |

Other chinaware

Platter (oval plate)

Salad crescent

Hot water jugs

Coffee pots

Milk jugs

Cream jugs

Consome cup and saucer

Hot milk jugs

Sugar basin

Butter dishes

Ashtrays

Egg cups

Soup bowl/cup

Chinaware should be stored on shelves in piles of appropriately two dozen. Any higher may result in them toppling down. They should be stored at a convenient height for placing on and removing from the shelves without any fear of accident occurring. If possible keep covered to prevent dust and germs settling on the china.

### Some Tips on Chinaware

1. Vitrified chinaware is stronger.
2. It has a high breakage rate and therefore needs careful handling.
3. It should be stored in shelves.
4. It should be stored carefully so that it does not topple over.
5. It should be stored at a convenient height to avoid accidents.
6. It should be kept covered to avoid dust and germs.

## DISPOSABLE

The new improvement in the quality design and durability of disposable equipment has made its use much more common. In restaurants these equipment are also much acceptable to the public because of advesnt of fast food operations.

This includes:

1. Serviettes and napkins
2. Place mats and coasters
3. Slip cloth sand banqueting roll
4. Knives fork and spoons
5. Cups for beverages and glasses for drinks

6. Plates and dishes of all sizes

There are some advantages and disadvantages of disposable items such as:

**Advantages**

1. It reduces the number of staff and amount of equipment needed for washing up.
2. Improves the standard of hygiene.
3. It reduces the amount of capital investment in the long-term.
4. Eliminates losses due to breakages and pilferage.
5. It takes up less storage space and easier to transport.

**Disadvantages**

1. Customer acceptability may be poor.
2. Disposables can be more expensive than some conventional equipment.
3. Backup quantities are required.
4. There is heavy reliance on supply and delivery time.

## LINEN

Linen is perhaps one of the most costly items within overheads, and therefore, its control is of utmost importance. The generally recognized routine in majority of the restaurant is an exchange of one.

This is one of the most important jobs in the preparation and is usually undertaken by one of the chefs de range. A surplus linen stock is usually held in the food service area in case of emergency.

At the end of the service dirty linen is send to the house-keeping department to be exchanged for clean.

In general terms the factors to consider when choosing a table cloth and napkins are as follows. Appearance colour and pattern should be integrated with the décor and style of the restaurant, durability and resistance to wear are important and so the ease and cost of cleaning is also important. The quality of the product particularly in the case of linen, the edging of cloths should remembered.

Linen should be stored on paper lined shelves, the correct sizes together and with the inverted fold facing outwards, which facilitates counting and control. If the linen is not stored in a cupboard it should be covered to avoid dust settling on it.

There are many qualities of linen in present day use, from the fine Irish linen and cotton to the synthetic materials such as nylon and viscose, the type of linen used would depend on the class of establishment, type of clientele and cost involved and the style of menu and service to be offered. The main items of linen normally to be found are:

(a) Table cloths

(b) Slip cloths

(c) Serviette

(d) Buffet cloths

(e) Trolly cloth and side board cloths

(f) Waiters cloths or service cloths

(g) Tea and glass cloths.

## SERVICE EQUIPMENT

Service equipment means those equipments which are handled by the staff only. Service equipment includes: service spoon and fork, ladle slicer and so on.

These equipments are used in silver service or guerdion restaurant as well as in self-service and tray systems restaurant also. These service utensils are sued as a precise means of portion control as well as a means of serve the food.

**SPECIAL FOOD**

**Service equipment**

(a) Ashtrays
(b) Bread boats
(c) Flower vases
(d) Fruit stands
(e) Tea strainers
(f) Candle stands
(g) Wine cradles
(h) Wine funnels
(i) Drip bowl
(j) Sundae coups
(k) Cheese dish
(l) Oil, cinegar bottle
(m) Oval au gratin
(n) Cocotte dish
(o) Jam pot
(p) Toothpick stand
(q) Straw stand
(r) Chaffing dishes
(s) Burner for dishes
(t) Copper pans
(u) Irish coffee burners
(v) Shaker
(w) Stirring spoon and bowl
(x) Punch bowl and ladle
(y) Supreme bowl.

Before purchasing service utensils following points should be considered:

1. Service utensil in the shelve be of similar, if not identical quality, to the tableware in sue.

   For example silver service equipment should be sued with silver cutlery.

2. Silver-service restaurants should have at least three service spoons and forks for every cover to ensure that staff always have equipment available for service. One of the basic standards of good silver service is that different food items are served with a different spoon and fork.
3. Ladles should have the correct capacity with deep rather than shallow bowls.
4. Items of specialist equipment such as asparagus trays, grape scissors and so on should be available so long as they are likely to be used on a regular basis.

## OTHER EQUIPMENT

Apart from the above-mentioned equipment, there are some other equipment are also found in a restaurant such as, table, chair, sideboard, tray etc.

### A. Tables

Tables generally come in three shapes: round, square and rectangular. A restaurant may have a mixture of shapes to give variety of tables of all one shape according to the shape of the room and the style of service being offered. These tables have two or four seats, sometime two tables may be pushed together to seat larger parties, luncheons, dinner, wedding etc. by using extensions a variety of shapes may be obtained allowing full use of the room and getting the maximum number of covers in the minimum space.

### Sizes

**Square:** 76 cm (2 ft 6 in) square to seat two people.... 1 m (3 ft) square to seat four people.

**Round:** 1 m (ft) in diameter to seat four people... 1.52 m (5 ft) in diameter to seat eight people.

**Rectangular:** 137 cm × 76 cm (4ft 6 in × 2 ft 6 in) to eat four people to which extensions would be added for larger parties.

## B. Chairs

Chairs come in an enormous range of designs, materials and colours to suit all situations and occasions. Because of the wide range of styles the chairs vary height and width but as a guide a chair seat is 46 cm (18 in) from the ground. Height from the ground to the top of the back is 1 m (39 in) and the depth from the front edge of the seat to the back of the chair is 46 cm (18 in).

Additional purchasing considerations are the size, height shape and the variety of seating required-banquette, armchair, straight backed padded chairs, giving the guest a choice.

## C. Sideboards

The style and design of a sideboard vary from one restaurant to another. It is depend upon:

...The style of service and the menu offered.

...The number of waiters working from one sideboard or work station.

...The number of table to be served from one sideboard.

The amount of equipment it is expected to hold.

## D. Trays

Trays are used throughout food service operations, they are used for carrying equipment and food to service table.

Additional considerations in the purchase of trays includes:

(a) Lightness and straighness - trays should be carried out when fully loaded and not become misshapen when weight is placed upon them.

(b) Stackability
(c) Heat resistance
(d) Ease of cleaning
(e) Resistance to slippage
(f) Resistance to damage from split items or damp.

## MAINTENANCE AND CARE OF EQUIPMENT

The maintenance and care of all food service equipment is a major task of restaurant operation. The restaurant needs effective and efficient cleaning facilities and procedures because:

1. in the restaurant the restaurateur has a duty in law as well as a moral obligation to ensure that food items are served in hygienic manner.
2. the appearance and polish of table siting and equipment is large so that effective working life must be maximized by ensuring proper use and care.

The items that must be cared for metal, ceramic glass and wood.

### 1. Metal

Metal items can be washed by machine although forks and cutlery may be more effectively washed by hand. Stainless steel should be thoroughly rinsed to prevent pitting, while self-drying is to be avoided since it can lead to spotting. Stainless steel will also be permanently discoloured if placed in a naked flame or at temperature above 204°C. Metal equipment must also be regularly polished to prevent tarnishing.

### 2. Glassware

Glassware can also be washed by machine. Glasses should be washed in warm water with a detergent specifically designed for glassware and rinsed in clear warm water and then inverted on a surface that allows the free circulation of air into the bowl of the glass. They may then be polished with a linen glass cloth to ensure a proper sparkle. Where glasses are in frequent use it may be advisable to store them in shelves to avoid dust and debris falling into stored glassware. Glassware, not in use, should always be stored in compartmentalized storage containers or cardboards boxes.

### 3. Wood

Cheese boards salad bowls and so on are of wooden equipment. They should never be machine washed, but always rinsed in tepid water and dried thoroughly. Oiling the wood with edible oil also helps to improve the appearance of wood as well as to prevent cracking.

### 4. Ceramics

Ceramic equipment may be washed in dish washing machine, although, it is likely that any on-glaze decoration will eventually be worm away with repeated washing.

These machines also depend on a detergent that produces little or no foam but which is more corrosive than other type of detergents. For this reason it is recommended that wash cycle temperature should not exceed 60°C.

Crockery that is in constant use should be stored in shelves in the serving area. It should not be stored in hot plates or plate warming cupboards or dispenser but should be placed in them approximately one hour before service. Crockery should be placed in proper containers with each items separated from the next to it by cardboard or paper filler and each box clearly marked to identify what to contains.

## DESIGN AND CONSTRUCTION OF EQUIPMENT

Equipment must be so designed, constructed and finished that it can be easily cleaned and disinfected. Equipment such as slicers, mixers and processors etc., which do require dismantling for cleaning must be easy to take apart and reasonable, all edge must be smooth and rounded, rough and sharp edges constitutes a serious hazard to cleaners.

The buyer should also observe that all joints and welds are smooth and thus nuts, bolts and screw heads are absent from food contact surfaces.

## CONCLUSION

Restaurant equipment is a major capital and operating cost of the business. Very often the people employed to handle and clean the equipment are untrained and unskilled, therefore it is essential that as part of their induction or training they are made aware of the cost of the equipment. It is common practice in fact, especially in large restaurants to display prominently in the wash up and storage areas the main items of crockery along with their price to reinforce daily this fact. In addition to keeping the running costs to a minimum, great case must be exercised in the selection of equipment to ensure value for money and a quality of product suited to the style of the establishment. By establishing the correct leaves of stock for each items of equipment, capital investment can be minimized, but this must not be at the expense of operational efficiency.

## CHAPTER 5

# RESTAURANT DECORATION

In a restaurant on a client first impression is of great importance. A customer may be gained or lost on these impressions alone. The creation of atmosphere by the right choice of decoration is therefore a contributing factor to the success of the restaurant. A careful selection of items in terms of shape, design and colour enhance the overall décor or theme and contributes towards a feeling of total harmony. The general considerations on décor are:

1. Appropriateness to the type and style of operation.
2. Sufficient flexibility especially where the shape has multi-usages e.g., function rooms.
3. Functional reliability.
4. Ease of maintenance including refurbishment.
5. Industrial rather than domestic quality.
6. Ease of cleaning and general house-keeping needs.

The decoration of restaurant is a combination of various aspects such as:

1. Lighting
2. Colour
3. Furniture
4. China

5. Earthenware
6. Stoneware
7. Porcelain
8. Tableware and
9. Glassware

**1. Lighting**

The atmosphere created through lighting in a restaurant is very important. Ideally it should be flattering both to the faces of the diners and the food before them, conducive to pleasure and conversation.

In the past, decorators have tended to neglect lighting, concentrating instead on the colours and patterns of a fabrics and wall papers and the styling and arrangement of pieces of furniture.

By and by, the situation become changed. Developments in lighting unlike other areas of interior decoration depends on development in technology. While todays lighting designers tends of two work with light itself creating fittings to produce chosen effects the designers of the post had little control over the quality of the light and mostly concentrated on making and mostly concentrated on making decorative objects. It is important for a restaurant to begin planning a scheme by carefully assessing the different types of ambience required.

Modern designs tend towards a versatile system of lighting by which a food and beverage service area may have bright lighting at lunch time and a more diffused form of lighting in the evening. It is also an advantage to be able to change the colours of the lights for special functions, cabarets etc. The restaurateur must find a lighting scheme which will attract and please as many people as possible, basically restaurants may select from two main kinds of interior illumination - incendescent and fluorescent. The former is warmer in colour but less efficient to operate than fluorescent bulbs of the same wattage. Incandescent can be easily directed to specific spots such as a particular table or pointing, however, its warmth appeal can cause a colour problem. It may makes surroundings cheerful and inviting, but the yellowish hue of its bulbs, especially when dimmed, makes meets and lettuce appear muddy colour. Warmer bulbs such as pink light make red meats look natural but salads unappetizing.

The main virtue of fluorescent lighting is a lower operating cost, but it is often criticized for given a dull an lifeless illumination. Food may be made to look appealing by using blue white light from fluorescent fixtures but the blue white glow may also detract from a warm romantic atmosphere.

So a balance is essential for both warmth and good food appearance, many experts recommended a lighting system made up of 70% cool or blue white fluorescent bulbs and 30% incandescent. This will give mood and a pleasant and natural appearance for food. But it should be never forgotten that a restaurant needs more than proper décor lighting, functional lighting is a must, meaning proper illumination for cooks to prepare food, staff to serve it and eat it. Functional lighting may amount to as much as 75% of a restaurants total lighting system. In the dining room two basic areas require functional lighting, the table and the room as a whole. The aim, therefore, is to mix the right blend of décor and functional lighting at the lowest possible cost. Now-a-days, CFL bulbs are widely used.

Table lighting is most flattering to guests when it shines down from the ceiling. Incandescent ceiling lights serve the purpose well here; care must be taken, however, to ensure that the bulbs used do not give off too bright a light creating too much contrast between dark and light spots. Clean and well polished silver, glassware and china on a dining table or a well polished reflective table top in the lounge will gently bounce light upwards, acting as a softener to overhead lights.

There are a number of purposes which are served by the functional lighting in the dining room. They are as follows:

(a) Fixtures directing light onto ceilings and walls indicates to guess the dimensions of the room together with any special attraction such as picture old oak beams and so on. Low wattage incandescent bulbs are best suited for this purpose.

(b) It projects a subdued atmosphere with contrasts between bright and dark areas and table tops capturing much of the light whilst ceiling sand upper walls remain dark.

Generally, it is accepted that the food and beverages service needs to select for its own purposes the correct mix of décor and functional lighting. Brighter lights subconsciously tell the guests to sit more quickly and leave.

Thus, the lighting system is of much importance in a restaurant decoration, it is the heart of restaurant decoration.

## 2. COLOUR

It is well-known that there is a close relationship between food and beverage colour. It should not be overlooked. For a restaurant a few special colours are regarded as most acceptable, pink, peach, pale yellow, clear green, beige, blue and turquoise. These colours reflect the natural colours found in good and well presented food stuffs. The specific aim of the proprietor must be borne in mind when considering a new colour scheme. These would include the type of restaurant and style of services. The colour scheme should assist in reflecting the character of the restaurant, for a restaurant colour scheme should be considered together with lighting scheme because a badly planned lighting system can easily spoil a well designed colour scheme. It should be remembered that the restaurant surroundings can contribute a great deal towards the price quality relationships in the minds of potential guests. It is realized that what may be suitable for a fast food operation would be entirely unsuitable for a restaurant operation catering for an executive market. A bar may be bright illumination with light colour on the walls but food service areas are better with dinner illuminations and warmly coloured walls giving a more relaxed and welcoming atmosphere. Colour should also contribute to a feeling of cleanliness.

It is clear that colour is an important factor as lighting which reflect the character of the operation.

### 3. FURNITURE

Furniture plays a great role in restaurant decoration. Within the restaurant, furniture varies according to an establishment's nature. Floors may be covered with costly carpeting polished wood or in simpler restaurants, in linoleum or plastic floor covering, chairs similarly vary in upholstery and covering according to the degree of luxury sought, items such as curtains, table lamps and other lighting fittings are similarly variable in quality and design.

Furniture should be according to the needs of the establishment. Very often by using different materials designs and finished and by careful arrangement one can change the atmosphere and appearance of the food services areas to suit different occasions.

Generally, wood is used in dining room furnitures. There are various types of wood and wood grain finished each suitable to blend with a particular décor. Wood is strong and rigid and resists wear and stains. It is found as the principal materials in chairs and tables in use in all food and beverage service areas with exception of canteens, some staff dining rooms are cafeterias. Todays apart of wooden furnitures more metals mainly aluminium and aluminium plates steel or brass are gradually being introduced into restaurants, aluminium is light weight, hard wearing and has a variety of finished, it is easily cleaned and the cost is reasonable. It is very common in a restaurant to find a wooden topped table with a metal base of the frame of a chair being light weight metal with a plastic finish for the seat and back.

Formic or plastic coated table tops may be found in many restaurants, these are easily cleaned, hard wearing and eliminate the use of linen. The table top comes in a variety of colours and designs suitable for all situations.

Plastics and fibreglass are also being used extensively to produce dining room chairs. These materials are easily moulded into a single piece, seat and back to fit the body contours. As these are durable, easily cleaned, light weight, may be stacked, available in a lager range of colours and designs and relatively inexpensive so they are useful for a small type of restaurant.

Furniture purchasing is the responsibility of management. There are points which must be considered when purchasing equipment furniture for a restaurant. They are as follows:

1. *Design:* It includes functional quality such as:
   (a) Durability
   (b) Ease of cleaning
   (c) Ease of storage
   (d) Colour suitability
2. *Style*: Its appraisal and reappraisal in terms of customers, menu and form of service.
3. *Budget*: that is funds for initial purchase and subsequential upkeep and/or replacement.
4. *Flexibility in use*: For example cutlery size afford no knives and spoons suitable for varied purposes.
5. Type of service to be offered
6. Type of customers
7. Ease of maintenance
8. Stackability
9. Availability in the future-replacement

10. Rate of breakage in china
11. Psychological effect on guest
12. Shape
13. Storage
14. Delivery item.

**Chairs:** Chairs come in an enormous range of designs, materials and colours to suite all situations and occasions. As chairs vary in height and width due to range of their styles it is sufficient to that, as a chair seat is 46 cm form the ground, and minimum of 46 cm wide. The height form the ground to the top of the back is one metre (39 in) and the depth from the front edge of the seat to the back of the chair is 46 cm. A leather or wool fabric is much easier to sit on than PVC which tends to make one uncortable around the back and seat.

**Tables:** There are three accepted shapes of tables: round, square and rectangular. A restaurant may have a mixture of shapes to give variety. These table will seat tow or four people and two tables may be push together to seat large parties or extensions may be provided in order to cope with special parties, luncheons, dinners wedding etc., by using these extensions correctly a variety of shape, may be obtained allowing full use of the room, and getting the maximum number of covers in the minimum space. In many, instances the tabletop may be found to have a plasticised back or green booze covering which is heat resistant, non-slip, so the table cloth will knot slide about as it would on a polished wooden top table and deadens the sound of china and cutlery being laid. (For china, earthenware, stoneware, porcelain, tableware and glassware see Chapter 4.)

## INTERIOR DECORATION

The interior decoration of a restaurant will contributes greatly to the success of a food service outlet.

It has both capital and running costs.

*Capital costs*: The investment in creating the right interior must be such that a satisfactory return on capital will be achieved within a prescribed period of time. Such investment is only justified if sales and turnover consequently increased substantially in order to pay back this investment.

*Running costs*: The design of the interior will also affect the running costs of the operation, some these can easily be established. Energy use i.e., heating and lighting, cleaning costs of floors wall surfaces etc.

## REPLACEMENT COSTS AND DEPRECIATION

### Factor affecting décor

There are mainly five factors which are responsible for affecting the décor in restaurants. They are as follows:

***(a) Market profile:*** The type of customer using the establishment according to such criteria as age income level, frequency of visit and so on.

***(b) Operational planning:*** The maximizing of operational efficiency by the accurate positioning of every element in the design.

***(c) Maintenance:*** The incorporation of features that will reduce running costs and minimize maintenance.

***(d) Style of restaurants:*** Design will reflect the function and style of the unit, as well as the menu of specialties of the operation.

***(e) Life expectancy:*** The length of time that the décor will expected to last until it replaced.

### Elements of interior design

There are mainly three elements relating with interior decoration of a restaurant.

**(a) Colour:** The colours used in the décor of the room can have several effects for example dark colours make a room appear smaller than it is, while bright colour expand it.

Blue is a 'cold' colour while red is 'warm'. Similarly it has shown that the blue end to the spectrum will produce in people a desire to withdraw whereas the red end to the spectrum induces feelings of expansion and sociability.

**(b) Patterns:** Patterns too can affect people and great care must be taken to ensure that patterns are well established. At first everything must blend together to form a whole. People have an instinctive desire for conformity and uniformity, for instance most people will straighten a picture if it is crooked or will straighten the cutlery on a table in a restaurant. Secondly too many pattern in wall paper can be distracting rather like sitting inside a kaleidoscope. Lastly patterned, wall paper can make a room seem smaller with large patterns, taller with striped patterns, and so on.

**(c) Texture:** The texture of wall hangings, curtains floors and furnishing also contribute to the customer sense of security. According to Newell, "The use of fabrics in relation to the other decorative features is one of the basic principles of design and is important to the customer, not only because of its visual impression but because he finds it more pleasurable to touch than hard walls or wood surfaces.

## CONCLUSIONS

It is quite true that the atmosphere created by wells integrated interior will contribute greatly to the success of a food service outlet. Design, furniture and décor are the important part of catering operation which create the image of the establishment and ensure its smooth operation. Restaurants manager must do their part in maintaining this image by ensuring that the intentions of the designer are recognized and the maintenance of furnishings and fittings in carried out irregularly. Relatively small points such as replacing light bulbs as soon as they wear out with a bulb of an identical design and wattage may appear trivial but if the organization has paid a designer a considerable sum of money to develop the décor than the operators must be prepared to accept this expert advice. Likewise, a shabby of scruffy interior will not attract customer. The restaurant manage must supervise the regular cleaning of all furnishing and furniture making sure the cleaning operative are using the correct cleaning agents and materials.

# CHAPTER 6

# MEALS AND MENU PLANNING

## ORIGIN OF MENU AND MENU PLANNING OBJECTIVE

A menu is a list of prepared dished of food which are available to a customer, and its content and presentation should attract the customer and represent value for money.

Originally the 'bill of fare' as it is termed in English or 'menu' in French was not presented at the table. The banquet consisted of only two courses each made of a variety of dishes, anything from 10-40 in number. The first 10-40 dishes were placed on the table before the diners entered - hence the word *entrée* these when consumed were removed or relieved by 10-40 other dishes hence the word relieves and removes.

It is said that in the year 1541 Duke Henry of Brunswick was seen to refer to a long slip of paper. On being asked what he was looking at he said it was a form of programme do the dishes, and by reference to it he could see what was coming and reserve his appetite accordingly. Thus, we may presume that the menu developed from some such an event.

The bill of fare was very large and was placed at the end of the table for everyone to read. As time progressed the menu became smaller and increased in quantity allowing a number of copies per table. Depending on the establishment and the occasion the menu may be plain or artistic in its presentation.

Menu planning is one of the most important jobs of a caterer and there are a number of factors that must be taken into consideration before any menu is written. These factors are as follows:

***(a) The kind of menu:*** It must be clearly understood what kind of menu is required whether a special party menu, table d'hote or a la carte.

(i) *Special party menu*: These are menus for banquets and parties of all kinds.

(ii) *Table d'hote*: This is a set menu forming a complete meal at a set price. A choice of dishes may be offered at all courses; the choice and number of dishes will usually be limited.

(iii) *A la carte*: this is menu with all the dishes individually priced. The customer can therefore compile his own menu.

***(b) The season of the year:*** If menus have to be compiled for a long time in advance of the actual date of production the season of the year should be considered. It is necessary because the weather may be hot, cold or mild and certain dishes which would be acceptable in hot weather would be most unsuitable in cold weather. Apart from this reason seasonal foods should be included in menus where possible as they are usually in good supply of good quality and a reasonable price.

***(c) The capabilities of the kitchen staff:*** The capabilities of the cooks should be also considered. There are many excellent cooks male of female, whose training is such that they can cope with simple dishes but who might be at a lose if asked to produce highly complicated foreign dishes. On the other hand, if a staff of well trained cooks capable of a good standard of international cookery is available, they should be given a chance to produce dishes that can express their skill and pride of craftsmanship.

(d) ***Size and equipment of kitchen:*** The size and equipment of kitchen should also be considered, a good cook will usually manage to produce a required meal somehow in spite of any shortcomings of space or equipment. Nevertheless the writer of menus should be aware of such deficiencies and be vary of putting on dishes that might be difficult to produce because of shortages. Care should be taken to see that the method of cooking is not repeated otherwise certain pieces of equipment can be overloaded; for example, steamer.

(e) ***Capabilities of serving staff:*** The ability of persons who serves the meal should be considered. If the standard of the waiter is of the highest order than a high standard of well presented and garnished dishes can be used because the caterer can be sure that the prepared food will be correctly shown to the customer. If the waiters are untrained, care should be taken in the selection of dishes.

(f) ***Price of menu:*** The proposed charge per head is obviously an important factor to consider when selecting food for any menu when the caterer is asked to produce a meal to sell at a modest price per head, he cannot consider expensive foods.

(g) ***Type of customers:*** The type of customers to be served can sometimes affect the choice of foods. So the caterer should keep in mind their types as there are certain foods which would suit one group but not necessarily the others.

(h) ***Supplies:*** When considering foods for a menu it is sound policy to think of part prepared, ready prepared, and deep frozen food.

If large stocks of food are held, care should be taken where possible, to use foods on the menu which are already in store before ordering fresh supplies.

The cold room or refrigerator should be inspected to see if there are many cooked food that may be incorporated into menu's. This is an important point and as there are many ways in which cooked food can be used to produce attractive dishes.

***(i) Balance:*** This is particularly important when compiling special party menus and the following points should be considered:

1. *Repetition of ingredients* - Never repeat the basic ingredients on one menu. For example if mushrooms tomatoes, peas bacon etc., are used in one course of a menu then they should not reappear in any other course of the same menu.
2. *Repetition of colour* - Where possible avoid repetition of colour.
3. *Repetition of words* - Avoid repeating the same words on a menu.
4. *Overall balance of a menu* - If many courses are to be served, care should be taken to see that they vary form dishes of a light nature to those of a more substantial nature and finish up with light dishes.
5. *Texture of course* - Regard should be given to the texture of courses; some food should be soft, some should require chewing crunching, biting, some should be swallowed and so on.
6. *Seasonings* - If strong seasoning like onion, garlic of pungent herbs such as thyme, sagea or bay leaf are used, ensure that they are not repeated in more that one course.
7. *Sauces* - If different sauces are served on one menu the foundation of the sauces should vary e.g., demi glace, veloute tomato, butter thickened, arrowroot or cornflower thickened.
8. *Garnishes* - If traditional names are used for garnishes than the garnishes must be correct and they should bot be repeated.

9. *Food values* - Special attention should be paid, however, to the nutritioned balance of meals for people engaged in light or heavy work. It is usual to prepares such menus a week or two in advance and it necessary to see that the food provided over the period is satisfactory from the point of food value.

***(j)*** **Colour**: This is a most important factor to consider in the presentation of food. The sensible use of colour will always help the eye appeal of a dish. If it is sometimes necessary to use a little artificial colouring in order to finish certain foods correctly, care must be taken to see that these colours are used in moderation. Deep vivid colouring of any food should be avoided; the aim should be to use natural tints.

Plate appeal in term which refers to the appearance of a course when it is served on a plate. The attractive appearance of each course is essential to the successful meal and foods of each course is essential to the successful meal and foods such as carrot, tomato, peas, watercress, parsley, truffis, oranges, cherries etc., can give colour to the dullest coloured dishes.

***(k)*** ***Wording of menus***: Following points should be considered before writing a menu:

1. Consider the customer to be feel and select language which will be easily understood.
2. If using French for menu writing give an English translation as a simple description under or by the side of each dish.
3. Having selected all language for the menu avoid using a mixture of language on the same menu except in the case or certain national dishes which are best kept in the language of the country of origin.

4. When writing menus a decision has to be made regarding the use of capital letters for the name of dishes.

As we say above the menus, the most important part of the caterers work and its compilation is regarded as an art. The aim of the menu planning is to give the customer what he wants and not, what the caterer thinks. In general, it is better to offer fewer dishes of a good standard rather than having a wide choice of dishes of mediocre quality.

Menu is a link between the establishment and the customer. Thus, this important link - the menu should be compiled by a number of people in liaison with one another, namely the chef de cuisine, maitre d'hotel and the manager. In this way the menu should list a well-balanced appetizing meal.

## BASIC TYPE OF MENU

There are many types of function carried out at different times in various forms of establishments. There are only two basics classes of menu namely:

1. Table d'hote,
2. A la carte, and
3. The carte du jour menu.

### 1. Table d'hote

The definition of table d' hote menu is covered with the following points:

(a) The menu has a fixed number of courses.

(b) There is a choice within each course.

(c) The selling of the menu is fixed.

(d) The dishes provided will all be ready at a set time.

This type of many may be offered by itself or in conjunction with as a la carte du jour menu. It is more popular and simpler form of menu, being easier to control and operate and giving less wastage of food. The set price of table d'hote menu is charged whether or not the full menu is consumed.

**2. A la carte**

The term a la carte may be translated as 'from the card'. An a la carte menu may be defined by the following points:

(a) It gives a full list of all the dishes that may be prepared by the establishment.

(b) Each dish is priced separately.

(c) A certain waiting item has to be allowed for each dish.

(d) It is cooked to order.

This type of menu may be offered on its own in a first class establishment or in conjunction with a form of table d'hote or carte due jour menu in a smaller catering establishment.

The dishes on an a la carte menu may be changed according to season - oysters, melon, asparague, game but each item will remain individually priced.

Another form of a la carte menu is the plat du jour or 'specialist of the house'. This consists of dishes individually priced which may be changed from day to day or remain for a certain period of time. The dishes concerned here are normally main courses. Usually the plat du jour supports or is supported by a table d'hote menu, and in some cases a limited a la carte menu. This form of a la carte menu will normally be offered in a medium size establishment.

**3. The carte du jour menu**

Many large hotels and restaurants carry this form of menu which is printed daily, one for lunch and one for dinner. This form of menu combines the table d'hote, a la carte and plat du jour menu each being priced according to its type.

Smaller establishments for economy reasons may offer this form of menu or just an a la carte menu for a number of weeks until the season change. Where only a table d'hote menu is offered it will normally be altered day-by-day.

## SEQUENCE OF COURSES AND PLANNING MENUS

The number of courses offered at luncheon, dinner or supper varies according to the types of restaurant, numbers to the catered and for prices charged. The 'build up' from appetizer to heavier dishes has been indicated for the sequence of dishes. This applies no matter how long or short a menu may be.

At one time, the meal's quality tended to be judged by the number of courses served.

In those days the order in which dishes are served is:

1. Huitres (oysters)
2. Potage (soup)
3. Hors d'œuvre (dainty fish)
4. Poisson (fish)
5. Entrée
6. Roti (roast)
7. Sorbet (punch)
8. Gibier (game)
9. Dessert
10. Coffee

Today the normal order in which dishes are served is:

1. Hors d' oeuvre
2. Soups
3. Eggs
4. Farinaceous

5. Fish
6. Entrée
7. Joint
8. Vegetables
9. Poultry or game
10. Salads
11. Sweets
12. Savouries
13. Dessert
14. Coffee.

**Sequence of courses at luncheon menu**

Luncheon menus do not follow a pattern as strict as those for dinner. They are usually short with fewer courses but offering more choice within each course. Emphasis is on stews, roast joints, grilled meats cold buffers and hot puddings.

Many dishes served for lunch are considered to be less fine and therefore beneath the standard require for dinner. Luncheon is normally a more quickly served meal. Dinner taken more leisurely allow time to prepare more complicated a la carte dishes.

**Sequence of courses at dinner menu**

Dinner regarded as the principal meal affords an opportunity for artistry in menu composition. At dinner guests have come for relaxation, to enjoy food, dining rituals and the atmosphere.

Usually, with item to spare customers can better appreciate a longer menu with a choice of more exotic or esteemed dishes. At dinner, dishes chosen may be classical. Menu language should be perfect. Menus will often be a la carte but many will be compiled for functions. The same basic rules apply in composing a meal.

## DINNER MENU - SEQUENCE OF DISHES

| *Order of courses* | | *Dishes available* | *Notes* |
|---|---|---|---|
| 1. First Course | (a) | Cocktails: fruit, shellfish | General: formal dinners used to open with soup but single hors d'œuvres and appetizers, especially the fine and costly ones, increasingly appear |
| | (b) | Fruit: melon, fresh figs, avocado pears | |
| | (c) | Delicacies: caviar, oysters, seagulls eggs, snails, potted shrimps, prawns, frogs' legs, foie gras, timbales | |
| | (d) | Smoked: salmon, trout, ham, salami, sausages, sprats | Traditionally these were not served cold at dinner, though recently appearing on menus |
| | (e) | Hors d'oeuvre varie: hot and cold | |
| 2. Soup | (a) | Clear: Consomme and consome based, turtle, petite marmite, etc. | |
| | (b) | Thick: creams, veloutes, bisques | |
| 3. Fish | (a) | Deep poached: salmon, turbot, blue trout (truite au bleu) | |
| | (b) | Shallow poached: prime fish, with classical garnishes and sauces | Including cold consommes |
| | (c) | Hot shellfish: lobster, crab, crayfish, crawfish scampi, scallops, (rarely mussels) | |
| | (d) | Meuniere: sole, trout, salmon, red mullet | With garnishes (other fish appear rarely fried or grilled for dinner) |
| | (e) | Fried: whitebait and, nowadays, seampi, sole (sometimes en goujon) | |
| | (f) | Grilled: lobster, sole, salmon, red mullet, turbot | |

(contd.)

| Order of courses | | Dishes available | Notes |
|---|---|---|---|
| | (g) | Cold: salmon, salmon trout, trout, sole, usually in aspic | |
| 4. Entree Lighter dinner dishes invariably garnished and usually individually porioned | (a) | The sautes: tournedos, noisettes, cutlets, veal collops, etc. (not Viennoise), saute of chicken, etc., Filets mignons, sweetbreads\ kidneys, saddle of hare | Never stews or ragouts served with a minimum of rich sauce |
| | (b) | Vol au vent, fried chicken | |
| | (c) | Hot : mousse, timbales, souffles meat) Where an entree is followed by a releve, vegetables and potatoes are not served separately | |
| 5. Releve Large dishes (Not roasts, grills or the smaller entrees) which usually have to be carved | (a) | The poeles: chicken (casserole, cocotte, poele), saddle of lamb, veal, whole fillet, sirloin (usually boned as contrefilet) | Butcher's meat which, in classic menus, never appears as a roast at dinner, is poele to serve as a releve. Normally garnished. |

## Sequence of Courses of Supper Menu

Today, supper menus are usually a la carte, with a customer choosing as many or as a few dishes as desired, only occasionally, there will be found a set of supper menu. At supper there are fewer courses. Dishes are lighter than those served at dinner.

Normally set supper menus consists of three courses only, with many choices in the second or main courses. A la carte menu may include egg dishes when informal and consumed some time after supper meal time, towards the end of a floor show or during dancing.

## Sequence of courses of 'Dating Menus'

A breakfast menu is usually dated only for special parties or events. Table d'hote luncheon dinners and suppers which change daily, should always bear the date. This is usually printed or typed at the bottom right-end, corner.

## TYPES OF MENUS

### (a) Indian

Fruit juice

Or

Eight boy curry (shrimp, beef or chicken curry with rice, eight condiments from which the guest makes his choice)

Or

Hard cooked egg, chopped

Or

chutney

Or

fresh grated coconut

Or

Green peppers, diced

Or becon, crisp, crumbled

Or current jelly

Or

Pickles, chopped

Or

Salted peanuts chopped

Or

Rice

Mixed vegetable salad French dressing

Or

French bread and butter

Or

Salad

Or

Ice cream

Or

Kulfi

Coffee, tea

**(b) English type menu.**

Egg mayonnaise

Or

Half fresh grape fruit

Or

Chilled fruit juice

Or

Cream of onion soup

Or

Consomme brucise.

Deep fried fillets of haddock only

Or

Toast leg of lamb, mind sauce

Or

Madras curry chicken, Patna rice

Creamed sweds, garden peas

Or

Boulangers and parmentiere potatoes

Ox tongue, cheese roast hem, grosvenour pie

Or

Salmon mayonnaise, roast beef

Or

Fresh salads in season

Black current stream cheese cake

Baked rice pudding

Or

Gooseberry pie and custard sauce

Or

Assorted ice cream

Or

Cheese and biscuits.

**SUPPER MENU - SEQUENCE OF DISHES**

| *Order of courses* | | *Dishes available* | *Notes* |
|---|---|---|---|
| 1. First Course | (a) | Cocktails: Particularly, shellfish | |
| | (b) | Delicacies: caviar, oysters, sea-gulls, eggs, snails, potted shrimps, etc. | |
| | (c) | Smoked: salmon, trout, ham, salami, sausage | |
| | (d) | Consomme and consomme base soups, particularly turtle and soupe a loignon | |
| Second Course | | Fish: deep poached: salmon and particularly smoked haddock dishes. | |
| | | hot shellfish: the lighter dishes only | |
| | | fried: whitebait, scampi, sole (sometimes). | Crabs rather than lobster |
| | | grilled: kippers, salmon, sole (sometimes) | |
| | | Entrees: the sautes as at dinner (not hare) but with simpler garnishes. | Kippers particularly in the early hours of morning. |
| | | Calves liver, minced chicken dishes | |
| | | Roasts: very seldom, and then the smaller birds like quail. woodcock, snipe | |
| | | Grills: all grilled meats including chicken and kebab and other skewered grills, kidneys | Grills particularly featured at supper |

| | | |
|---|---|---|
| Served with vegetables | Where applicable, but most supper dishes of fish, well garnished entrees or grills do not require a dish of vegetables to accompany them | |
| and potatoes or | Most varieties are served but frequently fried kinds for grills | |
| Cold Buffet | Cold fish: salmon, lobster, trout, crab, prawns. | |
| | Cold meat: all the cold joints and poultry, game, pies | |
| served with | terrines | |
| salad | Most varieties of salad. | |
| Thid course | | |
| Sweets | Hot: souffles, pancakes, fritters | |
| | Cold: souffles, bombes, biscuit glace, fruit coupes | |
| | (perhaps accompanied by petits fours, friandises, etc.) | |
| Savoury | All varieties served | |
| Cheese | All varieties served | As for dinner |
| Dessert and Coffee | As for dinner always | As for dinner |

CHAPTER 7

# DINING SERVICE

The provision of dining service is one of the oldest services associated with loging establishments. At most restaurants the profits from operating a dining room and cocktail lounge are relatively small compared to those from room sales. In fact, some properties do not expect to earn a profit from dining service.

A good dining service operation provides a service both to guests of the hotel and to the community. Many travellers judge the overall quality of a hotel by its food and beverage services. If the quality and services are good, members of the community will also patronize the dining room, helping to supplement food and beverage sales.

There are several methods which are employed to enable the customer to receive the meal. The mode of service will depend on the type of establishment, and in some places more than one kind of service will be used, often from one kitchen. The cost of operating these methods varies but the final objectives is the same that is the food when presented to the customer, should look attractive should be of the right temperature it should be as ordered and give value for money.

## MISE-EN-PLACE

The term mise-en-place is the traditional term used for all the duties that have to be carried out in order to have the room ready for service. In other words the term mise-en-place means preparation for service. A duty rota showing the jobs to be completed before service, and which member of staff is responsible, is drawn up by the reception head waiter. It is important to drawing up the duties at the end of service to be completed in order to leave the room in readiness for the service of the next meal.

## DAILY DUTIES

The daily duties can be stated as follows:

### 1. Head waiter

(a) Check the booking diary for reservations.

(b) Make out the seating plan for the day and allocate guests accordingly.

(c) Make out a plan of the various stations and show where the chef and commis will be working.

(d) Go over menu with staff immediately before service is due to commence.

(e) Check that all duties are covered and that a full team of staff is present.

### 2. Restaurant cleaning

a) Brush and dust the tables and chairs.

b) Polish all sideboards window, ledgers and cash desk.

c) All brasses to be polished.

d) Clean and polish the reception area.

e) Commence again as for Monday.

### 3. Linen

Collect the clean linen from the house-keeping department, check items against list; distribute to the various service points, lay tablecloth and fold serviettes spare linen to be folded neatly into the linen basket.

### 4. Hot-plate

Switch on the hotplate. Ensure all domens are closed. Items to be placed in the hot-plate would be according to the menu offered. For example; soup plates, consomme cups, fish plates, joint plates, sweet plates, coffee cups.

Set out the required kitchen silver on top of the hot-plate. Stock up after each service with clean and polished china in readiness for the next meal service.

**5. Silver**

To be cleaned daily.

a) Spirit and electric heaters.

b) Flare lamps, spirits and gas.

c) Ashtrays

d) Carving trolley.

**6. Accompaniments**

Write out a stores list of any dry goods required.

Polish and refill, crults, oil and vinegar stands, sugar basins, peppermills and cayenne pepper pots.

*Prepare accompaniments:* Tomato ketchup, French and English mustard, ground ginger, radish, mint sauce, worcestarshire sauce etc.

Distribute the cruets to the tables and the accompaniments to the sideboards. For the number of accompaniments and sets of cruets to prepare, check with the head waiter the number of side boards and tables that will be in use.

**7. Sideboards**

Items to be placed on the sideboard after ensuring it is polished and clothed up.

a) Assorted tableware from right to left; service spoons and forks, desert spoons and forks, tea and coffee spoons, fish knives and forks, joint knives, side knives.

b) Assorted china join plates, fish plates, side plates, sweets plates coffee saucers, consomme saucers, etc., according to the menu.

c) Service plate and service slaver.

d) Soup and sauce ladles.

e) Under-flats for vegetables and entrée dishes and for sauce boats.

f) Spirit or electric heater after it has been cleaned.

g) Roll basket.

h) Check pads, service cloths menus Gueridon may have to be laid up in conjunction with the sideboards according to the type of service offered.

**8. Dispense bar**

Clean bar, restock the bar with items sold the previous day, polish glasses; clean cocktail equipment and display on the bar counter, prepare lemon slices, cocktail cherries etc. Prepare stock control sheets, ensure that necessary wines have been chilled ready for service and that an adequate supply of ice is available.

**9. Still-room**

Make out an order for any dry goods required form the dry goods store; prepare melba toast and butter, pre wrapped portions of curled portions made from fresh butter, coffee in still set of according to the method used in the particular establishment concerned; hot milk or cream according to the policy of the establishment prepare butter dishes and the appropriate services for melba toast; coffee services to include coffee pot, milk or cream jug, sugar basins on a service salver; any special requirements, to be ready such as lemon tea and so on.

**10. Miscellaneous**

Prepare and lay up the carving trolley; sweet trolly and hors d'œuvre trolley. Polish the sideplates and fish plates required for laying up.

As the necessary preparation work is completed the staff are to report back to the head waiter who must check that the work has been carried out in a satisfactory manner than reallocate the member of staff to work involving the laying up of the room.

## SEQUENCE OF DUTIES

Duties should be proceed in a certain order that the duties may be carried out efficiently. It is unnecessary to point out that the dusting would not be done after the tables are laid or the tables and chairs all put in place. Therefore the suggested order of work according to the duties shown on the duty rota would be as follows:

a) Dusting
b) Stacking chairs on the table
c) Hoovering
d) Polishing
e) Arrange tables and chairs according to the table plan
f) Linen
g) Accompaniments
h) Hotplate
i) Still-room
j) Sideboard
k) Silver cleaning
l) Misc. trollies

## DUTIES AT THE END OF SERVICE

Following are some of the duties done at the end of service:

1. The head waiter to supervise all the clearing up and to see that it is done properly.
2. Responsible for clearing the cold buffet to the larder, collect and wash all carving knives and assist in dearing the restaurant.
3. Collect all linen both clean and dirty. Check that the correct quantities of each item of linen are

returned. The serviettes to be tied in bundles of ten. Place all linen in the linen basket and return with the linen list to the linen room.

4. Switch off the hot-plate.
5. Return all the silver together with the tableware trollies to the silver store.
6. Collect all cruets and accompaniments. Return to their correct storage place.
7. Check all the sideboards are completely empty. Hotplates are switched off and the dirty linen compartment is empty.
8. Clear down the bar top, put all the equipment away. Wash and polish used glasses. Put them away in their correct storage places. Remove all empty bottles etc., complete consumption and stock sheets. Lock up.
9. Put away all equipment that has been used. Empty all coffee pots and milk jugs. Wash and put away. Put all perishable materials in their correct storage places. Empty still set and milk urns and wash out, leave standing with cold water in them.
10. Empty and clean all trollies and return to their appropriate places. Any unused food items form the trollies should be returned to the necessary department, any silver used on the trollies to be cleaned and returned to the silver room.

**Duty rota**

The exact nature of duty rota varies, with every establishments according to the duties to be performed, the number of staff, time off and whether a split/straight shift is worked.

The object of a duty rota is to ensure that all the necessary duties are covered in order that efficient service may be carried out. At the same time it allows every member of staff to have a chance to carry out each duty in turn.

Mis-en-scene in the restaurant will include the following tasks:-

1. Cleaning of furnitures, fixtures and fittings.
2. Placing of furniture including tables and chairs.
3. Brusing/vacuuming of carpet.
4. Table light/wall lights have funcitoning bulbs.
5. Menu cards/tent cards are presentable and attractive.
6. Opening the windows/doors after some time to freshen the restaurant. Closing the windows/doors after some time to allow air-conditioning temperature to be maintained.
7. Exchange dirty linen for fresh linen.
8. Discard wilted flowers and replace with fresh.
9. Laying of table cloth and mats on the table.
10. Pest control measures as required.
11. Ensure no-smoking boards are properly placed.
12. Lying tables and different meals.

Table lying is usually a group exercise for a brigade of waiters. Each waiter will take an allotted table throughout the room. The procedures involved in laying the tables are outlined below.

## Laying of the tablecloth

Before laying the tablecloth, the waiter must ensure that the tables and chairs are in their correct position. Secondly, he must see that the table top is clean, thirdly that the table is level and finally see that it does not wobble. If the table wobbles slightly then a small wedge or an old menu folded up will correct the fault.

Next the waiter must collect the correct size of table cloth for the table to be clothed up. The waiter must stand in the correct position to lay the tablecloth properly, that is between the legs of the table. This is to ensure that the corners of the tablecloth cover the legs of the table and do not fall between of the table and do not fall between the table legs. The table cloth folded in the screen fold ahs one inverted fold and two single folds and should not be opened out across the table in front of the waiter with the inverted and two single folds facing him and with the inverted fold on top.

The tablecloth should then be laid in the correct manner. Following are some of the points which should be noted to lay the tablecloth correctly:

1. Corners of the tablecloth should cover the legs of the table.
2. The overlap should between all round the table: 30/45 cm (12-18 in).
3. The creases of the tablecloth should all run the same way in the room.
4. If two tablecloths are necessary to cover a table for a larger party then the overlap of the two table cloths should face away from the entrance to the room.

Nothing is more attractive in the room than tables clothed-up with clean, crisp and well starched linen tablecloths, the tablecloth should be handled as little as possible and this will be ensured by laying the tablecloth in the correct manner.

## LAYING THE TABLE

Once the table is clothed up it would be laid in readiness for service. If the cover being laid is an a la carte cover then the first item set on the table is the fish plate in the centre of each cover. If it was a table d' hote cover being laid then the first item to be set on the table d hote cover being laid then the first item to be set on the table would be the serviette or side plate in the centre of each cover. If the sideplate was laid in the centre of each cover it would be moved to the left hand side of the cover once all the cutlery and flatware has been laid. The purpose of initially placing something in the centre of the covers is to ensure the covers are exactly opposite one another and that the cutlery and flatware of each cover are the same distance apart. Cutlery and flatware should be laid down from a service salver or service plate. An alternative to this is to use a service cloth and hold the items being laid in the service cloth, giving a final polish before setting the item on the table. In some instances a cutlery trolley is used for storing the cutlery and this would be pushed around the tables and then the cutlery and flatware laid after a final polish with the waiters cloth. When laying a table d'hote cover the cutlery and flatware should be laid from the inside to the outside of the cover. The purpose of this is that it ensures even spacing of the cover and normally lessens the chances of having to handle the items laid more than necessary. In other words the order of laying should be:

a) Joint knife
b) Fish knife
c) Soup spoon
d) Joint fork
e) Fish fork
f) Dessert fork

**Dessert spoon**

The waiter must ensure that where applicable, all cutlery and flatware is laid 1.25 cm form the edge of the table and bandaged crockery with the bandage at the head or top of the cover. The glass after polishing would be placed upside down at top right hand corner of the cover. Once the covers have been laid the table accompaniments would be placed on the table according to the fashion of the establishment.

**Re-laying of tables**

It is very often the case in a busy restaurants or dining room that a number of the tables have to be relaid in order to cope with in the inflow of customers. Where this is the case the table should first of all be completely cheared of all items of equipment. It would then be crumbled down. At this stage if the table cloth is a little soiled or grubby a slip cloth would be placed over it. It will then be relaid in the approved manner. It is essential that this procedure is carried out as quickly as possible to ensure maximum turnover of guests in the limited amount of time available for service. This will then allow for maximum sales which, in a well-run establishments will mean more profit.

## PROCEDURE FOR SERVICES OF DIFFERENT MEALS

The procedure for service to a guest may change and vary according to the establishment the type of menu and service offered and the time available. It is generally accepted that as far as possible food is served from ht e left, alcoholic and non-alcoholic beverages are served from the right and dirty linens are cleared from the right. There are one or two exceptions to this general rule, for example depending on the position of a table and the guests seated at the table and when clearing sideplates, which, being on the left hand side of the place setting or cover, are more easily cleared from the left thus avoiding stretching in front of the guest. Following points are during meal service in a restaurant.

1. Guest enters, greeted by reception head waiter. Check if, they have a reservation. If not see if a table is available.
2. Ask from the reception head waiter what will the guests would like and aperitif in the lounge or reception area.
3. Take guests to table and indicate who is the host to the station head waiter. Hand over to the station

head waiter who will pass the item of the day with guests and help to seat them.

4. Unfold serviette and place over guests lap and turn wine glass up the correct way.
5. Sommelier comes to table to offer wine list for choice of aperitif. Takes order.
6. Rolls and melba toast are offered. Butter placed on the tables.
7. Menus presented to host and guests. Allow time for party to make their choice.
8. Recognition of the host is most important.
9. Station head waiter takes orders of party through host. Stands to left of host and should be ready to offer suggestions and advice on the menu, or translate any items if necessary.
10. Sommelier comes to table to see if any wine is required with meal. Takes order through host.
11. Waiters change covers where necessary for the service of the first course. Place accompaniment on the table.
12. Lay plates and service of first course.
13. Clear first course in approved fashion.
14. Lay covers for the fish course. Place any accompaniment required on the table.
15. If wine is to be served with fish course the correct glass would be placed on the table.
16. Wine presented to host and opened. Host to taste. Serve guests ladies first. Serve host last. It is well to remember here that one can get approximately three glasses of wine from a half bottle and six glasses of wine from a full bottle, white wine served chilled and red wines served at room temperature.
17. Lay fish plates and serve fish course.
18. Clear fish course.

19. Lay covers for main course. Place any accompaniment required on the table.
20. If a wine is also to accompany the main course the correct glasses would be placed on the table. Clear dirty wine glasses.
21. Wine presented to host opened and then toasted by host. Serve guests ladies first. Serve host last.
22. Lay joint plates and serve main course. The station head waiter must ensure everything required on the sideboard before commencing service of this course. Otherwise this can disrupt the service and may mean the food is getting sold. All cold dishes should be served before hot dishes.
23. Underplates should be used under vegetables dishes and sauce boats, all hot food being served should be piping hot and served into hot joint plates. The meal will be served first and placed on the part of the plate nearest the guest or at the bottom of the cover. This will be followed by the potatoes, vegetables and any hot sauces and accompaniments that have to be offered.
24. Sommelier to top up the wine glasses when necessary. Station head writer to offer more rolls, melba toast and butter as required.
25. Clear main courses to include side plates and side knives, cruets, butter dish, accompaniments, everything should be cleared in the appropriate manner.
26. Crumb down.
27. Change ashtrays if necessary.
28. Offer menu to guests to choose a sweet dish. Take order.
29. Lay sweet covers and accompaniments,
30. Sommelier to clear wine glasses and wine bottles.
31. Clear sweet course.

32. Clear sweet course.
33. Take coffee order.
34. Sommelier to present liqueur trolly. Serve liqueurs as required.
35. Coffee service placed on the table service of coffee offer more coffee at the appropriate time.
36. Presentation of the bill payment to waiter who has bill receipted by cashier and it is then returned with any change to host.
37. Station head waiter see guests out of restaurant.
38. Clear down table.

## RESTAURANT RESERVATION SYSTEM

In restaurant table reservation starts before guest arrive. This is because many guests reserve their seats, usually by telephone, in advance. Reservations are normally registered on a 'diary' basis that is in a page in a full scape size register reserved for the day's lunch and/or dinner seating. In such cases, regular customers or those making reservations who are known to the restaurant are likely to be given priority and to have their wishes met in regard to their seating. It is vital not to let new guests or less favoured guests be aware of any priority accorded to others.

Reservation system in the restaurant will include the following tasks:-

1. Receiving, accepting or rejecting reservations.
2. Dealing with enquiries.
3. Noting the guests requirements.
4. Entering the reservations.
5. Writing the 'reserved' cards.
6. Placing the reserved cards on the tables with the guest's name.
7. Informing the appropriate departments.

### Table allocation

Where a guest is seated in a restaurant is important to him. Actual table allocation depends on whether a table is pre-booked otherwise it is conditioned by the number of vacant places at the time of entry, the size of the party and as far as possible, at the time of entry, the size of the party and as far as possible. The wished of guests themselves. It is very common that some customers may prefer quiet corners, others to be near an orchestra or by a window. A good head waiter ascertains the wishes of guests or gauges them. He also uses his discretion, so that guests who are well mannered and pleasing in appearance may have more conspicuous places than those who might appear to have undesirable qualities or not well groomed.

Many restaurant operators today question the desirability of putting up a fully trained head waiter on the reception task and modern brigades may increase the responsibilities in all directions of the section waiter. In America a hostes or greater may be assigned restaurant reception work on the basis of personality intelligence and aptitude rather than skill of head waiter type duties.

But, whoever receives customers at the door does so with a courteous greeting in a clear an affable tone of voice and smile.

### Greeting on arrival

Only a stranger need the old traditional greeting; good morning or good afternoon or good evening. How many are there in your party, please 'where guests' names are known they may be used.

## RECEIVING THE GUEST

Receiving of guest go a long way towards selling an establishment and making a guest feel at home in a friendly and relaxed atmosphere. This aspect of service is very often neglected and all employers should impress upon their staff at regular intervals the great importance attached to customer contact. It must be remembered that a pleasant welcome to a guest can gain a sale, a poor welcome will loss a sale. It is always first impression that count.

Today, guests in many restaurants are first received at the entrance to a restaurant's cocktail bar or lounge, here an aperitif is taken and the meal and accompanying wines may be selected. Flexible interpretation of the procedures which are outlined below must take this possibility into account.

Today, guest in many restaurants are first received at the entrance to a restaurants cocktail bar or lounge. Here and aperitif is taken and the meal and accompanying wines may be selected, flexible interpretation of the procedures which are outline below must take this possibility into account.

## Who receives?

Previously in large first class establishments, there were usually greeting phrases may, of course, be varied to suit the occasion. Having received an answer the head waiter leads the way to a suitable table-if he guestures towards a table or to indicate a direction she should do so with open palm to avoid any impression of pointing. He then helps the ladies to be seated and calls the head wine butler and section head waiter to attend to the guests.

## Getting at table

A station waiter acknowledge a customer with a smile and greeting 'good morning (or good evening) Mr. C. Singh (or sir, or madam)'. After the first use of a guest's name he should be addressed as sir, unless it is clear from the established relationship that he prefers his own name to be used. A waiter aims to make sure that guest feel welcome and gain the impression that staff are glad to look after them.

In America, a captain or station waiter customarily introduces himself by name saying for example, 'I am 'A' and I am your waiter for tonight'. Sometimes indeed and American introduction of this kind can be most informal such as 'Hi! I am 'M' from Missluri, and I am your waiter for tonight.

In India such informality is not yet widely practised, but social condition today make anything acceptable, it makes guests feel welcome and they are aware that a waiter is pleased to receive them and look after them.

However, a waiter should be guided by management and supervisor before developing informality.

Thus, the tasks of receiving guest includes following tasks:

1. Greeting guests correctly.
2. Dealing with enquiries.
3. Explaining the establishment's facilities.
4. Dealing with undesirable guests.

## METHODS OF SERVICE

Restaurants are mainly for food services. In the restaurant foods are served under certain procedures universally accepted. The potential customer has to be attracted towards a restaurant and this may be done through the various attractive and methodical styles of food services.

Generally one restaurant offers one type of food service depending on the demand. But the trend today, however, seems to be towards the multi-restaurant, offering various forms of food service. This means that under one roof may be found a bar serving draught bear and sherry together with snacks such as sandwiches and pies; a doubles bar with drink at slightly reduced prices and hot snacks. However, because of the style of restaurant and because of other conditions, same rules are not possible always to maintain but it is essential to have clean, decent and methodical service in small or big restaurants.

### 1. French service

In France itself service a la francaise is derived from that used in bourgeoise household and is found in both family pensions and in banqueting where the dish is presented to the left of each guest who serves himself.

Thus, a fundamental element of true French service is that is affords guests an opportunity to help themselves.

For small parties up to three guests dishes may be placed directly on the table, the main dish is positioned before the guest expected to be served first. The plates are paled conveniently near the dish.

For larger parties certainly for tables of four or more, a gueridon or side table should be used. In this case, the waiter brings plates and dishes to the queridon, sets the plates at guests covers and then presents the dishes to guests to help themselves.

Often, of course some preliminary treatment of portioning or carving may be required form the queridon. Thus French service can also enables guests to see food 'finished' by their table, for serving and portioning and salad mixing may be affected in front of them. Refinement or simplifications internationally depend on the grade of the restaurant.

Basic French service, as practised in France, has advantages in that it demands relatively staff and does not require great skill but it can be slow and less 'sure' because of possible guests ineptitude in serving themselves.

Although this is called French service in France Switzerland and elsewhere on the continent, some British people think that the custom of guests helping themselves from offered dishes typifies an English form of service because this style survives in private houses in this country when dishes are passed by servants.

### 2. English service

On the continent a 'l'onglaise is used especially in function service, fixed price table d'hote and in travel catering, in this style the dish is presented to the left of the guest and served by the waiter. It is thought to have originated in the British tradition of the 'master' or family head carving or portioning and serving all at the table.

In restaurant English services, the waiter fulfils this rate, that is, the fundamental element is that he serves and at the same time, in effect, decides the portions as distinct from the quest taking his own. Again refinements or simplifications depend on the grade of the restaurant.

Generally, English service is also a 'silver' service with portioning largely effected in the kitchen so that food, particularly when it involves a varied or complicated garnish, may be easily separated and carved by the waiter.

The waiter brings plates and dishes to the sideboard, places a plate before each quest at his own cover, presents thc main dish to the host or guests and then passes around the table serving each customer.

English service has the advantage of conveying a stylish or up market impression with relatives speed and efficiency but it does require skill from staff. It is, for example, difficult to apply successfully to fragile food, for example fish fillets, omelettes.

This form of service also can be affected from the gueridon. In this case the waiter places the dishes with the required number of plates on the gueridon. He serves by completing one plate at a time which is immediately placed before the guest. Gueridon service is greatly facilitated by the use of an assistant waiter to aid in passing the completed plates.

### 3. Russian service

This form of service is almost not-existent today. The principle involved was to have whole joints, poultry game and fish elaborately dressed up and garnished which would be presented to the guests who would help themselves. Display and presentation was a great part of this form of service. Today it may still be seen to some extent in the form of the now popular 'cold buffet'. The other aspects still seen is when gueridon service is involved and whole chickens, ducks, game and fish are presented to the guest and then carved or filleted on the gueridon.

### 4. American service

Fundamentally, American service evolved more recently than French, English and Russian services. It depends on preplating and the pre-setting of tables with silver needed throughout the meal plated food is brought by waiters from the kitchen by tray which is then placed on a tray stand by the guests' table. American service may be slightly elaborated by fine table equipment and by ancillary serving procedures such as dispensing by separates waiters of hot rolls and trolley on cart service for salads and so on.

American service is, therefore, plate service adapted to restaurant usage. Its advantage lies in its economy of equipment, speed an simplicity. Hence it can be learnt easily by inexperienced staff.

### 5. Buffet service

Modern restaurants increasingly adopt a buffet service which involves guests, self service. Guests helps themselves to most items and these can include hot dishes. Carveries are a form of buffet service.

For buffet service, food is arranged on a buffet table in trays on chafing dishes, oval flats, entrée dishes, etc., plate hot or cold are stacked at the head of each line or table. Napkins and silverware are normally located at the end of the buffet line, a qualified member of the waiting or kitchen staff is available to deal with carving or portioning and is in attendance even in self carving operations.

Cold buffets are usually embelished with decorative dishes such as ham or chaufroid, salman and poultry but centre piece can be of flowers, ice carvings, butter mouldings or company insignias or other relevant features.

Spot lightings to a buffet table is an effective finishing touch especially when high lighting a centre piece.

U shape, L shape, V shape and other shapes of tables arrangement can be assembled to accommodate the food to be served and the numbers to be catered for. Some items for example soup or beverages are often set up separately so as not to cross the regular buffet lines and to increase traffic flow speed.

## 6. Banquet service

This is a very formal sit down service organized in special occasions like marriage ceremonies in honour of VIPs during visits of head of the states etc., special attentions are paid to the sitting arrangements and for suitable floral decorations. The shape of the table depends upon the size of the room. It may be T, round, oval, horse shoe or block shaped. For a banquet consisting of hors d' oeuvre clear soup, fish, a main dish with vegetables and salad, ice, biscuits and coffee, each cover is laid with a service plate, a large knife and fork, a dessert spoon for the soup, fish and desert knives and forks, a bread plate with a small knife, a water glass a wine glass and a champagne glass. Formerly it was customary to place five glasses on the table at banquets. Now the glasses are changed of more that one wine is served. Plates for the hors d'œuvre are laid, cups for the soups and plates for the fish and main dish are kept in the hot cupboard ready for use. A soup ladle, saucers for the soup, plates to place under the saucers and desert plates are kept ready for use on a separate service table. Cocktails or a glass of champagne are usually served in the lounge before the start of the banquet.

At a wedding the service always starts form the centre with the bridal couple, at banquets the most important guest is served first. The first course is served from right to left the second from left to right, the other courses alternatively, if ladies are present they ought to be served first but this is not customary everywhere.

**7. Silver service**

Today, in silver service food is placed on or in appropriate silver plated dishes in the kitchen by the chef for presentation for services by waiters.

The term 'silver' embraces stainless steel and also fire proof enamel dishes, china or earthenware. These latter dishes are normally presented on oval 'flats' of silver or stainless steel. Fish, for example is frequently so served.

Sometimes silver service has been called continental service in England.

**8. Plate service**

In this style the customer is served in the simplest manner with food already placed on table. Such service is used in canteens, many boarding houses and restaurants, where more personal silver service cannot be given.

Plating food requires case and supervision. For example, the plate should be the right size for the food item and adequate to accommodate its garnish and accompanying vegetables. In arranging the food, colour and consistency should reflect a chef's artistry or when done by service staff should aid or recreate such artistry.

In implementing plate service, metal plate rings enabling plated food to be stacked one plate on another may be used. Vegetable are not always plated or preserved but may be offered separately in a vegetable dish placed on the table with its serving spoon for guest self services. Trays are used by waiting staff for this type of services.

In some higher class operations otherwise using silver service, grills may be served on plates. This is only to speed service and ensure that they are hot when served direct from the grill without unnecessary manipulations.

**9. Cafeteria service**

Industrial and institutional catering make wide spread use of cafeteria service. The basic principles of cafeteria food service have remained relatively stable. Food is set out on one or more counters with heated, unheated and refrigeration sections. Customers pick up a tray at the entry to a service line and pass along the line selecting food as required. Cutlery and paper napkins are at the end of the line next to a cashier who receives payments. This may not be required in some institutional services where meals are prepared.

Commercial cafeterias may augment service by having staff at each station to assist or provide call-order service for grills, breakfasts or toasted sandwiches etc.

In institutional catering where meals are pre-sold to students or other types of institutional customer dishes are usually set up on the counter in order to consumption from soup through to sweet.

In cafeterias where each dish is individually priced the survey line is arranged with merchandising and maximizing sales in mind. Thus an attractive salads display, hors d'œuvres or side dish might be first in line for hungry customers are more likely to be tempted with such extra items when they are seen before main dishes.

**10. Family service**

In many clubs today a type of 'family service' is still carried out. Here the main dish may be either plate or silver served by the waiter. All the accompanying potato and vegetable dishes together with the sauces and other accompaniments are placed on the table for the members to help themselves. This form of service may also be carried out at functions where a large number of covers are being catered for and only a minimum of staff are available. Because there is less actual service for the waiter to do that enables them to serve an extra one or two tables, depending on size. A further variation is for the main dish to be placed on a small hot-plate on the table near the host together with the necessary hot-plates. The host then plates the main dish and passes it to the guests at the table. The guest in turns helps themselves to the potatoes, vegetables, sauces and other accompaniments.

**11. Snack bar services**

This is also a form of popular catering and there are many variations on this particular theme. For this form of services number of customers are seated at the actual service counter itself. The menu can offer a wide range of dishes which should come within the popular price range. A very quick turnover is necessary for this form of services and labour costs are reduced to a minimum because as many customers as possible are seated at the service counter. Therefore the counter hand can take the order prepare and plate up the dish required and serve it, in order to do this efficiently and quickly and to keep the number of staff employed a possible should be used. This would include tea/coffee making machines; salamander grill, cooling unit, refrigerators, deep frying unit bein marie, hot-plates and ovens, steam heat injection and mixers. There may be a number of tables sited around the service counter and if this is the case a waiter would be needed to take the order of customers seated at the tables, serve the dishes requested, receive the cash for the meal, served and keep all the tables clear. Most snacks bars are unlicensed unless incorporated within a larger concern as in Railway catering.

**12. Gueridon service**

This is a meal served to a great pleasure by the waiter form a trolley or side table. It is the most advanced form of food services and demands dexterity and skill on the part of the waiter who in turn must have good organizational ability. This is because he has to carry out such procedures as filleting, carving, fumbling and preparing and cooking specialty dishes at the table. The menu presented where this type of service is offered is what we term as a la carte menu, with all the dishes individually priced. This type of menu gives more scope to the professional waiter to display flair and skills than does the limited table d'hote menu a list of 'specialties of the house' which are all individually priced and enable the waiter to complete the dish at the table.

**Conclusion**

All the forms of service listed and variants of them are conditioned by general rules of serving and the preceding notes are intended merely to outline their basic forms. Restaurateurs, prompted by guests demand for convenience and tempered by common sense and good manners, have formed services styles in order to smooth or facilitate a meals progress. In the restaurant business these customs and styles are affected also by staffing and cost considerations so that restaurateurs are constantly seek to adopt style to modern needs and realities.

## CHAPTER 8

# FUNCTION CATERING BY RESTAURANTS

Function catering is the term used to cover the service of special functions in a restaurant which is separate from the normal service found in the grill room and on the floors and in the lounge. It would include functions such as luncheon parties, conferences, cocktail parties, weddings, dinner-dances and so on. In the large establishments all functions would take place with, in the banqueting suites and be under the administrative control of the banqueting manager.

In the smaller establishments these functions would normally take place in a room set aside for the purpose and came under the jurisdiction of the manager or assistant manager. Most of the staff available for function are employed on a casual basis. At busy periods there may be a number of functions running at the same time.

There are two main types of function:

1. Luncheons:

   Dinners

   Wedding breakfast

2. Buffet receptions:

Wedding reception
Buffet tea
Running buffets for dances etc.
Anniversary parties
Hunt balls
Conferences

A further breakdown of the types of function may be as follow:

A. *Social*

Dinners (old boys)
Luncheon (Rotarians)
Receptions
Cocktail parties
Charity performance
Fashion parades

B. *Conferences*

National and International sales
Industrial Training Boards

C. *Public relations*

Press party to launch a new product
Fashion parade
Exhibitions
Dealers meetings
Seminars

D. *Functional planning*

The nature of functions is of two types:

1. Contracted functions
2. Speculative functions.

In contracted functions, the caterer agrees to caterer for a specified and guaranteed number of customers. But in speculative functions the caterer is not assured of any customer but contracts to provide refreshment on a site for members of the general public attending the event. Keeping in view the individual nature of every function, the restaurant management attempts as far as possible to pre-plan functions in several ways.

The first element of planning is to provide the customers a selection of menus to choose from. The advantages to the caterer of this are that:

1. Pre-designed menus can be given a great deal of thought by the caterer to ensure that the principles of good menu planning are adhered to.
2. Menus that are planned in advance enable the banqueting manager to quote a price to the customer immediately, since they are pre-costed.
3. The quality of food service is likely to be higher if the kitchen staff are preparing dishes that they are familiar with and have prepared often.

The second element of planning is *space requirement planning*. It is generally recognized that the minimum space between sprigs is 2 metres (6 ft). This is made up of 2 chair widths from edge of table to back to chair (46 cm) plus a gangway of 1 metre (3 ft); allowing each waiter passing space. A total of 2 metre (6 ft) Tables widths are approximately 75 cm (2 ft + 6in)

The length along the table per cover should be 50-60 cm (20-24 in). The space from the wall to edge of the table should be a minimum of 1.4 metres (4.6"). This is made up of a 1 metre (3 ft) gangway plus 1 chair width of 46 fcm (18 in). The height of the chair from the ground will vary according to the style and design but is approximately 46-50 cm (18-20 in).

The length of the table used is generally 2 metres (6 ft) but 1.2 and 1.5 metre length (4 and 5 ft) may be used to make up a sprig.

Round tables would be 1, 1.5 or 2 metres (3,5 or 6 ft) diameter with the appropriate extensions.

Suggested areas allowances for sit down function per person is approximately 1/1.4 square metres (12-15 sq ft.), for buffets the allowance is 0.9/1 square metres (10-12 sq ft.).

The third element of planning is applied to seating plan. Of the total number of people attending a function it must be determined how many will be seated on the top table and how many on the sprigs, round or oblong tables making up the full table plan. All tables with the exception of the top table should be numbered. The table numbers themselves should be on stands of such a height that they may all be seen from the entrance of the banqueting room. The approximate height of the stands would be 75 cm (30 in). After the guests are seated and before the service commences these stands are sometimes removed. It left they are and aid to the sommelier when checking for cash wines. As far as possible when formulating the table plan; avoid seating guests with their packs to the top table. Normally there are three copies of the seating plan. These go to:

(a) *The organizer*: So that he may check all necessary arrangements.

(b) *The guests*: This seating plan would be placed in a prominent position in the entrance of the banqueting suite so that all guests may see where they have been seated and who else is seating at their table and the position of their table in the room.

(c) *The banqueting manager*: For references purposes.

(1) Seating plan using rectangular tables.

(2) Seating plan using square tables.

The fourth element of planning is table planning.

There are three main types of table plan, formal informal and cabaret style.

*Formal layouts* It involves lines of long tables. In some of them, 'sprige' run at right angles to a top table. Such sprigs may be flush against a top table but waiters can move and work more easily if space is left between them. Moreover, this facilitates draping and decorating front of the top table.

*Informal layouts*: Seats guests at separate tables.

*Carba ret layouts:* Arrange smaller tables often leaving a centre space for dancing or entertainment.

*Drafting plans:* A scale plan of the room with card templates of tables to the same scale is useful in table planning, especially if guest numbers are near the rooms maximum capacity. Cut templates to include both chair space and gangway space. Moving real tables involves unnecessary time and labour. It is simpler to move templates until the best seating is achieved. To be effective, a plan must show entries and exists and other factors related to room and seating such as pillars, alcoves and power points. Exits must be left unobstructed to meet local authority and safety requirements and service, and guest access aistes left clear.

### A. Table Plan Display

One or two copies of the table plan must be displayed for guests in the reception room. For a large function, each table on the plan will carry either a letter or a number. Beside this plan a list of guest in alphabetical order indicates where a guest is seated by letter or number. At the top table each guest is informed of his place, usually by a name card at his seat.

This information is previously advised by the organizers.

The types of table plan put into operation for a particular function depends upon a number, of major functions, these being:

1. Organizers wishes.
2. Nature of the function.
3. Size and shape of room where the function is to be held.
4. Number of covers.

For the smaller type of function 'A' or 'U' or 'T' shaped may be used or where the luncheon or dinner party is more informal there may be a top table and separate tables, round or rectangular for the various parties of guests where the function to be held has a very large number of covers there the generally accepted form of table plan is a top table and sprigs. However, before these various table plans can be shown to the organizer when a function is being booked, a great amount of consideration must be given to spacing. This is to allow a reasonably comfortable seating space to each guest and at the same time giving the waiter sufficient room for the service of the meal. Also the gangway space must be such that two waiters may pass one another during the service without fear of any accident occurring.

**SIZE OF TABLES TO SEAT VARIOUS NUMBERS**

| No. of Covers | Round (Diameter) | Square | Rectangular |
|---|---|---|---|
| 2 | 0.8 m | 0.75 × 0.75 m | 0.6m × 0.7 m |
| 3 | 0.9 m | 1.0 m × 0.75 m | |
| 4 | 1.0 m | 1.0 m × 1.0 m | 1.2 m × 0.75 m |
| 6 | 1.2 m | Not advisable | 1.5 m × 0.75 m |
| 8 | 1.5 m | Not advisable | 2.4 m × 0.75 m |

## Laying of clothes

The size of banqueting cloth is from 2 metres (6 ft) wide by 4 metres (12 ft) in length and then running upwards in length

i.e. 5½ metres (18 ft) and so on.

These cloths would be used on top tables and sprigs and therefore very often avoid the necessity of overlapping when smaller size table cloths are used. When laid the centre crease should run straight down the centre of the table. All cloths should be in the same fold and have the same pattern. Any overlap of cloths should face away from the main entrances so that the join is not visible to the guest as they look down the room on arrival. When laying the cloth it may require depending on its size, three or four waiters to manipulate it thus ensuring that it is laid correctly creasing or becoming dirty.

The fifth and final element of planning is ensuring the proper number of staff. Sometimes a function organizer asks the head waiter to check on numbers present at the function and to notify him of that number as soon as possible during the meal but the number of waiters and waitress required both for the service of drinks and food will have to be decided well in advance on the basis of forecast numbers.

### Service stations

Using silver services a waiter usually serves ten to twelve covers. A table seating such a number thus matches both the service dish made up in the kitchen and a waiter's station but with tables of varying seating capacity in informal layouts, waiters should still serve similar numbers. At long tables waiters also serve similar numbers. The sprigs should be made up to seat guests in multiples of ten or twelve or whatever figure each waiter is to serve. Otherwise waiters work successfully along rows of diners serving their allotted number. Waiters may serve more guest up to sixteen or even more when simpler services are introduced.

One wine waiter is allocated even more if wine is prepared inclusive in the function.

### Staffing examples

For a function for 300 in a high class restaurant four

course dinner menus plus coffee, with table wines to include sherry with consomme a white wine with fish, a red wine with the main course and brandy/liqueurs with coffee, pre-war staffing would have been in nature of:

Banquet manager

Assistant banquet manager

Head waiters

20 waiters

10 commis waiters

9 wine waiters

Today such a function might be staffed

Banquet head waiter

Assistant banquet head waiter

20 waiters

6 wine waiters.

**Instruction to staff**

The purpose of the staff instruction sheet is to ensure that all duties are covered and that a particular function is laid up and everything is in order in the shortest possible time.

When all the necessary mise-en-place has been completed, and all the staff are assembled, and all the staff are assembled together the stations are allotted to the waiters and wine waiters. Care must be taken in the allocation of the top table and usually one of the more experienced and proficient member of the brigade will be given this job. One must bear in mind the age and agility of the staff when allocating stations, giving the older members of the brigade the stations nearest the service doors. When the waiter queue up at the hotplates for each course this should be done in an orderly fashion with the waiter for the top table at the head of the queue and then the various waiter in order according to the distance of their station from the service hotplate. This order must be maintained throughout the service. After the service of each course the brigade should remain outside the banqueting room and in readiness to clear and serve the next course.

## B. MANAGEMENT OF FUNCTIONS

In some operations organizing and selling functions will be in the hands of an executive reporting to the general manager. Such an executives needs sound catering knowledge and function experience in substantial restaurant operation.

Large restaurants may also have a senior banqueting head waiter or function head waiter who reports to the banqueting manager. This head waiter supervises other staff and engages them according to the demands of business.

### Communicating to staff

Following information should be provided to the waiting staff a few days before the function:

1. Date and time of function
2. Number to be served
3. Where to assemble
4. Where to serve
5. Menu detail
6. Plan of tables
7. List of guests
8. Drinks, aperitifs, wines, liqueurs, spirits and whether preordered or cash
9. Cigar, cigarettes.

#### *Where to assemble*

Aperitifs and appetizers are served in a reception room. A few chairs should be placed around the walls so that the elderly may sit down. Small tables, with ashtrays, for guests to deposit their empty glasses must be provided.

### *Where to serve*

This information is supplied with table plan.

### *Menu details*

This consists of the menu for the actual function as served in the dining room and also information of any appetizers to be served during the evening. Soup on departure may also be required in certain cases.

### *Quoting for functions*

Normally a catering establishment's function prospectus takes care of many customers need for detail and helps to eliminate possible misunderstanding and queries. The function order form records the customer's demands; the prospectus details what is to be provided.

### *Mall confirmation*

Lengthy letters should not be necessary where a good prospectus and order form are used. Butifs forms and standards literature not be available then a letter of quotation or confirmation for a function seek to cover all aspects.

## C. FUNCTION STAFF

In large first class restaurant there is generally a small nucleus of permanent staff dealing with function above. These would include banqueting managers, one or two assistant banqueting managers, one or two barmen and a secretary to the banqueting manager. In smaller restaurants where these are fewer functions the necessary administrative and organizational work would be undertaken by the manager assistant manager and head waiter.

### 1. Sales Administrative Manager

The main object of the sales administration manager is to sell the function facilities of a restaurant to a client

## FUNCTION ORDER FORM

Brassington, Barchester

Telephone

Organization. . . . . . . . . .
Address . . . . . . . . . . .
In charge . . . . . . . . . .
Telephone No. . . . . . . . . .

Function . . . . . . . . . .
Day . . . . . . . . . . . .
Starting time . . . . . . . .
Receptipon . . . . . . . . .
Meal time . . . . . . . . . .
Vacated . . . . . . . . . . .

☐ Guarantee

Gurantee figure

Guarantee means the number of meals to be served. We will be prepared to serve 10% more without delay. Should the number served be less than the guarantee, the minimum change will be for 95% of the guarantee.

Banquet room

Lobby bulletin board posting

Menu
Starter . . . . . . . . . .
Entrée . . . . . . . . . .
Potato . . . . . . . . . .
Vegetable . . . . . . . . .
Salad . . . . . . . . . .
Dessert . . . . . . . . .
Coffee, tea, milk - rol ls and butter included all regular meals
Price per cover Rs./$ . . . . . .
Plus VAT and 15% gratuity

**Tables and seating**

Top table Yes ☐ No☐
No. of persons at top table . .
Double set-up - separate tables for meeting and dining
Yes ☐ No ☐
Other instructions

**Coffee break**

| | tea/coffee | rolls | biscuits |
|---|---|---|---|
| . . . . .am | ☐ | ☐ | ☐ |
| . . . . .pm | ☐ | ☐ | ☐ |

**Special needs**

Movie screen ☐ Rostrum ☐
PA system . . . . . . . . . .
Blackboard ☐ Piano ☐
Stages . . . . . Easels . . . .
Others . . . . . . . .

**Bar Requirement**

Prtable bar Yes ☐ No ☐

Please Sign. . . . . . . . .

Bill to . . . . . . . . . . . . . . . . . . . . . . . . . . . .
. . . . . . . . . . . . . . authorised representative date
. . . . . . . . . . . . . . . . . . . . . . . .
. . . . . . . . . . . . . . Banquet Manager date

**Fig. An example of a function order form.**

and where necessary make the initial approach and contact. After this the client is referred to the banqueting manager concerned. Because of the varied made up of each banqueting suite in the various restaurants the sales administration manager must have an extensive knowledge of room specifications, size, light switches heights of doorways, maximum floor loads etc. This enables him to give positive and negative answers to any requests at the initial meeting with a client without causing any dealy to either party. The sales administration manager must be a person of ideas. For every function he should be able to make suggestions for that function.

Polydor Hotel,
London.
W4

The Secretary,
The Meat Cleavers' Assciation,
London,
NW 22

6th November 1987

Dear Mr Carver,

Following, our recent talk, I have pleasure in confirming that a tentative reservation has been made of the ballroom for your annual dinner dance for approximately 250 persons on Friday 27th January, 1988.

Our ballroom will accommodate a maximum of 300 persons for this type of function.

I enclose menu samples for your consideration at the price levels (.... to ....) you indicated. The price quoted per head are exclusive of reception drinks which I gathered you wished served on a cash basis to all except official guests.

The charge includes hire of private accommodation, floral decoration, dinner, coffee and, at a set time later in the evening, light refreshment of achoice of tea, sandwiches, pastries and ices.

Ten per cent is added to the total of the account to

include staff gratuities, with the exception of wine waiters who, where drinks are served on a cash basis, may receive gratuities at tables at the time of service at guests' discretion. Special cloakroom accommodation from part of the ballroom suite and will be available for guests, and this is included in the above charge.

We can supply and print menu cards similar to the enclosed sample at a charge of per hundred. Should you need the services of reception and dinner only, or until 11.30 p.m.

You may wish to make your own arrangements for an orchestra but, should you wish, we shall be happy to have our musical director quote to you.

We serve dinner to members of the orchestra and to the toastmaster at a charge of per head.

I do hope we shall have the pleasure of catering for you. We shall spare no effort to ensure the complete success of the occasion.

Yours sincerely,

A. Merrythought
Banqueting Manager

**2. Banqueting Manager**

He has the entire administrative responsibility. He meeting the prospective clients, discussing arrangements with them concerning menus, table plan, costs, wines, bands toastmaster etc. The banqueting manager must send to all the departments concerned a memo telling them the date of function numbers and any further details that might be applicable to a certain department. He works with the banqueting manager and is responsible for handling all incoming and outgoing mail for seeing any memos dictated are sent to the appropriate departments and for the correct filing of any correspondence. The secretary should handle all telephone calls and in the absence of the banqueting manager may take provisional bookings for functions.

**3. Banqueting Head Waiter**

He is in charge of the banqueting suites. He may also be responsible for the engaging of staff, on a casual basis to cover the various duties at a function. The banqueting head waiter would normally have a list of name and addresses and telephone number of best casual staff and will ensure that they are well employed.

**4. Barman**

If he is a member of the permanent banqueting staff he will be responsible for the allocation of bar stock for various functions, the setting up of the bars, the organization of the bar staff, control of stock and cash during service and for stock taking when a function is completed. He would also be responsible for the restocking of the banqueting dispense bar.

**5. Banqueting Head Wine Butler**

He may work in conjunction with the dispense barman or if there is no permanent dispense barman he may take over the latter's duties together with those of organizing the banqueting wine waiters and allotting them stations, giving them floats if there are cash wines and discussing the service with them.

**6. Permanent Waiting Staff**

These are usually experienced chefs derange who can turn their hand to any job concerning banqueting and who generally do most of the miss-en-place before the function that is the laying of tables. Their job during service is mainly wine waiting. They may also help to clear after service is completed.

**7. Casual Staff**

Casual staff normally report approximately 1 hour before a function commences. They would be allocated stations and given a brief talk with regard to the procedure for the service of a particular function. After service they would e paid and then dismissed.

## 8. Porters

There are generally two or three porters on the permanent banqueting staff. They are essential members of staff as here is a great deal of heavy work to be carried out.

## 9. Booking a Function

At the initial meeting of the banquet manager and the client a file must be opened recording all points mentioned concerning this particular functions and to hold all correspondence received. If the enquiry is not made immediately a firm booking then the provisional details are only penciled in until the booking is confirmed. It would then be linked in. The banqueting manager should have available specimen luncheon and dinner menus with the costs per head and photographs of the various table layout for different numbers. This gives the client a clear picture of the facilities available in the price range he can afford.

After the initial meeting and the booking having been confirmed the following basic points should have been noted:

1. Type of function
2. Date
3. Time
4. Number of covers
5. Price per head
6. Menu, method of service
7. Wines, inclusive or cash
8. Type of organization
9. Table plan.

Sequence of Service

1. Dinner announced by the toastmaster

2. Grace
3. Guests seated, chairs pulled out by waiters, Serviettes across laps.
4. If first course is not already on the table proceed to hotplate to collect first course.
5. Line up as previously mentioned. Top table first.
6. Serve first course-top table waiter to commence service first.
7. All waiters (food) to leave room after each course is served.
8. Take in fish course plates.
9. Clear first course and lay fish plates.
10. Take out dirties and collect fish course.
11. Serve fish course. Leave room taking dirty silver.
12. Take .in meat plates.
13. Clear fish course and lay meat plates.
14. Take out dirties and collect potato and vegetable dishes.
15. Deposit on sideboard or sideplate.
16. Return to hotplates and collect main meal dish.
17. Present on each table and serve.
18. Serve accompanying potatoes and vegetables.
19. Leave room taking dirty silver.
20. And so on until the end of the meal.

## CONCLUSION

Function catering is a specialized sector of the food services industry covering a wide range of functions and events. It is a risky business that requires a great deal of fore-thought and planning down to the last details with regard to all aspects of the operation. And once the functions is underway it is essential to control very closely the movement of stocks and performance of staff for without strict control the potential profit form an outside catering function may not be realized. In many respected this type of catering provides a real challenge to the professional caterer and a great deal of job satisfaction is to be gained from the diversity of operations and difficulties surmounted.

CHAPTER 9

# GUERIDON SERVICE IN RESTAURANT

The most elaborate form of silver service in restaurants today is called gueridon service.

A gueridon is a table or trolley placed beside the customer's table at which the waiter prepares fillets, carves and sometimes cooks the dishes to be served. This style of service is flamboyant and emphasis the personal attention and service that a customer receives. It is associated with menu dishes that are of highest quality and very expensive, being based on classical French cuisine.

## A. HISTORY

Gueridon service first became popular in the Edwardian era. The first claimed flambe dish was creps suzette which was supposedly invented by Henri Charptentier when working as a commis at the cafe de paris in Monte Carlo (1894). The origin of gueridon service itself is hard to trace. It includes carving, salad preparation, filleting, preparation of fresh fruit etc.

## B. DEFINITION

The definition of the term gueridon is a movable service table or trolley from which food may be carved, filleted, flambed or prepared, then reheated and served. It is in another words movable sideboard carrying sufficient equipment for the immediate operation in hand, whatever, it may be, together with a surplus of certain equipment in case of emergency. It should also carry any special equipment that may be necessary. The gueridon itself may come in various forms *i.e.,* Colour gas trolly specially made for the purpose; plain trolly specially made for the purpose; plain trolly or even a small table.

## C. MISE-EN-PLACE FOR GUERIDON

Where necessary the top and under shelf of the gueridon should be covered with a foled tablecloth. For convenience of working the cutlery lay out should be similar to that of the sideboard. This saves time and speeds up the service from right to left.

1. Service spoons and forks.
2. Dessert spoons and forks.
3. Soup tea and coffee spoons.
4. Fish knives and forks special equipment including a soup and sauce ladle.
5. Joint and side knives.

The hotplates or table heaters are generally placed on the left hand side on the top of the gueridon. These heaters may be gas electric or methylated spirit. If the latter then coffee saucers should be placed under burners.

Also on the top will be found a carving board, knives for carving and filleting and a selection of basic accompaniments such as oil and vinegar, worestershire sauce, English and French mustard and castor sugar.

Underneath will be found a service plate and service salver, sideplates and some joint plates for dirty cutlery when an operation is being carried out. There should also be some silver underflats of assorted sizes for the service of vegetables and sauces. A selection of doilies etc., are useful for the presentation of sauces and other accompaniments.

Any other mise-en-place required such as coffee saucers, accompaniments, check pads, etc., will be on the waiterssideboard together with a surplus of all the gueridon equipment in case of emergency.

## D. GUERIDON SERVICE EQUIPMENT

### 1. Flare lamps

These are an essential item of equipment for gueridon service and are used in reheating, cooking and flam being dishes. The maintenance of the flare lamp is very important and should be carried out very carefully ensuring each part is fitted together correctly that it is filled to the correct level with mythylated spirits and that the wick is of sufficient length to give adequate heat when in use. The flare lamp should be cleaned regularly with the aid of plate powder. Regular trimming of the wick is essential to avoid methylated spirit fumes leaking out and spoiling the aroma of the food. The lamps are usually 20-25 can high with a grid diameter of 15-20 cm. In a specially made gueridon trolly the lamp is incorporated in the trolly, thus giving the same working highest all along the trolls' top. This is much safer for the as he works since there is less chance of accidents. Care over its use is essential as it is a costly item.

### 2. Chaffing dish or suzette pans

The true chafing dish is rarely seen now a days. This was deeper had a lid and made to into its own individual heating unit. The shallower pans which are used today are called suzette pans. They resemble frying pans in shape and size and have a diameter of 20-30 cm without a lip. The Lip is usually found on the left hand side. The pans are generally made of silver plated copper as this gives an even distribution of heat.

### 3. Hotplates

These are always positioned on the sideboard, but may often be found on both the sideboard and the gueridon. There is a vast range in sues and they may be heated by gas, electricity, methylated spirits, and there are even infra-red ones available. The majority of hotplates in present day use heated by methylated spirits and therefore, as with the flare lamps, care should be taken in cleaning, filling and trimming the wicks.

The hotplates main function is to keep food hot before it is served to the guest. The wicks in both hotplates and flare lamps should be long enough and adequate for the service.

## E. SEQUENCE FOR SERVICE

Presentation of all dishes for all courses is very important both before the actual service commences and in placing the meal upon the plate especially when filleting and carving.

### 1. Hors d' œuvres or substitutes

These are served in the normal way except for speciality dishes. Such as pate de foie which may have to be cut into slices. Accompaniments passed in the normal manner.

*Soup:* Always served from the gueridon whether in individual soup bowls or in soup tureene with a ladle. All accompaniments passed.

*Fish:* filleted when necessary and served from the guaridon.

*Meat:* carved when necessary and served from the guerid on.

*Vegetables:* sauces and accompaniments served as previously mentioned.

*Sweet:* served from gueridon if a flam be type dish of from the cold sweet trolly. All accompaniments passed.

*Savoury:* served from the gueridon.

*Coffee :* Normal silver service. Order of Service of Guests.

(a) The host is always last except at dinners and banquets where he is served first.

(b) If there are ladies in the party serve the lady on the hosts, right, and then follow round the table.

Then serve the males round the table starting from the first male on the host's right and round the table last.

(c) Where the party is all the female, the eldest lady is served first and the hostest is served last.

(d) Where the party is all male the same principle applies.

(e) Where there is a family party serve mother first then daughter then son and the father last.

## Method of Serving a Dish at the Table

First present the dish to the customer then return to the gueridon. Place the hotplates on the side of the trolly with the food for service standing on the hot-plate. The food for service is then carved or filleted if necessary and is placed onto the plate of the guest. Unlike silver service when the spoon and fork are used together in one hand, gueridon service requires that the spoon and fork are used together one in each hand. The vegetables are then placed onto the plate by the waiter while the plates are still on the gueridon. The sauces are also place onto the plates by the waiter and the plates are then placed in front of the guests. It should be noted that when there are more than two people at one table than two people at one table the main dish is served as described but the vegetable are served as for normal silver service, and will be kept hot and in readiness for service on the hot-plate on the waiters sideboard. During this operation it will be the commis or debarrasseurs' function to keep the gueridon clear of dirty dishes and equipment.

## F. DISHES INVOLVING WORK ON THE GUERIDON

### 1. Hors d' oeuvre or substitutes.

***(a) smoked eel (anguille fume)***

***Cover***

Fish knife and fork—cold fish plate accompaniments.

Horseradish sauce/cayenne pepper/peppermill/segment of lemon.

Brown bread and butter.

Equipment for gueridon

Smoked eel on a board.

Small sharp knife and a joint fork

Sapre plate for skin and bone

Spare plate for dirty cutlery

Service spoon and fork.

***Service***

1. Commence at the tail end.
2. Cut a section about 10 cm long.
3. Insert the knife between skin and flesh on one side and loosen the skin.
4. Insert the skin between the pronge of the fork and roll up on the fork towards the backbone.
5. Cut round the backbone.
6. Roll skin off the other side and cut free with the knife.
7. Fillet each side removing the backbone.
8. Place onto a cold fish plate and serve.

**(b) Smoked trout (Truite fume)**

***Cover***

Fish knife and fork and cold fish plate.

Accompaniments:

Horseradish sauce/cayenne pepper/pepper mill/ segment of lemon.

Brown bread and butter.

Equipment for gueridon.

Smoked trout dressed on a silver flat service spoon

and fork.

Spare plate for dirty cutlery.

Service spoon and fork.

Service

1. Present dish to customer-return to gueridon.
2. Place little crips lettuce leaves and tomato on the fish plate.
3. Place the smoked trout onto a cold joint plate before removing the head and tail.
4. With the aid of trhe service spoon and fork remove both the head and tail.
5. Get the smoked trout neatly onto the cold fish plate and serve.

**(c) Smoked salmon (saumon fume)**

***Cover***

Fish knife and fork, the cold fish plate.

Accompaniments:

Cayenne pepper/pepper mill/segment of lemon.

Brown bread and butter.

Equipment for gueridon:

Smoked salmon on a board.

Carving knife and a joint fork.

Service spoon and fork.

Spare plate for dirty cutlery.

**Service**

1. Remove the black line in the middle of each slice by making a small 'V' shaped incision in the side of smoked salmon before carving.
2. Carve each slice wafer thin, giving 2/3 slices per portion.

3. Insert the edge of the slice of smoked salmon between the pronge of the joint fork and roll up.
4. Lift over to the cold fish plate and unroll neatly serve.

**(d) Caviare: This is the roe of the sturgeon**

***Cover***

Caviare knife on the right hand side of the cover.

Cold fish plate.

Accompaniments:

Hot breakfast toast/butter/segment of lemon/sieved hard boiled white and yolk of egg/chopped shallots.

Equipment for gueridon

Caviare pot in a dish of crushed ice on an unerfalt.

Sweet spoon-or-two teaspoons for service.

Spare plate for dirty cutlery.

***Service***

If a sweet or desert spoon is used than generally one spoonful, which will weigh a approximately 30 grams, is recognized as being a portion. If two teaspoons are used, the caviare is moulded in the two spoons, ¾ teaspoonfuls per portion. When served direct from the pot in this fashion the caviare is usually weighed before and after service and charged according to the amount served.

**(e) Whole melon (Melon frappe)**

Main varieties.

Contatoupe/honeydew/charentais

***Cover***

Dessert spoon and fork or dessert spoon and fork plues a small (side) knife. This is in case the melon is a little unripe.

Cold hors d'œuvre or fish plate.

Accompaniments:

Ground ginger and caster sugar.

Equipment For Gueridon:

Melon is small container of crushed ice cutting board.

Sharp knife.

Clean serviette.

Spare plate for dirty cutlery.

Soup plate for pipe from melon.

Service spoon and forks.

Cocktail cherries in small silver or glass dish.

Cocktails sticks in a holder.

***Service***

1. The melon should be in a small container of ice. Ensure all mise-en-place required is to hand before commencing the service.
2. Lift the melon with the aid of a clean serviette onto a board. Trim both ends.
3. Stand on end and cut out the required portion.
4. Place the cut portion on your clean serviette and hole firmly in left hand. Scoop out any pipe with the aid of a service spoon into remainder of the whole melon. If there is less than half the melon lift then scoop the pipe straight on to a soup plate.
5. Trim base of each portion so it stands squarely on the cold fish plate and will not roll or slide about.
6. If required the waiter may cut the flesh of the melon from the rind and slice.
7. Decorate with a cocktail cherry on a stick serve.

**2. Soup**

Real turtle soup (in tortue vraie).

***Cover***

Sweet/dessert spoon. Hot consommé cup on consomme saucer on an under plate.

***Accompaniments***

Brown bread and butter. Segment of lemon in a lemon press, placed on a side plate at the end of the cover.

Cheese straws:

Measure of warm sherry : added by the waiter at the gueridon.

Equipment Required for the Gueridon:

Portion of soup in a soup tureen, measure of sherry, sauce ladle lamp.

***Service***

1. Serve from the gueridon.
2. Reheat on the lamp and then pour into the consomme cup, which will be sitting on the consomme saucer on an underplate.
3. The measure of sherry may be warmed and added to the soup at the last moment in the kitchen or it may be heated in a ladle over the soup.
4. Serve immediately.

**3. Fish**

***(a) Sole (sole grillee ou meuniere)***

***Cover***

Fish knife and fork and a hot fish plate.

Equipment for the gueridon.

Silver flat with the sole service spoons and forks, hot joint plate for filleting, spare plate for dirty cutlery, spare plate for dirty debris, lamp.

***Service***

1. Present dish to the customer. Return to the hot plate.

2. Remove from the silver flat onto the hot joint plate.
3. With the aid of a service spoon and fork remove the side bones.
4. Run the tip of the spoon down the backbone.
5. Place two large forks back to back at the head of the fish and on the backbone. Press the forks down so that the tips of the fork pierce the flesh on either side of the backbone. Now ease the fillets slowly away from the backbone.
6. Continue to do this working the forks gradually down the backbone towards the tail.
7. Lift out the bone.
8. Place the fillets back together in their original shape on the silver flat. Reheat as necessary.
9. Coat with beurre foundue, or replace garnish and serve.

***(b)* Sole poche(with sauce over it) *i.e.,* Bonne femme veronique)**

**Cover**

Fish knife and fork. Hot fish plate.

Accompaniments

According to garnish

Equipment required for gueridon.

Hot joint plate for filleting, service spoon and fork, two joint forks, lamp, spare plate for dirty cutlery.

**Service**

1. Present dish to guest. Return to gueridon.
2. Remove sole from silver flat onto hot joint plate.
3. Remove side bones with the aid of the joint fork.
4. Run the tip of the service spoon down backbone of the sole.
5. With sid of two joint forks, fillet sole as in sole

grille ou meuniere, disturding the glazed sauce coating the fillets as little as possible.

6. Replace fillets together in the shape of fish on the silver flat.
7. Rocat with sauce and serve.

### (c) Sole frits

***Cover***

Fish knife and fork and a hot fish plate.

Accompaniments:

Sauce tartare and segment of lemon.

Equipment required for gueridon:

Service spoon and fork, hot joint plate for filletring, spare plate for debris, spare plate for dirty cutlery lamp.

***Service***

1. Ensure gueridon is laid up fully with all required mise-en-place.
2. Present dish to guest.
3. Lift sole onto hot joint plate.
4. Remove side bones as for sole grills.
5. Run the point of the spoon down centre of the sole.
6. Cut off tail approx 2.5 cm (1 in) from end.
7. Hold the spoon curved side upwards and insert the point between the fillet and the bone at the tail end of the fish.
8. Hold the sole firmly with the fork and push the spoon up towards the head, lifting off one top fillet.
9. Reheat for other top fillet, and then lift the two loosened top fillets off the backbone.
10. Lift out the backbone.
11. Replace top fillets on the bottom ones on the silver flat and reheat and then place onto a hot fish plate for service.

12. Add garnish of lemon and serve.

### (d) Saumon poche ou grille (cutlet or 'dame' of salmon)

This type of dish is generally served in an earthenware dish and therefore it is not necessary to remove it to a hot joint plate for skinning and filleting.

***Cover***

Fish knife and fork and hot fish plate.

***Accompaniments:***

According to the garnish *i.e.,* hollandaise doria

Equipment required for gueridon:

Service spoon and fork, lamp, spare plate for debris, spare plate for dirty cutlery.

***Service***

1. Present to the customer. Return to lamp on the gueridon.
2. Hold the salmon firmly in place with the fork.
3. With the point of the spoon, curved side outwards, run round the edge of the cutlet removing the skin.
4. As an alternatives to this method of removing the outer black skin, one may use a joint fork, inserting the skin between the prongs of the fork. Now twist the fork around the outer edge of 'dame' rolling the skin up on the fork as you proceed.
5. Insert the point of the spoon between the flesh and the center bone and push the fillets away from the bone.
6. Remove the bone.
7. Lift the two fillets onto the hot fish plate being careful not to break the flesh and add the garnish serve.

### (e) Blue trout (Truite au bleu)

***Cover***

Fish knife and fork and hot fish plate.

Equipment required for gueridon

Fish knife and fork, service spoon and fork, lamp, spare plate for dirty cutlery, spare plate for debris.

Accompaniments:

Hollandaise sauce for beurre fondu.

***Service***

1. Ensure gueridon is correctly laid up.
2. Present dish to customer and return to gueridon. This dish should come from the kitchen in an individual copper fish kettle.
3. Lift out on draining tray.
4. Remove out on draining tray.
5. Remove garnish of sliced carrots and onions.
6. With the point of the fish knife make an incision from head to tail on the thin line showing on the side of the trout. Only cut the skin and not the flesh.
7. Lift off the skin below that line with the knife and also above the line to the backbone.
8. Turn fish over and repeat process of removing the skin on the second side, remembering to remove the finns.
9. Lift trout carefully on to a hot fish plate and decorate with a few slices of carrot and onion. Moisten with a little stock.
10. Serve and then offer the appropriate accompaniment.

## 4. Steaks

### *(a) Entrecote double (Double entrecote steak) canning from the boned sirlion.*

***Cover***

Steak knife and a joint fork. Hot joint plate.

Accompaniments:

English and French mustard.

Equipment Required For the Gueridon:

Silver flat with the double entrecote steak on it.

A board for portioning the entrecote steak.

Sharp knife for carving.

Service spoons and forks.

Two side plates for pressing the trimmed ends to extract all juice.

Spare plate for dirty cutlery.

Lamp.

***Service***

1. Present dish to the customer return to gueridon.
2. Lift the double entrecote steak from the silver flat onto the board.
3. Trim the ends.
4. Cut on the slant into two portions. Place back on the silver flat on the lamp.
5. Press the trimmed ends between two hot sick' plates allowing the juices extracted to fall over the two portions of steak.
6. Place the portions of steak onto the hot joint plates and add the garnish. Set it out attractively. Serve.

### (b) Chateaubriand (Double fillet steak)

Although the chateaubriand is commonly termed a double fillet steak it may be large enough to serve a party of 2, 3, 4 or 5 guests as required.

The cover, accompaniments, equipment required for gueridon and service are as for entrecote double with a few exceptions.

### (c) Porterhouse steak or 'T' steak

This is a steak made up of part sirloin and part fillet, the whole being held together by the backbone and with a rib separating the sirloin from the fillet.

***Cover***

Steak knife and joint fork. Hot joint plate.

Accompaniments:

English and French mustard.

Equipment required for gueridon:

Silver flat containing the porterhouse.

Steak.

Board for carving.

Sarp knife.

Spare plate for dirty cutlery.

Spare plate for Debris.

Service spoons and forks.

Lamp.

***Service***

1. Present dish in customer-return to gueridon.
2. Remove from the silver flat onto the carving board.
3. Cut out the 'T' bone to give two separate pieces to meat; one of sirloin and one of fillet.
4. Return the two pieces of meat to the silver flat; reheat quickly.

5. Dress attractively onto the hot joint plate with the garnish.
6. If the porterhouse steak is for more than one person then carve the fillets as for a chateaubriand.

### *(d)* Steak tartare

***Cover***

Joint knife and fork and a cold joint plate.

Accompaniments:

Cayeme pepper and pepper mill.

Equipment required for gueridon:

Soup plate.

Service spoons and forks.

Spare plate for debris.

Spare plate for dirty cutlery.

Containers for the various ingredients.

Ingredients.

Portion of chopped raw fillet steak moulded into a cake shape and presented on a round silver flat. The portion of raw fillet steak will be welled in the centee to hold a whole egg. Only the yolk of the egg will be used. Chopped, gherkins capers parsley and shallots.

Oil and vinegar.

Pepper mill.

Salt.

French mustard.

Worchestershire sause.

***Service***

1. Ensure your gueridon has all the necessary mise-en-place before proceeding to make the sauce.
2. Add the seasoning of salt, pepper mill and French mustard together in the soup plate. Mix well.

3. Separate the yolk from the white of egg placing the york into the soup plate and the white into a spare container.
4. Beat the yolk and seasoning together using a service (Joint) fork.
5. Add vinegar and mix in and then add a little oil and mix in according to the amount of sauce you wish to make.
6. Be careful of the quantity of sauce as the finished product should be most but runny or too liquid.
7. Add the chopped gherkins, capers, parsley and shallots and bind the whole well together.
8. Now place in the raw chopped fillet steak together with dash of worceshtershire sauce, incorporating the sauce and fillet steak well together.
9. Shape into a round flat cake and place on the cold joint plate serve.

**(e) Steak Diane**

***Cover***

Steak knife and joint fork. Hot joint plate.

Accompaniments.

English and French mustard.

Equipment for the gueridon.

Lamp.

Pan on an underplate.

Service spoons and forks.

Tea spoons.

Plate for dirty cutlery.

Ingredients.

Minute steak on a plate.

Chopped shallots.

Chopped parsley.

Fine herbs.

Jug of double cream.

Cayenne pepper and pepermill cruet.

Oil and butter.

Worchestershire sauce.

***Service***

1. Ensure the gueridon is correctly laid up with all the mise-en-place.
2. Enquire of customer how he or she would like the steak cooked.
3. Place some butter and a little oil in the pan and allow to melt. The oil will prevent the butter from burning.
4. Season the steak with cruet, cayenne, pepper and pepper mill.
5. Place the chopped shallots in the pan and sweat without colouring until cooked.
6. Place steak in the pan and cook as required.
7. Add a dash of Worchstershire sauce, and then sprinkle with some chopped parsley and fines herbs.
8. Add measure of brandy and flambe.
9. Serve immediately from the pan onto a hot joint plate at the table.
10. Before serving, a thickened sauce may be made by the addition of a little double cream. Bring up to simmering point but do not boil.
11. If a sauce is made for the steak, it must be kept on a hot joint plate on the hot plate and covered whilst the sauce is being prepared.
12. Coat the steak with the sauce and serve ensuring it is piping hot.

**5. Salads (la salads verte)**

Green or fruit salad is generally offered as an accompaniment with a main course dish.

The cover for a salad when offered with a main course dish will be a salad crescent shaped dish, or a small round wooden bowls with a small or dessert fork, or a small wooden spoon and folk. The pronge of the small or dessert fork should be pointing downwards to avoid tarnishing the silver with the acids in the dressing.

There are a variety of both salads and dressings which may be offered to the guest according to the choice.

Dressings: The five main types of dressing are as follows:

1. French dressing
2. English dressing
3. Sauce dressing
4. Requefort dressing
5. Acidulated cream dressing

Equipment required on the gueridon when preparing a salad dressing:

1. The ingredients depending on the types of dressing required.
2. Soups plate.
3. Service cloth.
4. Service spoons and fork.
5. Salad crescent or wooden salad bowl.
6. Dessert or small fork or a small wooden spoon and fork.
7. Glass bowl for tossing the salad.
8. Teaspoon for testing the dressing.

***Service***

The dressing required will be prepared by the waiter

on the guedon at the table. The dressing and salad are tossed togethem the glass bowl; the salad or fruit will then be dressed on to the salad crescent which is then placed at the top left-hand corner of the cover before serving the dish which it accompanies.

### 6. Poury

#### (a) Chicken (poulet roti)

***Cover***

Joit knife and fork. Hot joint plate.

Acompaniments:

Bred sauce, roast gravy.

Equipment required for gueridon:

Caving board.

Shap carving knife.

Service spoons and forks.

Plate for dirty cutlery.

Plate for debris.

Lamp.

Chicken on a silver flat.

***Service***

1. Present the whole chicken to host at the table-return lamp on gueridon.
2. With the service spoon and fork lift the chicken from the silver flat on to the carving board, draining off any liquid that may be inside of it.
3. Lie the chicken on its side on the board from the right to left in front of you and with a leg uppermost.
4. Holding the bird firmly on the board with the flat of the knife, insert the service fork beneath ~he leg joint and raise the leg until the skin surrounding is taut.

5. Cut around the taut skin surrounding the leg with the tip of the knife at the same time pulling the leg away from the joint and cutting the flesh where necessary.
6. Cut the leg into two pieces through the joint and also remove the claw end.
7. Place the two pieces of leg onto the silver flat.
8. Proceed in the same manner with the other leg.
9. Turn the chicken onto its back. Insert the joint fork into the base of the carcase to hold it firmly.
10. Carve part of the breast and down through the wing joint giving one piece made up of the wing and a little breast.
11. If necessary turn the chicken on its side and with the aid of the service. The carcase at the same time holding the chicken firmly with the flat of the knife.
12. Proceed in the same manner with the other wing.
13. Position the bird on its back. Cut down one side of the breastbone and lever off half the breast.
14. Proceed in the same manner with the other side of the breast.
15. Turn the chicken on to its breast holding it firmly in place with the service fork.
16. Insert the knife between the flesh and the wishbone and holding the whate breast on the board with the knife, lever the carcase away with the aid of the service fork.
17. Cut the whole breast into two portions lengthways.
18. Reheat the carved chicken on the lamp.
19. Serve the chicken giving some brown and some white meat per portion. Remember to add some game chips and watercress if these make up the garnish.

**(b) Poussin (Young chicken: 6 weeks old)**

***Cover***

Joint knife and fork. Hot joint plate.
Accompaniments:

As per menu garnish.

Equipment required for gueridon

Poussion on silver flat.

Lamp.

Board.

Knife.

Service spoon and forks.

Plate for dirty cutlery.

Plate for debris.

***Service***

1. Present to customer-return to the gueridon.
2. Lift the poussin from the silver flat onto the carving board with the aid of the service spoon and fork.
3. Insert the service fork into the base of the carease and hold firmly on the board with the breast uppermost.
4. With the tip of the knife cut the Poussin in half down through the breast.
5. Take the half poussin attached to the backbone and remove the backbone.
6. Place the two portions of poussin on the silver flat and reheat if necessary.
7. Present attractively on to the hot joint plate. Add garnish and or souce. Serve.
8. Game:

   *(i)* *Grouse:* Grouse is regarded as a particularly dish. If small it is generally served whole.

Otherwise it would split into two portions by carving down through the middle of the breastbone.

(ii) *Partridge:* Depending on its size the partridge may be carved into two or three portions. If large the three portions would consists of:

*(a)* One leg and one wing with a little of the breast attached.

*(b)* as for (a) above.

(c) The breast left on the bone. If split into two portions by carving down through the breast bone.

*(d)* Woodcock (Becasse) : Split into two portions as for grouse or patridge. Generally served on a croute spread with a pate made from the goblets of the woodcock.

*(e)* Snipe (Becassine) : Served whole as spine are too small for carving into portions.

*(f)* Pheasant (Faisan) : The flesh of the pheasant is very dry and the waiter should use a very sharp knife. Remove the legs as for chicken or duck. These are normally not served. Carve in thin slices on either side of the breast down to the wing joint.

*(g)* Wood pigeon : Carved in half through the breast to give two portions.

*(h)* Saddle of hare : Carved in slices lengthwise as in a saddle of lamb. Flesh is dark in colour.

9. *Joints* : These would be carved on the carving trolley at the table.

(a) *Co trefilet de boeuf (Baned sirloin of beaf)* : Carved in thin slices giving mainly leen meat and a little fat per portion. The beef itself should be a little underdone. The accompaniments offered would be roast gray and Yorkshire pudding from the trolley and English and French mustard and horseradish sauce placed on the table by the waiter.

(b) *Aloyan de bocuf (Sirloin of beef on the bone)* : The portions here should be carved in thin slices down towards the ribs. On reaching a rib bone the waiter must release the meat attached to the rib bone by running the knife along the rib bone and between the rib bone and the sirloin. This thin allows the slices of meat carved to fall free. The accompaniments offered would be as for a counterfilet.

(c) *Corre d' agneau (Best end of lamb)* : Carve two outlets per portion. Hold the carre firmly on the board by inserting a service fork into the base at one end of the carre. Hold the carre upright. Carve into outlets using the exposed end of the ribs to guide to the correct amount per portion.

(d) *Selle d' agneau (saddle of lamb)* : Remove the whole side loin from the saddle and then carve into slices parallel with the ribs and approximately 6 mm thick, give some lean meat and some fat per portion.

Accompaniments offered would be mint sauce and roast gravy.

(e) *Gigot d agneau (Leg of lamb) :* The waiter should remember here that initially he should carve onto the bone. Take a small V-shape portion of meat out just above the knuckle. Now proceed to grave your portions of meat by carving on to the bone form the V-shaped cut. This part of the joint is known as the nut and is the most choice part. After the initial portions have been carved from the nut of meat the succeeding portions should be carved a slice from the nut and a slice from the underside.

The accompaniments offered are roast gravy and mint sauce. When carving a leg of lamb to hold it steadily on the board the waiter should hold the knuckle in a clean serviette.

(10) Service of flambe sweet dishes and dessert at the table.

(11) Peche flambe.

***Cover***

Dessert spoon and fork and a hot sweet plate.

***Accompaniments:***

Castor sugar.

***Equipment for gueridon:***

Lamp, pan on an underplate, sauce ladle, matches spare plate for dirty catlery, service spoons and forks on a service plate, one measures of brandy, castor sugar, portions of warmed peaches in peach syrup in a timbate.

***Service***

1. Place peach syrup in pan and heat.
2. Heat the portion of peaches.
3. Pierce peaches with a fork to allow the heat to penetrate more quickly.
4. Baste the peaches occasionally allowing the peach syrup to reduce right down until it is almost caramelizing.
5. At this stage sprinkle with caster sugar. This speeds up the carmelising effect and side flabeeing.
6. Ensure the hot sweet plate is now placed in front of the guest.
7. Pour over brandy and flambee.
8. Serve from the pan on to hot sweet plates at the gueridon.

### (b) Poire flambe

As for above using pears and pear syrup instead of peaches and peach syrup.

### (c) Banana flambes

***Cover***

Dessert spoon and a fork and a hot sweet plate.

***Accompaniments:***

Caster sugar.

***Equipments for gueridon:***

Lamp, pan on an underplate, butter in a butter dish on a doyley on a side plate, butter knife, matches portion of banana, coaster sugar, measures of rum, fresh orange juice, service spoons and forks on a service plate, spare plate for dirty equipment, board, small carving knife.

***Service***

1. Place a banana on a board. Trim both ends of the banana.
2. Slit the skin down the length of the banana through to the flesh.
3. Remove the skin.
4. Cut the banana in two lengthways.
5. Place the butter in the pan and melt.
6. Pierce both halves of the banana with a fork to allow the heat to penetrate more quickly.
7. Place the banana in the pan and heat. Baste with the butter occasionally.
8. When golden brown add a little fresh orange juice and blend well. This produces you sauce and take away the surplus fat from within the sauce.
9. At this stage place the hot sweet plate on the table in front of the guest.
10. When heated sufficiently, flambe with the rum or brandy.

11. Serve at the table from the pan on to the hot sweet plate or serve on to the hot sweet plates on the gueridon.

**(d) Cerises flambe au kirsch**

**Cover**

Dessert spoon and fork and a hot sweet plate.

***Accompaniments***

Castor sugar.

***Equipment for gueridon:***

Pan, lamp, matches, spare plate for dirty cutlery, portion of cherries-n-syrup in a timbalte, sauce ladle, services spoons and forks on a service plate, castor sugar, measure of kirsch.

***Services***

1. Place the cherries and cherry syrup into the pan and heat.
2. Reduce the cherry syrup to a minimum.
3. Sprinkle with caster sugar to help caramelize the remaining syrup and to aid flambeeeing.
4. Place the hot sweet plates on the table in front of the guests.
5. Add the kirsch and flambee
6. Serve at the table from the pan on to hot sweet plates or serve on to hot sweet plates on the gueridon.

**(e) Cerises flambes an glace vanilla**

As above with the vanilla ice cream being served immediately before the cerises flambee.

**7. Dessert (Fresh fruit and nuts)**

***Cover***

Fruit knife an fork, fruit plate, are finger bowl on a doyley on an underplate with cold water, or a small glass bowl if more than two portions of grapes are to be served, a second finger bowl on a dayley on an underplate containing warm water and a slice of lemon, spare sideplates for shells and skins etc., spare serviette nutcrackers grape scissors.

***Accompaniments:***

Castor sugar and salt.

***Service***

Present the fruit basket to the guest allowing him to make his choice. If the guest choose grapes the required portion will be cut from the main bunch and held in the grape scissors, will be rinsed in the finger bowl or glass bowl containing the cold water before being placed onto the fruit plate. If the pineapple, oranges, pears or bananas are chosen then these may be prepared on the gueridon by the waiter.

**General points to note**

(a) Gueridon service is essentially a chef and commis service. Therefore, there must be complete liaison and teamwork between them and every member of the brigade.

*(b)* Always push the gueridon and never pull it. This helps to avoid accidents as one is able to see more easily where one is going.

## CHAPTER 10

# RULES AND REGULATIONS FOR RESTAURANT

For putting up a restaurant project, an entrepreneur has to weave his way through a labyrinth of rules and regulations, requiring sanctions of the central and state governments and local authorities. There are many regulations that a restaurant project has to comply with prior to construction after constructions but before commissioning and those that it has to encounter during operations. There is virtually no action that could be independently taken by the industry as each of these are governed by some law or regulation.

**REGULATIONS PRIOR TO COMMISSION OF RESTAURANT**

| Nature of regulation | Regulating authority | Remark |
|---|---|---|
| Approval of project | Govt. of India | Required prior to starting the project. |
| Approval of floor | Local bodies | Required before taking up construction. |
| Approval of Hotel's height | Local bodies and civil aviation ministry | For restriction height of the hotel. |
| Approval of plumbing/sanitary systems | Local bodies | |
| Sanction for connected electrical load and maximum demand | Local bodies | |
| Sanction for water supply requirement | Local bodies | |
| Sanction of LPG furnance oil | Ministry of petroleum, IOC | |
| Sanction for garbage disposal, sewage systems etc. | Local bodies | |
| Approval for raising capital | Controller of capital issues | To obtain approval for raising of funds from public for construction of restaurants |
| Obtaining of import licence | Dept. of tourism, Reserve bank of India, DGFT | To obtain approval for import of equipment required for restaurant projects. |
| Clearance under Urban land | State Govt. (Under Central and State legislation) | To ensure that land used by hotel is not covered under any restriction of acquisitions under the ULC act. |

(contd.)

| Nature of regulation | Regulating authority | Remark |
|---|---|---|
| Approval for electrical and installation | Local bodies | |
| Approval for lift installation | Local bodies | |
| Approval for cold storage installation | Local bodies | |
| Approval for free safety installation and NOC | Local bodies | |
| Approval for operation of laundry | Local bodies | |
| Approval for boiler installation | Local bodies | |
| Approval for D.G. set installation | Local bodies | |
| Building completion certificate and occupancy certificate | Local bodies | Before occupying restaurant. |
| Approval of restaurant | Deptt. of Tourism | For operating a restaurant to be able to avail of various incentives. |

## LABOUR REGULATIONS

| *Labour regulations* | *State or Central legislation* |
|---|---|
| **Act/Rules** | |
| Industrial Disputes Act, 1947 | Labour department |
| Rajasthan Shops and Commercial Establishment Act, 1958 | Labour department |
| Minimum Wages Act, 1948 | Labour department |
| Payment of Wages Act, 1936 | Labour department |
| Payment of Bouns Act, 1956 | Labour department |
| Payment of Gratuity Act, 1972 | Labour department |
| Contract Labour (Regulation and Abolition Act, 1970) | Labour department |
| Industrial Employment (Standing Orders) Act, 1946 | Labour department |
| Maternity Benefit Act, 1961 | Labour department |
| Trade Union Act, 1926 | Labour department |
| The Employees Provident Fund and Misc. Provision Act, 1952 | Regional P.F. Commissioner |
| Employees Family Pension Scheme, 1971 | Regional P.F. Commissioner |
| Employees State Insurance Act, 1948 | E.S.I. Corporation |
| Equal remuneration act, 1948 | Labour Deptt. |
| Moter Transport Worker Act, 1961 | Labour Deptt. |

## REGULATIONS DURING OPERATIONS

| *Nature of regulation* | *Regulating authority* | *Remark* |
|---|---|---|
| Approval of storage furnance oil and HSD | Deptt. of Explosives | To store furnace and diesel, oil |
| Approval for operation of paging system, walkie, talkie etc. | Ministry of Communication and local Police Deptt. | |
| Availing of fiscal incentives | Deptt. of Tourism | Approval under Sections 32, 33 and 80 of the Income Tax Act. |
| Exchange of foreign currency foreigners arrival | RBI Foreign Residents Registration officer | To obtain money changers licence: For entimation of all arrivals of foreign tourists. |
| Prevention of food adulteration Act | Local bodies | To ensure that hotels are not using (under central legislation) adulterated raw materials for food preparation. |
| Boiler inspection | Boiler inspectors | For operating a boilder. |
| Liquor licence | Excise authorities | Transporting, storing and selling of spirits, wine and beer. |
| Sales tax act | Central and State Govt. | To regulate collection and payment of sales tax on sale of food, liquor etc. |
| Entertainment tax | Local bodies | Collection of tax on floor and shows entertainment shows musical nights etc. |
| Weight and measurement act | Central Govt. | To monitor weights and measurement regulations of all kinds of weighting |

| *Nature of regulation* | *Regulating authority* | *Remark* |
|---|---|---|
| Land and building tax | State Govt. | scales, measurements etc., relating to payment of goods and items sold. |
| Luxury tax act. | - do - | To impose and collect luxury tax from guests staying at the hotel on the premise that expenditure on the hotel is conspicuous luxury. |
| Property tax, water tax, sewerage tax | Local bodies | For collection of tax on hotels for the purpose of maintaining public utilities. |
| Release of foreign exchange | Deptt. of Tourism and RBI | For controlling outflow of foreign exchange involved in promotional tours developments and prospectus training of personnel import of raw materials etc. |
| Not to sell panner, khoya and milk based sweets | Local bodies | |
| Classification of the hotel | Deptt. of Tourism | For classifying hotels into various star categories on the basis of predetermined norms. |
| Renting of rooms | Local bodies | |
| Running of restaurant | Local bodies | Issuance of licence. |
| Sales and manufacture of tea and other eatables | Local bodies | |

CHAPTER 11

# TIPS REGARDING RESTAURANT MAINTENANCE

The growing demands of business traveller, the increasing cost of energy, a growing awareness of safety and environmental issues, both at the guest and employee ends, has resulted to take up these issues seriously. So, the engineering department of the restaurants incorporated many new ideas to realise these issues. They have implemented a number of innovative and technological advancements in the area of '**Restaurant Engineering**'.

By implementing these techniques, a restaurant can become a trend-setter and can establish a new benchmark in the following areas of restaurant engineering:

A. Energy Management

B. Environmental engineering

C. Fire, safety and security.

D. Connectivity and value addition

## A. ENERGY MANAGEMENT

A restaurant can save electricity, fuel, oil and water by implementing various innovative technological measures. The various measures adopted by a restaurant are as follows:

**Electrical**

1. Building automation system for HVAC.
2. Automatic voltage stabilizer for lighting.
3. Variable frequency drives for air handling units and water management system.
4. Automation and modification of the cooling tower by FRP fans.
5. High yield low energy pumps for cascades, sewage and storm water transfers.
6. PLC controlled water management system.
7. Energy efficient lighting like CFLs.
8. Long life, energy efficient tube lights, fittings and chokes.
9. On-line sub-metering and auditing of electrical energy by VC-PRO and SEMS.
10. Shiftwise power budgeting energy conservation logos and award schemes.

**Oil**

1. Oil additives for boiler fuel by EF.
2. PID controllers to maintain hot water temperature.
3. Hot water generation by flash steam.
4. In-house energy audit of steam generation and supply system for better control.

**Water**

1. Automatic pressure reducing valves in basement and ground floor.
2. Uses of laundry and kitchen waste water for horticulture.
3. Recycling back wash water in the nursery.
4. Auto flush and auto taps in the wash rooms.

## B. ENVIRONMENTAL ENGINEERING

This is the another important area of restaurant engineering. The various environmental tips that should be followed are as follows:

1. Recycling of cooking oil for soap manufacturing.
2. Auto flush and auto taps.
3. Environmental awareness training programme.
4. Free pollution checking drive for vehicles during 'World Environment Day' (6th June every year).
5. Photo voltaic lighting for logos and welcome Environ Board.
6. Ozone injection for cooling tower and swimming pool - phasing out of chlorine.
7. Recycling of bath and wash-basin water.
8. Recycling of spent oil from kitchen for soap manufacturing.
9. Installation of biomethanation plant—In this plant, biodegradable food waste from kitchen is converted into bio-gas and cater to 50 per cent of the cooking gas requirement of the hotel.

## C. FIRE, LIFE SAFETY AND SECURITY

To make a restaurant the safest one, a lot of innovations and technological advancements are incorporated by a restaurateurs. Some of the measures are as follows:

1. Coverage of the restaurant by sprinkler system, smoke detector, heat detector, central annunciation with call back facility, deluge system for LPG installation and transformers, public address systems for evacuations.
2. Fire doors and panic hardware for the guest rooms.
3. Machine guarding, lock out, tag out and work permit systems.

4. Voice display unit workstation analysis.
5. Microprocessor controlled fire panel with pager interface.
6. Compartmentalisation with panic hardware.
7. State-of-the-art fire fighting systems equivalent to in house fire station of per Tariff Advisory Committee.
8. Special evacuation chairs.
9. Portable smoke extractors and hand held automatic dual pressure nozzles.
10. Tail end smoke detectors.
11. Fluorescent energy candle lights—Welcome light.
12. Remote operated holdup alarms with pager interface.
13. Battery back up emergency light with CFLs.
14. Installation of eye wash stations at strategic locations.
15. Surveillance system with video grabber, multiplexer and time lapse video recording at strategic locations to enhance security.
16. Multi channel two-way communication through motorola GP-300 for better connectivity of the security personnel.

## D. CONNECTIVITY AND VALUE ADDITION

A restaurant has to manage some formulas to maintain the technological superiority in the industry and to meet the wants and needs of the business traveller. Some of them are as follow:

1. Business video conferencing by pro share technology - Desktop or Boardroom video conferencing facility, both national and international locations.
2. Info Kiosk with touch screen facility - provides information about within the hotel or places of interest.

3. Multicolour building illumination—building illumination by seven different colours on seven different days.
4. Bar automation, that is, liquor control through Berg Technology.
5. Room status display for freshen up services.
6. International and domestic flight information system.
7. Computerisation of Engineering Operation—an interactive complaint management and various other engineering functions through the local area network—LAN. Thus reducing paperwork, human interference and enhancing the services.

## E. HAZARD VERSUS LACK OF INFORMATION

It is well known that among many factors safety and security of a restaurant are of prime importance. To ensure that the customers and avail themselves of a comfortable stay, it is important that all criteria of the same are maintained, especially if a good response is expected.

The safety of a restaurant means the security of a number of things. Following are some of the requirements that require attention.

### A. Storage of Goods

Hazardous and inflammable goods in should be stored in specified conditions in proper storage areas or store rooms.

The inflammable goods need to be stored away from the building, especially from hot areas like the kitchen. It should be strictly enforced that these goods must be handled by authorised and trained personnel only. They should be stocked in a neat and clean area.

### B. Lack of Maintenance of Machinery and Equipment

If machinery and equipment are not maintains properly, then chances of accident can increase. So smaller and especially complex machinery like boilers, generators etc., must be maintained and serviced from time to time.

### C. Lack of Knowledge of the Operations of Equipment and Machinery

Even no knowledge or half knowledge in the operation of machinery and equipment can cause damage to machinery or safety hazards to the hotel property and human life. It is very important that only authorised and trained staff be allowed to handle such specific tasks and operations of the equipment.

### D. Lack of Knowledge of Safety Rules

Even a lack of knowledge of the safety rules amongst the staff and guests can cause negligence on their part resulting in a safety hazard.

So, it is very important that all rooms and public areas have safety regulations displayed.

It is also very important for any hotel to ensure that the guest is assured with the security of their property while in the hotel compound, or while they are in their rooms or even when they are away.

A hotel also needs to ensure the following:

(a) All rooms and public area must display safety regulations.

(b) Safe deposit facilities to guests in the room should be provide or at least at the reception. Smaller hotels can provide the same with a manager in-charge.

(c) Maintain proper lighting in all area. So that the staff should be able to notice any kind of suspicious activity.

(d) Security guards must be provided to guard entrance. Exist at all probable areas where in entry of outsiders generally goes unnoticed.

(e) Training of all staff for crisis management and safety systems.

(i) A communication system is also required, wherein employees are able to notify emergencies and suspicious characters without raising a false alarm or creating a panic situation.

(g) The movement of staff within the hotel must be controlled by the individual supervisors and managers.

## ENGINEERING OBJECTIVES AT A GLANCE

1. To be the leanest and meanest workforce and energy machine in the hospitality industry.
2. To be the most eco-friendly and safest hotel
3. Zero MTBF (Meantime between failure) through scientific methods.
4. To maintain the technological superiority in the industry.

*Source: Hotelier and Caterer 15th March, 1999.*

## CHAPTER 12

# MOTEL OPERATION

"Also called Motor Lodge, Motor Court, Tourist Court, or Motor Inn, originally a hotel designed for persons travelling by automobile, with convenient parking space provide. Motel serves commercial and business travellers and persons attending conventions and tourists. The automobile became the principle mode of travel by 1950 in the U.S. and by 1960s in Europe and Japan; and motel were built as near as possible to railroad stations. Most motels provide an informal atmosphere compared to hotels; often the guest transports his own luggage to and from his room. Most but not all motels have restaurant facilities and many have swimming pools, most rooms contain a television set.

Motels originated as a series of separate or attached roadside cabins, independently operated; but when professional management took over, their sized increased and the chain concept became popular. Franchising operations, in which an individual is allowed to go into business or himself under the widely advertised name of a chain of motel, thus realising the benefits of chain operations with relatively modest investment, has achieved remarkable growth for several chains."

Hotel located at highways to specially meet the accommodation requirements of road travellers are known as 'MOTEL'. In contrast with city hotels, the emphasis in motels is more on parking space, service station, petrol pump etc., which a road travellers needs the most. Sometimes, city hotels having large parking facilities also sell as motels. The sign of a motel atop a building is an indication to a traveller that he will get parking space for his vehicle there.

## HISTORY OF MOTELS

The motel is truly the inn-keepers's answer to the needs of the travellers - in the twentieth century, relating directly to the increased use and popularity of the automobile. The forerunners of the modern motels were small tourist cabins, usually a cluster of less than ten, mostly without baths, built by some farmers as a sideline along the road. They provide little more than a bed and overnight shelter for the passing travellers. As automobile traffic increased, these cabins grew in numbers, size and appointments became full-time business in themselves. Known as tourist courts, they consisted of detached frame cottages, clustered or spread over a sizeable tract of land, with heated rooms and private baths. Many ways, particularly on the outskirts of small cities and town or near resort areas. Most of them now have restaurant facilities, swimming pools, telephone service, television and air-conditioning improvements that make it difficult to continue classifying them as tourist courts They are not different from modern motels, except perhaps in design of the buildings.

The next development was the roadside or highway motel. Initially, these were one-storey building, spread over a large area, containing a central office and connecting rooms on one or both sides of it. As the needs for more rooms grew and land became more expensive, they became two and even three storeyed buildings.

All three types had one thing in common: very little, if any, service. The guests registered, were given they key to their room and then parked their own car in front of their room, carried in their own bags, and were free to leave the following day at or before check-out time. These establishments were geared to speed automobile travellers on their way conveniently and economically. As more facilities were added, restaurants and swimming pools in particular, guests may have lingered more but, with easy access to their room, were still free to come and go as they pleased. Motels usually provided soft-drink and ice-dispensing machine from which the guests helped themselves.

Thus, the primary difference between a motel and hotel, until recently, was in service. In a hotel, the guest, has his or her car parked by an employee and pays extra for the garage; another hotel employee takes the guest to the room; the freedom of movement, especially by car, that the motel guest has is restricted; and ice and soft drinks are available only from room service.

But in the early 1960s a new trend in motels began to emerge. They grew large and more elaborate and finally moved into the downtown sections of larger cities. Land there was very expensive, so in order to increase the number of rooms, the new motels were built ten, even fifteen storeyed high. No longer could a guest be given a parking space near the room, and the registration process became the same as in a hotel. All the facilities offered by a hotel - telephone, television, air-conditioning, room-service, coffee shops, restaurants, valet, laundry and shop of all kinds - are duplicated in such a motel. Perhaps the only difference is that every motel has a garage, and parking is usually free. Because they are more truly hotels, the larger ones have become known as "motor hotels". In fact, they are holds built primarily to cater to the motorist. However, with their large number of bedrooms, restaurants, and banquet and meeting rooms, they are in direct competition with the hotels.

In the 1970s, a new trend began. No longer are people migrating to the large cities; instead they are moving away from them, to the suburbs and the country. Crime, high taxes, the flight of industry, and the resulting loss in sobs were the principle reason fǫr this reversal. The travelling public, alarmed by the crime statistics published in newspapers and reported daily on radio and television began shying away from overnight stays in the city.

Still, the city has too many cultural attractions to keep people from visiting it entirely. Therefore, a new type of motel or motor hotel is emerging in the suburbs surrounding the big cities. There the travellers park the cars, stay at night, and each day travel into the city with the family by bus or train. They enjoy the city by day and return to the motel for the night.

Here again, economics comes into play. These motorists cannot fill the motel or make it a profitable business. The motels are built with restaurants and banquet and meeting rooms, many with luxurious appointments, to compete with the facilities offered by the hotels in the city. The better city hotels will survive, with large group and convention business and with the many visitors who stay in the cities in spite of all bad publicity; but the suburban and airport motor hotels are growing in number and popularity.

By the middle 1970s, the motel had come full cycle, from the small tourist cabins to the luxurious motor hotels in the resort areas, cities and suburbs. But a small crack had appeared in this headlong upward spiral of facilities and services. In California, a small chain was born with what is considered an entirely new concept of operation. The idea had been originally tried and discarded by the largest and one of the most luxurious chains of motels in the world, Holiday Inns, whose original properties were conceived as a group of low - to medium priced motels. As they grew in size and popularity, however, they added restaurants, meeting and convention room lobbies and recreational facilities, and upgraded the furnishing and equipment in the sleeping rooms, thus completely abandoning the original concept. The general public, during a prolonged period of prosperity, was not interested in economy.

However, in the late 1960s, inflation, recession, and the resulting increase in unemployment started to take their tall. The travelling public began to question, and many could not afford, the high room rates necessary to profitability operate these beautiful motels and motor hotels. The need grew, the time was right, and the concept started by Motel in California slowly spread across the country. Whatever name they go under - the operation of these budget motels are similar. Many are located in fringe areas, accessible to, but not on, the main highways. They are built at the lowest possible cost to provide lodging without frills, primarily for the commercial travellers and the family on vacation. For this purpose, the expenses of operation and the per-room cost of the building itself must be drastically reduced. Construction costs are kept low by using modular-type construction in which the entire rooms are built elsewhere, transported to the site, and placed side by side. The buildings usually have no lobbies, restaurants, banquet, meeting or convention rooms and the bedrooms are very small. Many have a small office and kitchen combination where guest can get themselves a light breakfast at a minimum charge. Furnishing in the rooms are down to the bare essentials. TV, where it is provided is coin operated and usually only in black and white. Although each room has a private bath, it is fitted with a small standing shower, rather than a combination services other than a maid to clean and make up, the room. All they offer is a clean comfortable room at a low rate.

The history of motels tells us that the increase in automobile travel produced a new phenomenon in the hospitality field, i.e., the motel industry. Today the motel became a method of providing low-cost accommodation for such travellers.

## THE MOTEL ASSOCIATION

The history of the hotel industry would be incomplete without some comments on the motel associations. The American Hotel and Motel Association came into being at a much later date than the New York City Association. Originally called the American Hotel Association, it began as a protective society whose purpose was to protect hotels from frauds perpetrated by guests. In the 1920s, however, it became actively involved in the educational and training field. It was because of action taken by the association that hotel schools and degrees in hotel administration were offered by an increasing number of colleges throughout the country.

Today, the American Hotel and Motel Association has related associations on Canada, Mexico, Bermuda, The Bahamas, Central America, The Caribbean, Europe, Asia, Africa, and South America. These associations collectively provide advice and direction to more then 8,000 individual hotels and motels. At the same time, they represents the hotels in the eyes of the public by providing advertising and public relation to support the industry. Furthermore, they act on behalf of the industry in various capacities where it must be represented at a governmental level.

## MOTLES IN INDIA

In a past few decades the tremendous increase in automobiles travel and the corresponding decrease in the use of railroads, has opened up many new areas that could not previously be considered proper sites for hotel development. As a result, newer hotels are frequently located outside the city at airports and on the highways. In particular, the increase in automobile travel produced a new phenomenon in the Indian hospitality field, the motel industry.

By the beginning of 20th century, Indian tourists travelled almost exclusively by rail and ship. The invention of the new transport medium, travel by a private car and coach received its first impetus in the ten yeats which preceded World War I. The entire shape of tourist industry was, therefore, transformed by the invention of this new transport medium. The growth of the private car may be identified as a major cause of the decline of the railways. The motor car gradually came to be the alternative means of transport for both short and medium range of journeys. Subsequently, with the growth of a fine network of fast and superfast national and international highway systems, long journeys were also performed by motorcar and motor coach.

The motor car revolutionlised by holiday habits. Although the motor cars had come into operation by the beginning of 20th century, after independence of the country their numbers jumped manifolds. It became increasingly important in the pursuit of leisure and tourism. The actual number of holiday-makers travelling by road increased tremendously as more and more people took holidays away from home.

Mobility can, perhaps, be considered as one of the major transport. The motor car had provided the actual mobility so that people are no longer anchored to a particular holiday centre as they tended to be when they mostly travelled by train. Speed is yet another important factor which economises on time, and, therefore, makes its possible for people with limited amount of time to travel to distant places. People with even one week of holiday consider it sufficient to travel. The gradual spread of the network of roads opened up many new areas and made many places hitherto not very accessible easy to get to. The gradual spread of the network of roads opened up many new areas and made many places hitherto not very accessible easy to get to. The railways, on the other hand, tended rather to concentrate and restrict movement to particular channels.

**SOME OF THE MAIN HOTEL-MOTEL GROUPS OF WORLD**

| Organization country | Type | Hotel/Motel Group | No. of rooms |
|---|---|---|---|
| 1. Holiday Inns (U.S.A.) | Chain | 1,755 | 303,578 |
| 2. Best Western (U.S.A.) | Consortium | 2,761 | 207,299 |
| 3. Sheraton (U.S.A.) | Chain | 418 | 107,966 |

(*contd.*)

| Organization country | Type | Hotel/Motel Group | No. of rooms |
|---|---|---|---|
| 4. Ramada (U.S.A.) | Chain | 635 | 94,000 |
| 5. Friendship Inn (U.S.A.) | Consortium | 1,080 | 78,500 |
| 6. Trust House Fort Britain | Chain | 810 | 72,299 |
| 7. Hilton Co. (U.S.A.) | Chain | 203 | 71,804 |
| 8. Federation, National, France | Consortium | 4,345 | 71,711 |
| 9. Supra National (Switzerland) | Consortium | 370 | 70,000 |
| 10. Howard Johnshon (U.S.A.) | Chain | 521 | 59,000 |
| 11. Golden Tulip (Holland) | Consortium | 350 | 55,000 |
| 12. Balkan Tourist (Bulgaria) | Chain | 684 | 51,443 |
| 13. Flag Inns. (Australia) | Consortium | 652 | 50,000 |
| 14. Days Inns (U.S.A.) | Chain | 315 | 44,000 |
| 15. S.R.S. Hotels (Germany) | Consortium | 159 | 43,900 |
| 16. Quality Inns (U.S.A.) | Chain | 350 | 41,415 |
| 17. H.R.S.I. (U.S.A.) | Consortium | 145 | 40,000 |
| 18. Clun Maditeranian France | Chain | 132 | 36,333 |
| 19. Novotel, France | Chain | 283 | 35,214 |

Road transport made striking advances in the subsequent years. Soon after, 1950, when the difficulties and restriction of the immediate post-war years had begun to make themselves out, there were rapid developments transport; whereas the car ownership multiplied, the motor coach appeared in increasing numbers and the coach tour became popular. Greater use of motor cars and coach is being made at present for the purpose of tourism.

Though economic conditions in the recent years as a result of increasing fuel costs and the energy crisis, have not favoured travel by private motor car, road transport remains the mode most used by visitors. Road transport is also used enormously by businessman. They send their goods mostly through trucks, lorries, small vehicles and so on.

Keeping in view these facts in mind emphasis is being give to the construction of new motorways and highways in India. An introduction of national highways is given below:

| | | |
|---|---|---|
| NH | 1 | Delhi-Ambala-Amritsar-Pakistan border |
| NH | 1A | Jalandhar-Jammu-Srinagar-Baramula-Uri |
| NH | 1B | Batote-Doda-Kishtwar |
| NH | 2 | |
| NH | 3 | Agra-Indore-Nasik-Mumbai |
| NH | 4 | Thane-Pune-Belgamun-Bangalore-Chennai |
| NH | 4A | Balgam-Ponda-Panji |
| NH | 5 | Baharagora-Bhubaneshwar-Vijaywada-Chennai |
| NH | 5A | Haridaspur-Paradwip Port |
| NH | 6 | Dhule-Nagpur-Sambalpur-Kolkata |
| NH | 7 | Varanasi-Nagpur-Bangalore-Kankakumari |
| NH | 7A | Palayankottai-Tuticorin |
| NH | 8 | Delhi-Jaipur-Ahmedabad-Mumbai |
| NH | 8A | Ahmedabad-Limbdi-Morvi-Kandla |
| NH | 8C | Chiloda-Ghandhinagar-Sarkhej |
| NH | 9 | Pune-Solapur-Hyderabad-Vijaywada |
| NH | 10 | Delhi-Fazilka-Indo-Pakistan border |

| | | |
|---|---|---|
| NH | 11 | Agra-Jaipur-Bikaner |
| NH | 11A | Dausa-Nanoharpur |
| NH | 12 | Jabalpur-Bhopal-Biaora-Kota-Jaipur |
| NH | 13 | Solanpur-Bijapur-Chitradurga |
| NH | 14 | Beawar-Sirohi-Radhanpur |
| NH | 15 | Pathankot-Amritsar-Jaisalmer-Samakhiali |
| NH | 16 | Nizambad-Mancherel-Jagdalpur |
| NH | 17 | Panvel-Mangalore-Kannur Edapally |
| NH | 18 | Kurnool-Nandyal-Cuddapah-Chittor |
| NH | 20 | Pathankot-Mandi |
| NH | 21 | Chandigarh-Bilaspur-Kullu-Manali |
| NH | 22 | Ambala-Chandigarh-Shimla-Rampur-Shipkila |
| NH | 23 | Chas-Ranchi-Raurkela-Talcher |
| NH | 24 | Delhi-Bareilly-Lucknow |
| NH | 25 | Lucknow-Kanpur-Jhansi-Shivapuri |
| NH | 26 | Jhansi-Sargar-Lakhnadon |
| NH | 27A | Allahabad-Mangawan |
| NH | 28 | Barauni-Muzaffarpur-Gorakhpur-Lucknow |
| NH | 28A | Pipra-Raxaul-Indo-Nepal border |
| NH | 29 | Gorakhpur-Ghazipur-Varanasi |
| NH | 30 | Mohania-Patna-Bhaktiyarpur |
| NH | 31 | Barhi-Shiliguri-North Salmara-Amingaon |
| NH | 31A | Sivok-Gangtok |
| NH | 31B | North Salmara-Jogigopa |
| NH | 31C | Calgalia-Baghdogra-Hasimanra-Bijni |
| NH | 32 | Gobindpur-Dhanbad-Jamshedpur |
| NH | 33 | Barhi-Ranchi-Baharagora |
| NH | 34 | Dalkola-Barasat-Calcutta |
| NH | 35 | Barasat-Bangaon-Bangladesh border |

| | | |
|---|---|---|
| NH | 36 | Nagaon-Deboka-Dimapur |
| NH | 37 | Goalpara-Guwahati-Jorhat-Sailkhoaghat |
| NH | 37A | Kuarital-Tezpur |
| NH | 38 | Mukum-Likhapani |
| NH | 39 | Num.aligarh-Imphal-Panel-Indo-Myanmar Borader |
| NH | 40 | Jorabar-Shillong-Bangladesh border |
| NH | 41 | Lolaghat-Haldai |
| NH | 43 | Raipur-Vizainagram-junction with NH NO.5 |
| NH | 44 | Shillong-Passi Badarpur-Agartala |
| NH | 45A | Viluppuram-Pondicherry |
| NH | 46 | Krishnagiri-Ranipettai |
| NH | 47 | Salem-Thrissur-Kanyakumari |
| NH | 47A | Junction with no. 47 NH-Willington Island |
| NH | 48 | Bangalore-Hassan-MangalOre |
| NH | 49 | Kochi-Madurai-Dhanushkodi |
| NH | 50 | Nashik-Junction with NH no. 4 near Pune |
| NH | 51 | Paikan-Tura-Dalu |
| NH | 52 | Baihata Charali-Pasighat-Saikhoaghat |
| NH | 52A | Bander Dewa-Itanagar |
| NH | 53 | Badarpur-Jirghat-Imphal-Sikhar |
| NH | 54 | Silchar-Aizwal-Tuipan |
| NH | 54A | Theriat-Lunglei |
| NH | 54B | Venus-Saddle-Saiha |
| NH | 55 | Shilliguri-Darjeeling |
| NH | 56 | Lucknow-Varanasi |
| NH | NE 1 | Ahmedabad-Vadodara |

From the above description it is clear that Indian roadways are too long. As we know that motel are mostly located outside the city limits in the countryside along with the main highways, so the developments of motels is linked with the development of motorways. The speedy growth of motorways has increased the number of motels in India.

The important services provided by Indian motels include parking, garage facilities, accommodation, restaurant facilities. With a view to provide the above services to the motorists, all the motels are equipped with filling stations, repair services, accessories, garages, parking space, elevator service to the automobile entrance, restaurants etc. There are also equipments and tools available which the guest can use himself if he wishes to repair his vehicle. The price charged for accommodation and meals/refreshment is much cheaper as compared to that in hotels.

Motels are of different types. Some motels provide just the minimum services while others are well furnished with comfortable accommodation and excellent facilities. The accommodation provided in a motel is of a type, with is furnished, having a dining hall and a fixed menu.

## CONCLUSION

The concept of motel and motel-hotel originated in the United States of America. Motel was meant for local motorists and foreign tourists travelling by road. Primarily designed to serve the needs of motorists, motels almost exclusively meet the demand for transit accommodation. They serve the function of transit hotel except that they are geared to accommodate motor travelling guests for overnight stay.

In India, many motels are located along with the highways. But these motels do not provide facilities like foreign motels. But the situation is being important. With the rapid growth of automobile travelling, Indian motels are also going to be increased in number and developed day-by-day.

## NAMES AND ADDRESSES OF SOME INDIAN MOTELS

1. HTDC Dabchick Motel, HODEL, HARYANA
2. HTDC Skylark Motel, PANIPAT. HARYANA
3. Motel Budgerigar. PINJAUR HARYANA
4. HTDC Parakeet Motel, NH No. 1, PINJAUR, HARYANA
5. HYDC Blue Joy Motel, SAMALKHA, HARYANA
6. Kwality's Motel Shiraz, Area Colony, Bhopal, M.P.
7. MPSTDC Tourist Motel, Durg Road, Raipur, M.P.
8. MPSTDC Santa Motel, Civil Lines, Santa, M.P.
9. MLSTDC Chinkara Motel, Mumbai Road, Shivpuri, M.P.
10. MPSTDC Shipra Motel, University road, Ujjain, M.P.
11. Suman Motels, Khopali, MUMBAI
12. PTDC Motel 'Amaltas', G.T. Road, Ludhiana, PUNJAB
13. RTDIT Mindway Motel, Barog, RAJASTFIAN
14. TRDC Midway Motel, Behror, RAJASTHAN
15. Utsav, National Highway No.8, Rajasthan
16. ITDC Motel Diamond, Ulundurpet, TAMILNADU
17. Neelkant Motel, Joshimath, U.P.
18. ATTIC Motel, 15/198, Civil Lines, Kanpur, U.P.

## CHAPTER 13

# BAR

Bar is traditionally defined as "a restricted or exclusive area in a tavern". The age old concept is still being carried for centuries. The purpose of making a restricted area was to provide separate identity and facilities for the exclusive customers who preferred their drinks to be shared with fellow drinkers closely and enjoy the cozy ambiance. This concept is being carried out till date almost in all countries. In many countries the sale of alcoholic drinks remained confined in the Bars only. Further there are many places where eateries and restaurants are allowed to serve alcoholic drinks from bar only. In Europe and in many other countries, gradually introduced excise rules and regulations. Such rules and regulations are also introduced in our country by the British rulers. Prior to that we had indigenous *Sarab Khana* or *Sari* where drinks were available to the visitors. During the British days, "*Desi*" *Sarab Khana* or *Bhati Khana* or country liquor bars were introduced. Functioning of these are now regulated by excise rules. In these places only locally brewed spirit are sold. As per excise regulation no women are allowed in these places. Gradually quality exclusive drinking places were established in major cities with different decor. Liquors, spirits; wines are stocked there for sale in retail style. No women were also previously allowed to have drinks in these places. But gradually permission were granted to women consumers as well if they accompany male companions. During British days - restricted drinking places were established inside clubs and cinema halls also. Some of them are still in operation in our cities - specially at Kolkata (Culcatta - the former British capital of India). With the change of time, the concept bar changed and it did not only signify restricted drinking "area". Bar is now understood as a place where drinks can be available on retail measures and foods and snacks may also be available along with drinks. It is a specific Indian habit to have some *namkins*, snacks etc. with drinks and food after post drinking sessions.

### Temporary Bar

In order to cater the demands for drinks in garden party, farm-house party, out door catering party etc., special day licence or function licence is available for restricted hours on specified dates. Licence holder are allowed to sale alcoholic products on such dates at specified venues.

In large establishments - bar also provides facilities for mixed drinks (cocktails) as well as non alcoholic fizzy drinks. However, such operation does not come under excise rules and regulation.

It is the house policy of the operator as to how he sales his products in a licensed Bar. In Europe, America there is no restriction for women to work in bars as bar tender or bar staff. But Indian excise provisions do not allow women to work in Bars.

### Bar Area

Traditional Bar designs - include counters of various sizes and designs - minimum height (36"). Bar stools for guests with comfortable leg rests etc. No back rests or hard rests are provided. At the back of the counter arrangements are provided for dispensing drinks, with ice, soda, tonic water cold water. Cold beer dispensing machine, granulated ice, ice cube machine, soda fountain etc. may also be provided when designing a modern bar. On the back wall of bar, products are suitably displayed aesthetically and functionally. Varieties of glasses of different sizes are needed for bar. These are well stoked properly. Bar design is a professional work and help from interior designers conversant with works should be called for. There is also arrangement for dealing cash. After the specified period of Bar operation, cleaning, cash counting, spillage and removal of empty bottles, should he organised for proper functioning of bar.

Proper stock taking as per excise rules are must. This is also necessary for collecting, fresh stock and new purchases.

## CHAPTER 14

# BAR OPERATION

In order to arrange a bar for full operation the following tools and equipments are necessary:

1. Corkscrew opener
2. Ice crusher
3. Cigar cutter
4. Ice shaver
5. Ice picks
6. Ice scoops
7. Ice bucket and tongs
8. Cocktail shaker
9. Mixing glass
10. Bar spoon
11. Decanter with stopper
12. Hawthorn strainer
13. Sprinkler pots
14. Peg measures 30 ml and 60 ml or as per state Excise Laws
15. Fruit knife
16. Juice extractor/squeezer
17. Cutting board
18. Cocktail/swizzle sticks

19. Huddler
20. Fine grater
21. Strainer/tunnel
22. Wine coolers.
23. Drinking straws.
24. Coasters.
25. Bottle/can openers.
26. Ashtrays
27. Doilies/paper napkins.
28. Silver/glass bowls.
29. Tray/salver cloths.
30. Glass cloths.
31. Serviettes.
32. "Dry day" display board/plate.
33. (a) Dusting cloths.
    (b) Waste bins.
34. Various types of glasses and capacity.
    Beer glass/tumbler/Mug
    High ball
    Collins
    Goblet
    Old-fashioned
    Brandy balloon/inhaler
    Cocktail glass
    Champagne saucer/ tulip
    Red wine/claret cup
    White wine glass
    Sherry glass
    Port glass
    Liqueur glass

Sour glass

Pony tumbler

Rolly-Polly.

35. Bar counter with top and shelves,
36. Bottle cooler,
37. Store room,
38. Ice cube machine,
39. Bottle display Rack,
40. Recharged battery,
41. Sink and Work space,
42. Bar stools and seating arrangements,
43. Billing machine/credit card handling machine etc. If there is control billing system.

**Wine glass capacity**

1. Water Goblet 10 oz,
2. Red Wine Glass 7 oz,
3. Champagne Tulip 9 oz,
4. Parfait glass 5 oz,
5. White wine glass $5^1/_2$ oz,
6. Wine goblet 6 oz,
7. Brandy Inhaler 9 oz,
8. Beer Goblet 14 oz,
9. Sherry 4 oz,
10. Beer mug 14 oz.,
11. Champagne saucer 6 oz,
12. Cocktail glass 4 oz,
13. Rolly-Polly 9 oz,
14. Liqueur cordial 3 oz,
15. Old fashion 9 oz,
16. Pool glass 10 oz,

17. Tom Collins glass 12 oz,
18. High ball glass $8^1/_2$ oz,
19. Pony tumbler/juice glass 5 oz. 1 fl. oz = 30 ml

## BAR CHECK-LIST

### Check points

1. Is the Bar name board distinct and well appointed?
2. Are the directional signs prominent and in proper places?
3. Is the entrance clean?
4. Is the door clean and well polished?
   A: Is the door glass clean and polished
   B: Has the glass door a painted sign
   C: Is the door in good working condition?
5. Is the bar air-conditioned?
   A: Is the AC working and effective?
   B: Are the AC grill clean?
6. Are the Light fixtures clean?
7. Are all the Light in working condition?
8. Are there light shades?
9. Do the curtains drape well?
   a. Are the curtains clean and in good condition?
   b. Are there bead conditions?
   c. Are the beads cleans and complete.
   d. Are there sheer curtains?
   e. Do they drape well?
   f. Are they clean?
10. Are the windows clean?
    a. Are they in good working conditions?
    b. Are the window glasses clean and polished?

11. Are there portions/screens
    a. Are they in good repair/ condition?
    b. Are they clean and presentable?
12. Are the objects d' Art clean?
    a. Are they well appointed and properly fixed?
    b. Are they catalogued?
13. Is the carpet clean?
    a. Is it well laid?
    b. Is it free of stains?
    c. Is it in good condition?
14. Is the Bar counter clean and polished?
15. Is the Bar foot rail clean and polished?
16. Are the Bar stools in good condition?
17. Is the refrigeration equipment in working order?
    a. Is the equipment clean and polished?
    b. Are the electrical connections right and safe?
    c. Are the door gaskets of the equipment clean and properly fixed?
18. Is the Bar counter sink clean?
    a. Is the hot/cold water supply satisfactory?
    b. Are the faucets leaking?
    c. Is the drain board fixed at the correct angle?
    d. Is the drain pipe leaking?
19. Is the Bar display counter/rack clean and polished?
    a. Are the mirror clean and polished?
    b. Are the bottle clean?
    c. Are all the labels on the bottle intact?
    d. Does the display look complete and impressive?
20. Is the bar adequately stocked?
21. Is the bar equipment and ingradients as per list

available and if yes, are they in good condition and sufficient quantity?

22. Are the bar cards/ wine lists clean?
23. Are the tables clean and well polished?
    a. Are they firm on legs?
    b. Are the table tops smooth?
    c. Is the table linen clean and unfaded?
    d. Is the linen in good condition?
    e. Is it of right size and well laid?
24. Are the chairs firm on their legs?
    a. Are they clean and polished?
    b. Is the upholstery clean?
    c. Is it in good condition?
25. Are the sofas clean and in good condition?
26. Is the upholstery of the sofas in good condition?
27. Is the bar furniture laid out as per plan?
28. Is the Bar staff well groomed and in clean and proper uniform?
29. Is the floor behind bar counter dry?
    a. Is it made of non slippery materials/tiles?
    b. Is it in good condition?
30. Are the control books for various purpose in good condition?
31. Is the excise register available and up to-date?
32. Is the bar par-stock store door clean and well polished?
33. Is the bar-stock store clean and neatly arranged?
    a. Is the store clean?
    b. Are the shelves clean and properly labelled? Is the refrigerator to store white wine?
    d. Is the store well lit and ventilated?

e. Is the store cool?

f. Are the bar-store records and registers up to date and in good condition?

As detailed out earlier, the bar operation is very critical though apparently approves to be simple.

Its operation has to be guided by many procedures and legal as well as excise provisions. All papers, registers and explanation for natural deviations has to be provided readily and to the satisfaction of the competent authority.

Bar is not only a service point for beverage but it has a special and silent responsibility to satisfy the consumers from their stress and other physical and mental tensions. Thus, the bar ambience, environment are of great value for those who gather around the place not only for simple drinks but also to socialize and relieve of their tension.

Hence, depending on the policy, size of the establishment. local demands, a suitable bar is established for business, entertainment and reputation.

The above check lists only provides guide lines for proper management and day to day check. Any laxity in any area should be dealt by the authority in time to maintain the reputation. Standardized business policy, honesty of service personal attention to regulars as well as for the first timers must be carefully handled to build business reputation.

In order to assess the guest satisfaction and proper management, a guest comment card with good quality paper having scope to note address, birthday etc. should be recorded by the Hostess, Maitre de' Hotel. The card should then be forwarded to the F and B manager.

## SAMPLE GUEST COMMENT CARD

**Dear guest**

It is our endeavour to provide you with quality service. You are requested to kindly fill up this card to help us serve you better.

Name: ____________________________________________

____________________________________________

Address: __________________________________________

____________________________________________

Phone Number: ____________ Cellphone Number: ______

Birthday: ________________________________________

Wedding Anniversary: ______________________________

Please insert you Visiting Card/Business Card

| | Excellent | Good | Poor |
|---|---|---|---|
| Decor | ☐ | ☐ | ☐ |
| Air-conditioning | ☐ | ☐ | ☐ |
| Ambience | ☐ | ☐ | ☐ |
| Entertainment | ☐ | ☐ | ☐ |
| Service | ☐ | ☐ | ☐ |
| Prompt | ☐ | ☐ | ☐ |
| Courteous | ☐ | ☐ | ☐ |
| Efficient | ☐ | ☐ | ☐ |
| Settlement of Bill | ☐ | ☐ | ☐ |
| Food | ☐ | ☐ | ☐ |
| Taste | ☐ | ☐ | ☐ |
| Portion | ☐ | ☐ | ☐ |

***We thank you for visiting us. It would be a pleasure to welcome you again.***

**PREPARING BAR AT THE OPENING TO CLOSING**

**Morning Shift: Bar opening tasks**

1. Cleaning all bar area including bar counter, furniture, glass etc.,

2. Stock drawn from main stores,
3. Any repairs required in the bar - report to maintenance department.
4. Linen arranged.
5. AC and Herpic system checked,
6. Display rack cleaned and Bottle displayed,
7. All bar requirements cleaned and kept in place.
8. Fresh fruits, cherries, cocktail olives, lemon slices, lemon juice etc. kept ready.
9. Stock of Ice cubes checked,
10. Bar stock checked as per stock register.
11. B. O. T. and Bill book made ready for use,
12. Dry-Day/closed board removed.

**Evening Shift: Bar closing tasks**

1. 'Closed" sign-board at closing time.
2. Totally clear all tables and counter. No dirties and left over to remain under any circumstances.
3. Wash and polish all equipments and store them,
4. Store all perishable items properly,
5. Take physical stock inventory and enter in bar register
6. Lock all liquor bottles.
7. Bottle cooler stocked with various bottles/can to be chilled.
8. Close Bill book and complete picking sheet.
9. Deposit cash collected
10. Lock Bar main door.
11. Deposit bar main key to security control or other authotised person.

## PREPARING BAR FOR OPERATIONS

Adequate care and pre-planning is necessary everyday for bar operation to begin in scheduled time. The work and service should be uninterrupted and guest should not made to wait for execution of his/her orders. Over crowding or clustering for getting orders at the counter should be prevented and should not be allowed to happen. Defective of wrong delivery must be immediately rectified end replaced.

Following are some standardised steps for preparing bar operation is an establishment:

- Obtaining supplies
- Laying Cloths
- Arranging bottles according to the plan.
- Squeezing fruits.
- Refilling and arranging juice and syrup bottles.
- Preparing cocktail decorations
- Arranging cutting boards and knives.
- Arranging cocktail making equipment
- Arranging trays and salvers.
- Preparing and arranging spices and bitters.
- Preparing and arranging mixers.
- Filling ice containers
- Arranging drinking straws swizzle sticks, bottle openers and cork screws
- Arranging service and glass cloths
- Arranging cocktail lists
- Refilling the cigar and cigarette stand and arranging cigar cutting equipment and match boxes.
- Starting the drought beer machine
- Arranging for waste disposal
- Arranging and laying of linen

- Operate drought beer wherever applicable
- Recognise and report malfunctioning of equipment and machine.

The above-mentioned are major steps of bar operation to be attended to. Therefore, other occasions where make shift Bars are required to be setup, for example at the banquet or at exclusive parties on the gardens or by the poolside or on roof top parties, adequate preparations are necessary in respect to glassware and products to be dispensed. There the host pre-negotiate the service arrangement product to be supplied thus there is no question of charging the customers/guest at the time of beverage service for these parties. Attention should be made to see pilferage/waste etc. Attention should also the given for proper washing of glasses and removal of broken glasses at once so that no injury takes place, to the customers in particular. Customers should not be kept waiting unreasonably during these large party gatherings. Adequate man-power is required to be planned before hand.

In order to clear the rush and avoid over crowding wine waiters with prepared drinks in glasses and separate mixes/ice etc. are rotated among guests for the convenience of the guests as well as for the bar operation.

In many restaurants, alcoholic drinks are served and there is no specific bar area is located within the dinning hall/ restaurant area. There, drinks are served from pantry bar in the same style, food is served from kitchen. Guests are presented with Drink list/Bar menu alongwith food menu and waiters take orders. In many Indian restaurants there are no special bar-waiter for easier and economic operation.

## Spirit/wine bottle capacities

Wines are usually served as full bottle because bottles once opened must be consumed unlike spirits etc. The practice is same with beer. However, presently small bottles of beer and can beers are now available in the market which are sold as such. In foreign countries, wines are available in retail in glasses and one can order one or move glasses if so liked.

The standard spirit bottle (full) contains 750 ml. Half bottle and quarter bottles are also available.

One litre, 2 litre, 5 litre magnums container for spirits are also available. There are miniature spirit bottles also on sale for tourists purpose and for airline beverage services.

Wine bottles are of 750 ml capacity. However, magnum size and 1/2 size bottles are also in the market.

The sizes, shapes and colours of wine and spirit bottles vary in accordance to the manufactures' trade practice. Wine bottles are usually dark green, whereas spirit bottles are made of white glasses. Amber colour bottles and blue colour bottles are also often used in bottling plants for spirits. For wine labelling with mandatory regulations, is essential exercise before marketing.

## CHAPTER 15

# BAR PROVISION

### ALCOHOLIC BAR PROVISION

It is synonymous that Bar provides alcoholic beverages. But one should understand that such old fashioned association with bar for alcoholic drinks is no longer there and there are milk bar, coffee bar as well in and around our cities. However, the major products associated with bar is still alcoholic beverages, in order to serve alcoholic beverages. In style and with appropriate mixture with other liquids for examples water, soda, aerated water, lemonade fruit juices etc. - the bar must be appropriately equipped and store provisions to satisfy the need of the customers.

In India, dispensing of spirits, beer etc. still dominate over dispensing wine varieties because of price constraints and drinking habits.

However, following are the major producers of alcoholic products with special reference to Indian market:

M/s Shaw Wallace and Co.

M/s United Breweries

M/s Mc-dowell and Co.

M/s Haywards and Co.

M/s Mohan Mekins and Co.

M/s Khodey Distilleries

M/s Kalayni Breweries

The above companies have their marketing and distribution all over the country. Some companies are also selling their products outside the country.

With proper import licences under excise rules, imported spirit, wines, beers, are also now freely available from "off shop and in licensed Bars".

These are comparatively costly and their demand is still restricted among high end customers. The whisky particularly manufactured in Scotland (UK) is popularly known as "Scotch" world over. Though, good whisky are manufactured all most in all parts of the world. Canadian whisky, Irish whisky, American whisky, Japanese whisky are also appreciated globally, Jamaican and Indian "Rum" Indian beer have good name in the International market.

## STRATEGY FOR PRODUCT PROCUREMENT

With varieties of Indian products and along side the availability of imported varieties, it is a hard job to formulate product procurement strategy for Bar operators. A detailed market survey as well as periodical review are essential for arriving at a strategy for product procurement.

A detailed market survey local purchasing power, socio-economic condition, urbanisation pattern, determine availability of stock in Bar. One should understand that Bar in a small district town may not consider it wise to store "Royal Salute" or "Chivas Regal" brands or wines from France or Germany. Thus, a judicious planning is essential before product procurement for Bar operation.

However essential description of popular alcoholic products sold from Bar are outlined as under:

### Beer

All beers are made by brewing process as shown in Fig. 2.

The colour variation in the product and flavours are due to use of various malts and their colour.

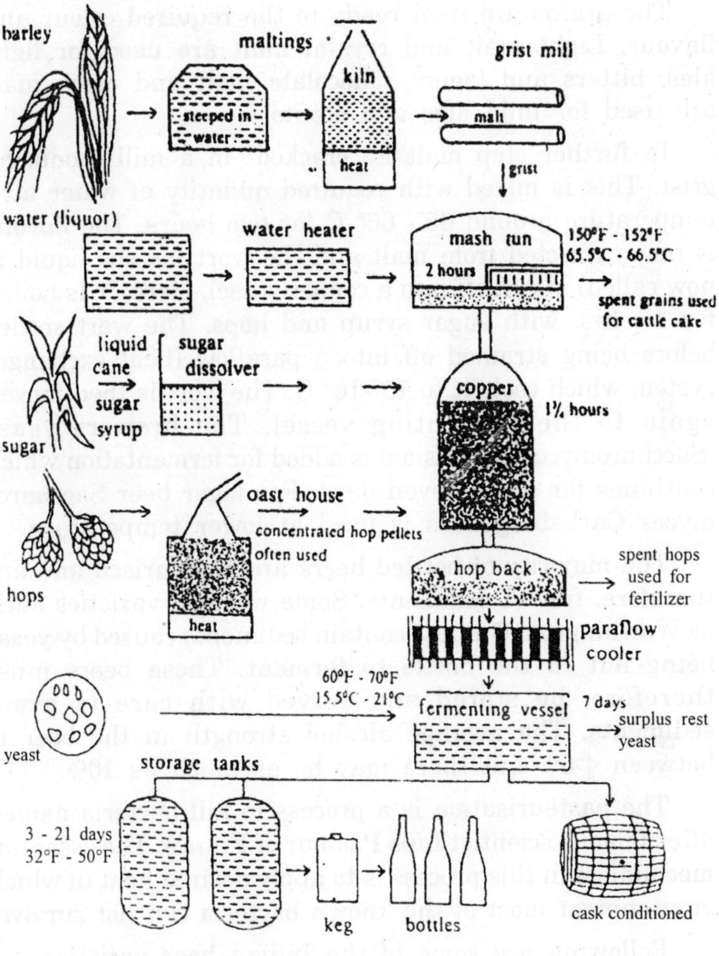


**Fig. 2: The beer making process**

## Malt

It is made by steeping barley in warm water for 2 to 3 days. Until it begins to germinate. During the germination process the starch is partly converted to sugars. The grains are then dried by hot air in a *Kiln,* which prevents any further germination.

The grains are then ready to the required colour and flavour. Light malt and crystal malt are used for light ales, bitters and lagers. Chocolate malt and black malt are used for mild ales and stouts.

In further step malt is "cracked" in a mill producing grist. This is mixed with required quantity of water at a temperature around 65°- 66° C for two hours. The flavour is now extracted from malt and the wort (as the liquid is now called) is run off into a copper vessel. Here, It Is boiled for 1¾ hrs. with sugar syrup and hops. The wart settles before being strained off into a paraflow (heat exchange) system which cools it to 15°-16° C. The wort is then moved again to the fermenting vessel. The brewers yeast (Saccharomyces Cerevisiae) is added for fermentation which continues for about seven days. For lager beer Saccharomyces Carl-sbergenees is used at lower temperature.

The majority of bottled beers are pasteurised and are therefore, free of sediments. Some western varieties such as Worthington, Guiness contain sediments caused by yeast being left in the bottle to ferment. These beers must therefore, be stored and served with care to avoid sediments. The average alcohol strength in the beer is between 4-6% but there may be as much as 10%.

The pasteurisation is a process to kill bacteria named after famous scientist Luis Pasteur of France. The essential mechanism in this process is to apply desired heat in which environment most of the known bacteria can not survive.

Following are some of the Indian beer varieties:

Sun Lager

Kingfisher (Light and Strong)

Haywards 5000

Haywards 200

Thunderbolt

Black label

Royal challenge

Pelican

Imported tin bottle beers

Heineken/Carlsberg, Amstel, Budweiser are also available

**Spirits:** Spirit is the distillate of fermented liquor. Generally the most common base ingredients for potable (drinkable) spirits are fruits, cereals, molasses and vegetable. Distillation concentrates the strength and flavour of the liquor by removing most of the water.

## FERMENTATION AND CHEMISTRY OF ALCOHOL

The alcohol, in the alcoholic beverages is the "Ethyl alcohol" chemical formula $C_2H_5OH$ by far the most important of any other alcohols in the chemical groups of alcohols. It is known in commerce as "spirit of wine" or "grain alcohol" and is manufactured by the fermentation of sugar solution with yeast. It is also produced from ethylene or acetylene. More than half of the world's supply of alcohol is now synthetic.

The yeast is a low from of plant life, fungus consisting of only one cell with a thin coating of Polysaccharides. Unlike green plants, yeast does not derive its food mainly from air and water but lives upon decaying animal and vegetable matter, energy necessary for its growth comes from decomposing of sugars.

Thus, if brewer's yeast cell be added to a dilate aqueous solution of glucose (grape sugar kept at 20-30° C, the liquid begins to forth shortly, carbon dioxide $CO_2$ evolves, which makes it appear boiling, though there is hardly any rise in temperature. About 95% of the sugar, is thus converted into ethyl alcohol and carbon dioxide through some ten (10) complex intermediate steps, Fermentation is thus a form of plant respiration which requires little or no oxygen.

The overall picture is broadly given by A. Lavoisier (1789) and expressed this reaction of grape juice = alcohol + carbon dioxide. This is the first chemical equation expressed by A. Lavoisier (1789):

$$\underset{\text{(glucose)}}{C_6H_{12}O_6} = \underset{\text{(Ethyl alcohol)}}{2C_2H_5OH} + 2CO_2$$

Such chemical change brought about by living cells is known as fermentation (Latin fermenter, means boil). The complex organic molecules are thus broken into simpler ones.

Fermentation has been used from the earliest times for making alcoholic beverages. The reaction is catalytic, the bio-catalyst here is a complex organic substance known as (derived from a Greek word enandzyme) secreted by plant and animals. In 1896 E. Buchner (German Scientist and Nobel Laureate) while experimenting with cell juice from yeast (which his elder brother, Hans, pressed out in an attempt to prepare medicinally valuable protein, used a concentrated sugar solution preservative for it. But he observed that a slow fermentation had started in the sugar solution. Later on, he thoroughly grounded yeast, all dust dry and pressed the mass wrapped in a strong cloth in a hydraulic press. The liquid obtained (which contained no yeast cell) fermented sugar solution. He, thus, separated the fermenting activity from the living yeast cells. The enzyme "Zymase" can also be separated from the dry powdered yeast cell with solvents. Fermentation is not directly a vital process as thought earlier by Luis Pasteur.

Zymase owes its origin to living matter no doubt, but itself devoid of life. Thus, Buchner proved that fermentation is purely a chemical process. During fermentation, there is liberation of energy which sustains the yeast plants, Yeast cells, added to a sugar solution grow, divide and multiply rapidly.

Enzymes which are protein in nature bring about most metabolic changes in plants and animal. They are soluble in water or dilute alcohol and precipitated by neutral salts. They are active between 20°-55°C and in pH 2-8, but susceptible to small changes of temperature and pH. Most of them become inactive above 80°C Enzymes are mostly hydrolytic but some are oxidising reducing also. Enzymes that acts on "Matose" is known as "Maltase" The enzymes act very selectively thus, maltase can not act on glucose Thus, Zymase can not act on cane sugar (Sucrose) to produces alcohol. Besides zymase yeast generally contains another enzyme sucrase or invertase which hydrolyses cane sugar into glucose and fructose. These can be decomposed by zymase into alcohol and carbon dioxide that is why if yeast is added to cane sugar solution, fermentation becomes visible after sometime.

Polysaccharides like 'starch' from cereals, potatoes maize etc. are thus hydrolysed first into glucose, this then, yields alcohol on application of yeasts. The starch breaking enzyme Diastase is obtained from Malt. In the alcohol making industry Diastase, Amylase are also obtained from some other fungi like Aspergillus and Mucor.

$$2(C_6H_{10}O_6)_m + nH_2O \xrightarrow{Diastase} nC_{12}H_{22}O_{11} \text{ (maltose)}$$

$$C_{12}H_{22}O_{11} + H_2O \xrightarrow{Maltase} 2C_6H_{12}O_6 \text{ (glucose)}$$

$$2C_6H_{12}O_6 \xrightarrow{Zymase} 4C_2H_5OH + 4CO_2$$

Starch may also be hydrolysed to glucose by warm dilute $H_2SO_4$ (Sulphuric acid). The liquid is neutralised with lime and fermented with yeast. Only a dilute alcohol is obtained by fermentation as the enzyme becomes inactive when the alcohol content reaches about 15%. The fermented liquor (wash) containing 8-10% alcohol is distilled in a fractionating column (Coffey's still) and by one operation 80-90% alcohol is obtained.

Rectified spirit is 95.6% alcohol by weight. There are other impurities which are subsequently removed by fractionation. In India, majority of drinking alcohol is manufactured extensively by fermenting molasses and Mohua (*Bassica latifolia*) flowers which are rich in glucose and fructose, Under optimum condition, one gallon of molasses yields about 0.4 gallon of alcohol.

The process of distillation is essentially a laboratory technique where vapours of liquid are generated on application of heat and the vapours are then cooled to convert the liquid in purer form. Each liquid vapourises at a particular temperature alcohol water and other soluble impurities can be separated. A mixed liquid can be fractionally distilled and this process is known as fractional distillation.

For obtaining spirits, two types of distilling apparatus such as Pot still (Fig. 3) and the Continuous still are used.

This continuous still is also called the Patent Still or Coffey Still (Fig. 4) (to honour the name of inventor Aenoes Coffey in 1832).

## DISTILLATION IN POT STILL

A fermented liquor (wash) is put into closed vessels and boiled. The first vapour comes out is known as "heeds" or "fore shots" and is discarded. Alcohol (Ethyl alcohol) boils at 78°C and so it will vapourise before water. The vapour is passed along a closed pipe into a cold water tank where it is cooled and thereby condensed into liquid again (spirit) the spirit will contain a high proportion of alcohol and some other impurities like moisture gases and oils. The residue left in the still is known as tail or which is discarded.

Pure spirit can be obtained by modern distillation methods. For this reason the pot still is used to produce the fine spirit. Some whiskys rums and brandies are produced in pot stills and these are often double distilled.

The still comprises two columns as in the above figure. One column is the analyser where the wash is vapourised and the other is called rectifier where the vapours are condensed. The wash is heated in the analyse by superheated steam, whereas the pot still uses direct heat. Continuous still are designed specifically for the individual spirit required. For example, a grain whisky still will allow more flavouring to remain in the spirit than a vodka still.

Line diagram for the of Pot still distillation principle is as under:

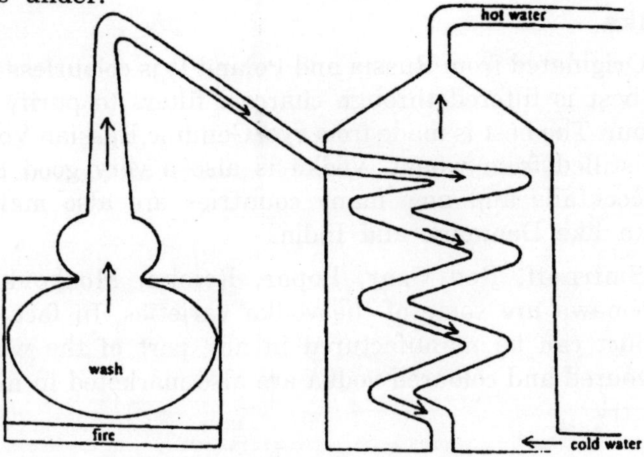


**Fig. 3: Pot Still**

## CONTINUOUS STILL OR COFFEY'S STILL

The technical principle of a Coffey's still is detailed as under by line diagram.

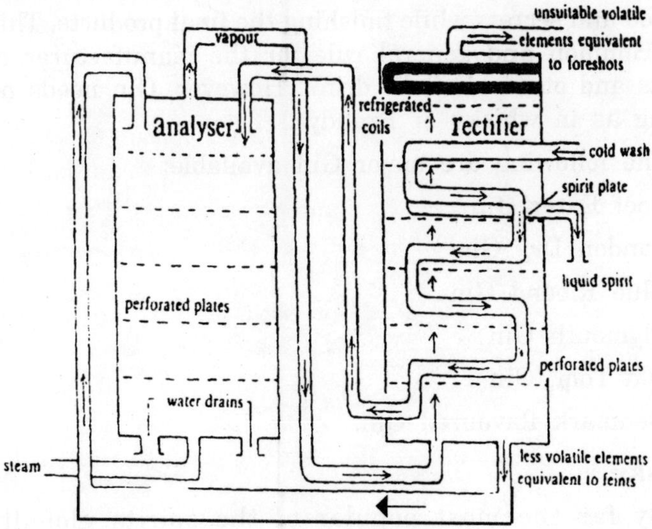


**Fig. 4 Coffey's still**

Following are examples of some well-known spirits:

**Vodka**

Originated from Russia and Poland It is colourless and the best is filtered through charcoal filters to purify the flavour. The best is made from rye. Genuine Russian Vodka is distilled from wheat. Vodka is also a very good base for cocktails and now many countries are also making vodka like Denmark and India.

Smirnoff, Red Czar, Popor, Reiska, Moskovkaya Wybonawa are some of the vodka varieties. In fact, the product can be manufactured in any part of the world. Flavoured and coloured vodka are also marketed in many country.

**Gin**

This variety of spirit originated from Holland. Gin is a spirit made from any source of sugar tasteless until readjusted with Juniper barriers angelic roots, coriander seeds, cardamon seeds, aniseed etc. are also use. In fact various breweries and distilleries have there own trade method and secrets while finishing the final products. This is a common and general rule for the manufacturer of spirits and other alcoholic drink. However, Gin needs no ageing as in whisky or Brandy

The following are major Gin available:

Beef Eater Gin

London Dry Gin

Blue Ribond Gin

Plymouth Gin

Old Tom, Gin

Denmark flavoured Gin.

**Whisky**

By far the most popular of the spirits globally consumed. Basically whisky is made from distillation of malted barley, nice, unmalted barley maize or rye. In fact, wherever raw materials water and distillation apparatus is available whisky can be made. However, several countries whisky became world famous brand and there are numerous manufacturer of whisky all over the world. Malt whisky from barley, grain whisky from Maize.

**Scotch Whisky (whisky made in Scotland)**

By far the best known whisky all over the world, like wines of some famous areas of France and Portugal. The climate, water, soil condition etc. make the Scotch whisky so very special and famous for generation. This whisky is made in Scotland (UK). Its average quality is governed by the type of cereal, the malting process, the peat used, the water, the distilling equipment and the skill of distiller and blender.

There are many distinct types of scotch. One is made from malted barley double and maize usually unmalted and distilled in continuous still this is called grain whisky the scotch on the market is either straight malt or a blend of grain and malt whisky. The cheaper whisky contain up to 70% grain and the best as little as 30% grain whisky.

*Scottish malt whisky generally comes from four districts*

A. The Highlands: which includes the famous river Spey and produces of Glenfivet Glenfiddich, Glengrant etc.

B. Northern Scotland which produces Glemnorangie and Dalmore

C. Western Isles : Whiskies from these area have a strong peaty smell.

D. Lowlands : Most of the whiskies from these area are used for blending purposes.

**Principles of making malt whisky**

Barley is malted by seeping in water and then spreading it out on a concrete floor in warm atmosphere. The grain germinate converting the starch to sugar. The germination is stopped by heating the grains over a peat fire. The peat smoke adds to the flavour of scotch. The malt is added to the boiling water in a mash tin and the sugars and flavours are extracted. The liquid is drawn off and fermented with addition of yeast. This wash is then double distilled in a pot still. In Scotland Scotch must be matured in cask for a minimum of three years by law. Ten years is a good age for high quality malt whisky but during this long ageing as much as 25% may be lost by evaporation. The most casks for malting Scotch are old Sherry casks.

**Whiskey for Ireland**

Equally well known in Europe and the Irish 'whiskey'. This whiskey is distilled mainly from a wash containing a minimum of 51% rye.

**Bourbon whiskey**

The popular "Bourbon whiskey" is an American whiskey which is made from maize rye and malted barley. 'Bourbon' takes its name from Bourbon county Kentuky (USA).

**Old No 7**

The product of M/s Jack Daniel Distillery, Tennensse 37352, USA, namely 'Old No 7' whisky is very famous and awarded. It is a product of oldest Registered Distillery in the USA. For more history and products visit www.jack daniels.com.

**Japanese Whisky**

The most famous brand is "Suntory". It is claimed that this variety is very much equivalent to the quality of high class scotch.

**Indian whisky**

There are different variation of Indian whiskies. These are made from varieties of grains and also from mixture of grain and malted barley.

"***Feni***" traditionally produced in Goa (India) has attained special fame and popularity. It is widely consumed local spirit and often flavoured with coffee and produced from cashew and coconut etc.

Apart from Feni several local spirits are obtained from rice grains as well and locally consumed by poorer communities all over India.

**Rum**

This is a spirit distilled from fermented molasses. Molasses is a by product of the sugar industry. Thus, countries which manufacture sugar also produce Rum and the quality of Rum produced in our country is quite superior in comparison of world class Rum varieties.

The molasses from which no further sugar can be obtained is used as base material for Rum. The yeast varieties used in the fermentation has great influence on the resultant product. The other factors which influence quality of rum, are the methods of distillation, type and amount of caramel used and the mauration. As in whisky, rum must be aged for at least 3 years in UK and can be matured in uncharred or charred in OAK casks.

The Rum is traditionally the spirit of West Indies from where it has developed its reputation. The Dark Rum a rich and full bodied product and is known as Jamaican Rum produced there. There are more varieties and also White Rum.

Famous Indian variety in the market is Old Monk sold in a typical squarish dwarf bottles. Bacardi is another popular variety.

**Brandy (From Dutch word "Brandy wijn" meaning burst wine)**

Brandy is the distillate of the fermented juice of fresh grapes only without adding any other spirit.

French Brandy is by far the best. Worldwide accepted varieties 'Cognac' is produced in the region of 'Cognac'.

Grand Champagne is the best sub-region followed by petite Champagne and Borderies.

Brandy quality depends upon the grape quality as well as on blending, distillation process and maturing.

Grapes are harvested in one go and grapes, are then pressed and the must fomented for 7-10 days. The wine produced in the process is acidic and harsh and alcohol content is around 8% to 10% the more unpalatable wine seems to produce best Cognac.

Only copper pot still is used for Brandy distillation which by French law must be completed by 31st March of the year following harvest under Excise supervision.

The wine is heated slowly for two hours in the stills by open flames fuelled by coal or gas. At 78° C the alcohol vapourise and travel through the coiled pipes in the cooling tank where it condenses into brouillis. This contains all the alcohol and some water plus other trace impurities. Brouillis is about 30% alcohol about 1/3 quantity of wine which was subjected to distillation. The still is cleaned and the process is repeated with more wine.

When there are three (3) lots of "Brouillis" are obtained they are put together in a clean pot still and re-distilled. This second distillation may take 10 hours. Only the middle portion of distillation called the Bonne Chauffe is used. The fore shots (earlier distillate) or 'tete' and the last part of the distillate known as queue are not used for Cognac.

The bonne chauffe is run off into Limousin or Troncais oak to casks to mature. At this point the raw spirit is colourless and at 72% vol. of alcohol which is the maximum recommended strength of Cognac. It takes about nine cask of wine to produce one cask of bonne chauffe.

During the maturation period (3 years) minimum by law the Cognac absorbs tannin and some colour from the Oak cask and develops some of the fine taste. It evaporates about 2-3% per and this less is known as Angels share. The celler master blends brandies to produce house style and quality. Before being sold, brandy strength is brought down to 40-45% alcohol with distilled water and colour adjusted with caramel.

The age of Cognac refers to age in casks before b Cognac does not improve with age in the bottle.

Indication of brandy age is marked as under:

Three star (***) and Vs Cognacs must be minimum of three years old but in practice they usually are of average of five-year old.

VO Cognacs stands for very old brandy with an average age of 8 years and above.

VSOP and older Cognacs are termed as "liqueur brandy" and should be drunk on their own nothing added.

XO, Cordon bleu denote Cognacs 30 years old.

**Armagnac**

This is another well known French brandy produced in south-west France. The main grapes used here are also same as Cognacs, like St. Emilion, Folle Blanche and Colombard. Here the distillation must be completed (by law) before the end of April following the year of the harvest.

The traditional method of producing Armagnac is by using the travelling continuous still rather than the pot still. After distillation this grape spirit is placed in black Oak Casks - so-called because the leaves of the Oak trees are black in summer. No caramel or sugar is added to Armagnac as is done in some Cognacs, because Armagnac obtains all its flavouring and colour from the distillation and maturation processes.

**Marc/Asbach/Grappa**

These are some other European brandies. In fact where ever grapes are available brandy can be produced. In India we also produce some brand of brandies.

Marc brandy is made by distilling the fermented liquor obtained from steeping the grape pipes and skins left after the grapes have been pressed for production of wine. These brandies are usually have a slightly perfumed banquet and less smooth than Cognacs or Armagnac.

Asbach brandy is sold in UK, which is made in Germany from wine imported from France.

Grappa is Italian grape residue brandy. Following are examples of brandy brands

| | | |
|---|---|---|
| Cognac | Courviour | Armagnac |
| | Hennessey | Chabot |
| | Martell | Janneaue |
| | Remi Martin | De Mental |
| | Napoleon | |
| | Camus | |
| Indian brandy: | Beehives | |
| | Golconda | |
| | Cherry brandy | |
| | Pan brandy | |

### Other fruit Spirits

Some other fruits, other than grapes are also used for making fruit spirit in many countries specially in Germany, France and Switzerland.

#### Framboise

It is made from the distillation of fermented raspbrries and it is colourless.

#### Krisch

It is made from the distillation of fermented cherries and is a colourless product. It is used extensively in cooking purposes

#### Mirabelle

It is made from the distillation of fermented mirabelles which are small yellow plums. This spirit is colourless.

**Poire Willam**

This fruit spirit is made from the distillation of fermented pears and is colourless.

**Calvados**

It is made by distillation fermented apple juice (cider). It is apple flavoured and brown in colour.

The calvados must be made by a double pot still distillation and must be aged to for two years in wood and sold at the level of 40-50% alcohol, by volume.

## OTHER SPIRIT AND BITTERS

**Ouzo**

It is a Greek spirit flavoured with aniseed (saunf). All these aniseed aperitif are usually served with ice and water. The spirit turns cloudy with addition of water. Ouzo becomes milky when water is added.

**Angostura bitters**

Produced in Trinidad from rum with addition of vegetable spices and vegetable colouring matter.

**Campari**

It is well known bitters served as an aperitif. It is flavoured with herbs and species and is red in colour.

**Amer picon**

This is French bitters. It is oranged flavoured and light red in colour and usually served as aperitif.

**Aquavit**

This spirit is made mostly in Holland, Germany and Denmark. Aquait is a national drink in Scandinavian country. It is flavoured with caraway.

**Tequila**

This is a Mexicon spirit made from fermented juice of cactus (agave). This is named after the Mexicon town of Tequite.

The blue agave is carefully cultivated to produce best quality and having sufficient quantity of juice to make Tequila, the plants contains big fruits of maturity resembling pineapples called (PINAS). After trimming, the fruits are cut to pieces and then steamed in huge steam vessels until the starch contents is converted to sugar. After steaming they are crushed to extract the sweet juice known as honey water. The sweet juice is then pumped into fermentation tanks and combined with additional sugar and yeast. It is the distillers formula and style regarding addition of sugar quantity to have the varieties of finished Tequila Regulation requires that Tequila should be double distilled in pot stills and the distillate be 100° US proof

There are three major Tequila varieties:

A. Clourless or Silver Tequila

B. Golden Tequila

C. Anejo Tequila

Anejo is aged Tequila aged between 1 to 3 years in wood and thus, mellower and less harsh than other Tequila. Some major Tequila varieties are

**PEPE HOPEZ**
**Jose Curevo**

Tequila drinkers take it neat preceded by a lick of salt and followed by a bite into lime wedge. Neat Tequila can also be followed by a mixture of Tomato-orange pickle. The most popular Tequila cocktail is "Tequila sun rise."

**Feni**

It is a similar type colourless spirit. The distillation techniques were introduced by Portuguese in their occupied land Goa (now in India). It is a very popular spirit locally consumed almost neat by the Goans.

**Todi**

It is also a local INDIAN spirit confined in the southern

states in India. These are produced from juices obtained from palm trees.

**Neera**

It is a fermented local spirit sweetish and mild obtained from Date plum juice in Eastern part of India.

**Liqueur**

Liqueurs are sweetened and flavoured spirits.

The following are the major internationally famous fruits liqueurs varieties.

**Advocat**

This is a low strength yellowish sweet liqueur made from yolks and brandy produced in Holland.

**Amaretto**

Brown colour Italian Liqueur having flavour of Apricot, Kernel.

**Apricot brandy**

It is a golden colour liqueur made from apricots and brandy.

**Benedictine**

French golden colour liqueur produced at the Monastery at Fecamp in Normandy. It is made from a mixture of brandy and large number of herbs.

**Chartreuse**

A high quality French liqueur flavoured with herbs and produced by Monks at Grenoble. There are two strength Green Chartreuse at 55% alcohol and Yellow chartreuse at 43% alcohol.

**Cherry brandy**

A reddish brown cherry flavoured liqueur produced in many countries including India (SIKKIM in particular N-E states)

**Coconut Liqueur**

Malibu is a colourless low strength coconut flavoured liqueurs with a base of Jamaican Light rum.

Coffee Liqueur Tia-maria is a liqueur made from Rum coffee and spices. There are many other Coffee flavoured liqueurs made in various countries e.g. Creme de cafe.

**Cream Liqueurs**

Baiely's original cream liqueurs are blend of Irish Cream and Irish Whiskey. Devonshire Royal cream liqueur is a blend of whisky, brandy and Devonshire cream.

**Curacao**

This is made from spirit and orange peel. It is made in various colours-brown red, blue and green.

**Cointreau**

It is a French orange flavoured liqueur made in Angers. It is the named after the family produces it. It is colourless.

**Grand Marnier**

It is also orange flavoured liqueur using Cognac as its base and produced in France. There are two golden brown varieties

'Cordon Rouge' and 'Cordon Jaune'.

**Galliano**

It is an Italian herb flavoured liqueur. It is a popular cocktail base in UK for Harvey Wallbanger cocktail.

**Maraschino**

It is colourless cherry flavoured liquor produced in Italy. It is made from the distillate of fermented maraschino cherries.

**Mint Liquor**

Creme de menthe is a mint flavoured liqueur either green or colourless.

**Scotch Liqueur**

These are liquors using Scotch whisky as their base Drambuie Glayva and Glen Mist are all golden colour liqueur made in Scotland from Scotch whisky herbs and honey. These whisky must not be confused with whisky liqueurs which is old mature whiskey.

**Southern Comfort**

This is another golden coloured whisky liqueur (Bourban) whiskey, peaches and orange)

**Strega**

It is an Italian herb and dark favoured yellow liqueur.

From the above discussion of liqueur, they can be broadly classified into five categories

1. Herb Liqueur
2. Citrus Liqueur
3. Fruit liqueur
4. Kernel/Bean liqueur
5. Egg liqueur

Liqueurs are produced in the process of infusion, percolation and distillation in potstill.

## WHAT IS WINE ?

The Wine and Spirit Association of Great Britain has sponsored the following definition of wine: -

> "Wine is the alcoholic beverage obtained from the fermentation of the juice of freshly gathered grapes, the fermentation of which has been carried through in the district of its origin and according to local tradition and practice."

For general purpose wines may be divided into three categories: Fortified wines, Table wines and Sparkling wines.

**Fortified wines**

These, which include amongst, others, Port, Sherry, Madeira and Marsala, are usually drunk as aperitifs before a meal or as desert wines. Certain types of Sherry may, however, be drunk throughout a meal. In the production of fortified wines the grapes are first crushed and the fermentation of the resulting juice or 'must' produces wine. The wine is 'fortified' by the addition of grape-spirit, which is added during or after fermentation. The addition of spirits increases the strength of the wine and if added while the 'must' is still fermenting the fermentation will cease, and a sweeter wine will result as all the sugar will not have been converted into alcohol.

**Table wines**

As a category these comprise all wines which normally accompany a meal. They are of infinite variety and among them can be found wines to suit all tastes and occasions. No spirit is added to table wines. They may be red, white or rose and are made on similar lines throughout the world. There are, however, two distinct processes in the making of red and white wines.

The red grapes are brought into the cuverie, the large barn where the wine-vats are kept, and are immediately put through a simple machine that separates the stalks from the grapes themselves. The latter are transported mechanically by suction into large wooden vats in which the 'must' ferments in contact with the skins and pips. These gradually rise to the surface and form a thick layer over the liquid. It is from the skins that the wine obtains its colour.

White grapes are placed in large hydraulic presses which slowly squeeze out the juice and separate it straight away from the solid matter. Thus, white wine, by fermenting out of contact with the pip and stalks, does not possess to the same extent the tannin content which is typical of the red wine and so essential to its balanced development. In consequence white wine is never so 'hard' and raw as young red wine, and becomes pleasant to drink art at earlier stage.

The delightful colour and pleasant, fresh flavour of rose wine is obtained by allowing the juice of red grapes to remain in contact with the pip and skins for only a matter of hours. Such wine should always be drunk when quite young.

**Sparkling wines**

Chief amongst this last group is, of course, Champagne. The method of producing Champagne is described later in this book and many other sparkling wine is a comparative newcomer to the wine trade as the method of making Champagne was discovered early in the 18th century.

Champagne is unique amongst wines in that as a table wine it is suitable for drinking with all foods and at the same time it has and unrivalled position of its own as the "Wine of Celebration."

## PORT

Port is a fortified, blended wines made chiefly from red grapes grown in a certain part of the valley of the river Douro in North Portugal. This district may be divided into two, and the parts are known as the Baixo (lower) and the Cima (upper) Corgo. The latter generally produces a smaller quantity of higher quality wine than the Baixo Corgo.

The vineyards in the Douro are situated on the sides of the steep, mountainous banks and, before the vines can be planted terr-aces have to be dug out of the sides of the hills. These are built up by supporting walls which conform to the contours of the hills. Owing to the stony nature of the soil, a hole of several feet has to be dug with a crowbar before a vine can be planted.

The vintage takes place towards the end of September, when the grapes are picked during the day and trodden by men with, their bare feet the same evening until about midnight. By this means the maximum amount to colour - a most important feature of port extracted from the grape skins, which alone contains the colouring elements of the wine.

During the process of fermentation, which starts soon after treading begins, the young wine or 'mosto' is run off from the trough or 'lagar' into great vats and there mixed with a certain quantity of high -strength grapes spirit which is the fortifying agent used. The result of this contact of the 'must' with the spirit is that the fermentation, which is itself a natural process by which the grape sugar is turned into alcohol and carbonic acid gas, is stopped, and a certain percentage of the natural sweetness is retained in the wine.

During the winter following the vintage the wine is shipped in pipes (oak casks of about 115 gallons) from the Upper Dour to the Lodges or warehouses in Vila Nova de Gaia the city opposite Oporto near the mouth of the river. It is transported by sailing barges, which need very skilful navigation to negotiate the bends and rapids, of the upper reaches of the river. It is a curious anomaly that, although the wine derives its name from the city, there is no port in Oporto, as by law it has to be stored in Vila Nova, and must be shipped to the outside world over the bar of the Douro at Oporto.

The various styles of port that are seen are:

**Tawny Port**

These are matured in cask in Vila Nova. The wines are blends of different years to ensure their continuity of style and character and after several years in cask they assume a brownish or tawny colour to which they owe their name. They do nearly all their maturing in Portugal and are ready to drink shortly after clarification and bottling in this country.

**Ruby Port**

Wines that are blended in a similar fashion to th( Tawnies, but younger and therefore fuller bodied, more robust and deeper in colour.

**White Port**

A port made on the same lines as tawny port but from white grapes.

**Vintage Port**

Vintage port is blended from the best wines of the quintas (vineyards) where the shipper has made wine in particular year. It is normally bottled in third autumn (e.g. *2000)* in 2002) in the country where it is to be drunk although sometimes it is kept an extra year, in wood so that it may be ready for drinking earlier. Vintage port does most its maturing in bottle and alt time throws a erust. The wine should be carefully decanted before use and the method of doing this is described later in this book.

**Crusted Port**

Crusted port is wine of a similar character to vintage port, through of no declared year. It Is kept longer in cask than vintage port, but not so long as tawny and needs less time in bottle to reach maturity than—vintage. In fact, it is a medium between vintage and tawny. This wine will also throw a deposit or crust and as with vintage port, must be decanted before service.

## SOME PORT VINTAGES

Amongst the great port vintages of the last century are 1908, 1912, 1924, 1927, and 1934

1945 This is one of the really great vintages of modern times. The wines were bottled in Portugal. But being big and full are developing slowly. They will improve considerably with a few more years in bottle, and should eventually be superb.

| | |
|---|---|
| 1945 | A very useful vintage, the most advanced of post war years. The wines are showing promise and are becoming ready to drink. |
| 1948 | A classic vintage shipped in small quantity : it would repay keeping for several years. |
| 1950 | These wines, although of high quality, are generally light and are development quickly. Some of the are almost ready for drinking now, but none shows expectation of long life. |
| 1954 | Although this year was not generally shipped, a quantity of very fine wine was made, showing great Character. It should be kept. |
| 1955 | Declared a vintage by most shippers, good well -balanced wines of quantity were shipped, which Promise well. |
| 1958 | Declared a vintage by many of the leading shippers. The wines show promise and are fuller in body than those of the subsequent 1960 vintage. |
| 1959 | Most shippers have announced their intention of shipping this vintage. The wines appear to be elegant, fruity and will probably mature before the 1958's. |

## SHERRY

All Spanish Sherry is made from the juice of white grapes, of the which the most important is the Palomino, grown in the vineyards of a small defined area in south west Spain centred on the town of Jerez de La Frontera in Andalusia. It is fortified and blended wines from different vineyards and different years are blended together in order to maintain continuity of style and character. In consequence there is no such thing as vintage Sherry.

### The Vintage

At the vintage the grapes are gathered by hand and carried in baskets to the yard outside the vineyard building.

They are then dried in the sun for approximately 24 hours on esparto grass mats being covered at night to protect them from the dew. Next they are brought under cover, and emptied into wooden troughs about 10 ft. square standing several feet above the ground. When these, which are known as 'lagars' are about a quarter full of grapes, peasants with hob-nailed boots 'mark time' on them extracting the juice by the pressure of their feet. The nails are so set that the soles of the boots do not Crush the pip and stalks which contain unwanted oils and tannin.

When the peasants have pressed the grapes by this method the juice is collected into large wooden pails beneath the trough. The juice, which is known as 'mosto' is next put into casks. It is then taken to the Bodegas or storing warehouses in Jerez de Ia Fronter or one of the small towns nearby where it remains until fermentation is complete, usually in the earl)' spring.

**'Flor'**

By this time most of the new wine will begin to grow 'flor' a white organic growth which forms on the surface of wine and which in France and other wine growing countries is regarded as a disease, but which plays an important parts in the making of Sherry.

Broadly speaking there are two main types of Serry-Fino and Oloroso, Fino is allowed to develop more or less mentally for a number of years growing 'for' all the time. When drink it is pale in colour and dry to taste, never develop 'for' at all or which has had the growth of 'for' artificially checked by a somewhat larger addition of spirit than is put into other wines. Oloroso matures in its early stages more quickly than Fino and is richer and fuller to taste.

After fermentation the 'mosto' is by no means bright and indeed it does not become so until the first spell of cold weather. When bright it is racked off the miscellaneous collection of skins, stalks and pips which have sunk to the bottom of the cask. The first fortification now takes place: the wine is racked into casks containing a quantity of spirit, and the resulting wine has a strength of about 15% alcohol by volume.

It is during the next period after the wine has been removed to the Bodega that each cask "makes up its mind" without further treatment as to the type of Sherry it is going to become. Although, adjacent casks in the 'anadas', as the collections of wines of any one year are called, may contain wine from the same vineyard, it is quite possible for one to become a Fino and another an Oloroso. Potentaial Finos are left at a strength of 15" (the maximum at which 'for' will grow, while those likely to become Olorosos are raised to about 17°. At the end of this period the wines are absorbed into 'criaderas' or nurseries in preparation for their eventual entry into the Solera.

### The Solera system

The Solera is made up of a collection of butts (casks containing approximately 115 gallons-larger than the shipping butt of about 108 gallons) sometimes as many as 200 stacked three or four tiers one above the other. It is on these Soleras that the shipper depends for maintaining the quality and style of each particular brand of Sherry.

When the shipper receives an order for shipment he goes to the various Soleras making up the components in the blend he requires and draws off, according to the formula, the quantity needed from the bottom row of butts only. They are never emptied of more than a third of their contents and are immediately replenished from those above. The top row of butts is refilled with wine from the Criaderas.

### Sweetening and colouring

As all the grape-sugar in the 'mosto' is converted into alcohol during the fermentation and before the addition of grape spirit, it follows that at the time of entry into the Bodega all Sherry is dry to taste. This fact is not generally appreciated.

Many sweet and medium sherries are, however, exported from Jerez and this a brought about in various ways. The best known and highest quality sweetening agent is a wine known as "P.X.". These letters stand for Pedro Ximenez, which is the name of a small and naturally sweet grape grown in part of the district which is otherwise famous for Finos. The "P.X." grapes are allowed to dry in the sun for about a fortnight after picking and when pressed produce a small quantity of wine which has a very high sugar contact and is necessarily expensive. Cheaper wines are sweetened with the produce of various types of muscatel grapes known generally as 'dulce'.

The dark colour of brown sherries is obtained by blending with natural dry wine and "P.X." a small quantity of what is known as 'colour wine'. This is obtained by boiling down and concentrating a sweet wine, the fermentation of which has been prematurely stopped by the addition of grape spirit.

**Shipment**

The Soleras are built up according to the style of wine the shippers generally require. Harvey's Bristol milk and Bristol Cream are the produce of many Soleras which together make up the final blend and much fine Oloroso Sherry of great age is used.

## SOME VARIETIES OF SHERRY

**Manzanilla**

A fine pale wine made and stored at Sanlucar de Barrameda on the coast not from Jerez de la Frontera. It is extremely dry and possesses a salty character of its own due to being kept s to the sea. It has a low alcoholic strength and is best drunk after the bottle has been opened.

**Montilla**

A very dry wine which takes its name from montilla,

near Cordoba. The Pedro Ximenez grape is predominant in this district' which is now outside the strictly deliminated Sherry area.

**Fino**

Pale in colour and dry to taste, Fino is one of the two basic styles of Sherry.

**Amontilado**

In Spanish this means a Sherry made in Jerez to resemble Montilla. It is a Fino that has gathered colour and body through age in wood and as shipped to this country. It is normally considerably less dry than a Fino.

**Oloroso**

The second basic style of Sherry. This is a wine that has never developed 'for' or in which the growth of the 'for' has been arrested by increasing the alcoholic strength of the 'mosto'. When shipped, Olorosos are rich full bodied with a fine golden colour.

**Amoroso**

A medium sweet wine similar in style to an Oloroso, but with less body and richness.

**Brown**

A sweet, dark, full wine, especially suitable for desert use. It is usually made by blending an Oloroso with wine made from the juice of the Pedro Ximenez grape and a certain quantity of 'colour' wine. It was developed purely for the English market and is unknown in Spain.

**MADEIRA**

In Portuguese the name Madeira means 'wood', and when the island was discovered in the 15th century it was covered with dense primaeval forests. It was cleared by a great fire which burned for seven years and destroyed almost all the trees in the island. The already rich volcanic soil was greatly improved by this, and is now one of the most fertile in the world. The Portuguese introduced vines at an early stage and in particular the Malvasia (or Malmsey) grape from Crete. For a long time the island was famous for its Table Wines which were exported to America on a large scale by English and Scottish merchants who settled there. In the 18th century they evolved a fortified wine made on the Solera system and similar in type to Sherry. It is matured in a unique manner, since, after the first fermentation of the 'mosto, it is put in ovens (Estufas) and heated to a temperature between 90°F and 140°F for several months. After this it is fortified by the addition of spirit, and is then matured in wood for a very long period.

Madeira is one of the longest-lived of wines and in wood will continue to improve for anything up to a century, although much wine is lost by evaporation. It also benefits from age in bottle. There are many different types, all of which have a distinctive burnt flavour, some being suitable for drinking as aperitifis and others as dessert wines.

No vintage Madeira has been made since the disastrous attack of Oldeum in the mid-19th century but the date in which the Solera was laid down is sometimes quoted on the label.

The wines are normally known by the name of the grape. Malmesy is the most famous of dessert madeiras and is full-bodied and sweet.

Bual (or Boal) is also a dessert wine. It is sweet and delicate, but somewhat less rich than malmesy and often of higher quality.

Verdelho is lighter in colour and body and drier than Bual and may be suitable for drinking before or after a meal. It can live to a great age.

Sercial is a dry wine with an attractive bitter flavour and is the ideal aperitif Madeira.

## MARSALA

Marsala is the best known Italian dessert wine and comes from the district around the town of the same name on the west coast of Sicily. It is a fortified wine with a distinctive flavour always made in this district for centuries.

## CLARET

Claret has been drunk in England, since the middle ages, when, in the time of the Black Prince, Bordeaux and the surrounding country was English territory. Some of the Chateaux still retain their English names, e.g. Chateau Talbot and of more recent date Chateau Palmer. The ties between Bordeaux and ENGLAND are very strong, particularly those between Bordeaux and Bristol.

Claret, which is known under this name only in England is one of the finest red wines in the world. It is absolutely pure and is reputed to be the least acid of all wines. It is also the easiest wine for the amateur to study as the wines of one year from any one chateau should be same from whatever source they are purchased, and it is inexpensive.

The finest claret comes from four different districts in the Bordeaux area: the Medoc which is north of the town and where most of the really great wines are made; the Graves district which is south of Bordeaux; and from Pomerol and St.. Emilion which lie to the east. There is strict nomenclature control by the French Government which ensures that the wine is described authentically on the label of the bottle.

## THE MEDOC

This is a large area which produces a great produces a great deal of wine, and all the wine made from vineyards within its borders may be sold under the label of Medoc. This name usually denotes a sound ordinary table wine. The famous communes are situated in the Haut Medoc district.

The Medoc is divided up into many communes each of which usually produce wines having a family likeness. The best known are St. Estephe, Pauillac, St. Julien and Margaux. If a wine is labelled St. Margaux, it means that the wine comes from that commune and as a rough guide it should be of better quality than a wine simply labelled Medoc.

The minor properties bearing a chateau name are divided into Crus Artisans, Crus bourgeois and Crus Bourgeois Superieures and above them again are the Crus Exceptionnels de aut Medoc. In good vintage excellent wines are made at a great number of those lesser - known Chateaux.

The great wines of the Medoc come from about sixty Chateaux which, owing to their remarkable quality, were included in the famous Bordeaux classification of 1855. Those outstanding Chateaux were divided into five ascending groups, known as growth or Crus. Over the past hundred years there has been some variation of the relative ranking of these great wines, but it should be emphasised that a wine of the fourth or fifth growth of the Crus classes is nevertheless one of the leading clarets among many thousands of Bordeaux vineyards.

The general character of the wine produced by each commune is roughly as follows:

**St. Estephe**

Fine big fruity wines. Chateau Cos d' Estournel and Chateau Calon Segur are among the most famous properties.

**Pavillac**

Big wines with great quality and finesse and possessing a fine bouquet. From this district come many of the most famous wines such as Chateaux latour, Lafite and Mouton Rothschild.

**St. Julien**

These wines are renowned for the lovely fragrance of their bouquet. They have less body than the wines above but great delicacy and finesse. St. Julien is well represented by such edateux as the three Leovilles.

**Margaux**

Fine wines with a refind bouquet and of great quality, midway in weight between the wines of Pauillac and St. Julien. Such famous vineyards as the Chateau Margaux itself and Chateau Rausan Segla are in the commune of Margaux.

## GRAVES

So many white wines are sold under the label of Graves that one is scarcely aware of the splendid red wines that are made in this district. The red Graves have a good colour, a fine bouquet and good flavour. They have plenty of body and are distinguished by their great finesse.

They mature well in bottle and keep for a long time. They differ form the wines of the Medoc both in bouquet and flavour, owing perhaps to the gravel upon which the wines are grown. Such fine wines were produced at the Chateau Haut Brion that it was included with the first growths of the Medoc in the in the classification of 1855. The Chateau La Mission Haut Brion also produces wines of high quality.

## ST. EMILIONS

The St. Emilions have a deep colour and a fine bouquet. Rich, generous, full-bodied wines tending to mature earlier in bottle than the wines of Medoc they have been called Bugundies of the Gironde. Chateau Ausone and Chateau Cheval blanc are fine examples of the wine of this district.

## POMEROL

These are full-bodied wines with a good colour and bouquet. They are more mellow than the wines of St.

Emilion and usually mature earlier but they are less heady and strong. They may be said to be midway in style between the wines of St. Emilion and those of a second growth Medoc. Examples are Chateaux Petrus La Fleur and La Conseillante.

## BOURG AND BLAYE

Bourg and Blaye are two large districts on the right bank of the Gironde opposite the Medoc. They produce a large quantity of red wines and some white although never attaining the peaks of quality found in the districts mentioned above. The wines may be sold under the names of Bourg, Cote de Bourg or Bourgeais and Blaye, Cote de Blaye, and Blayais respectively.

### Classification of wines of the Medoc

**I[ST] GROWTH**

| | |
|---|---|
| Chateau Lafite-Rothschild | Pauillac |
| Chateau Margux | Margaux |
| Chateau Latour | Pauillac |
| Chateau Haut-brion | Peasc, Graves |

**2[ND] GROWTH:**

| | |
|---|---|
| Chateau Mouton Rothschild | Pauillac |
| Chateau Rausan – Segia | Margaux |
| Chateau Rauzan – Gassies | Margaux |
| Chateau Leovila – Lascases | Saint-Julin |
| Chateau Leovila – Poyferre | Saint-Julin |
| Chateau Leovila – Barton | Saint-Julin |
| Chateau Durfort – Vivens | Margaux |
| Chateau Lascombes | Margaux |
| Chateau Gruaud – Larose | Saint-Julin |
| Chateau Brane – Cantenac | Cantenac |
| Chateau Pichon – Longueville – baron – de – Pichon | Pauillac |

| | |
|---|---|
| Chateau Pichon – Longuevilla – | |
| Comtesse – de – Lalande | Pauillac |
| Chateau Ducru Besucaillu | Pauillac |
| Chateau cos – d' estournel | Saint – Julin |
| Chateau Ducru Beaucaillu | Saint – Julin |
| Chateau Montrose | Saint – estepha |

**3RD GROWTH**

| | |
|---|---|
| Chateau Kirwan | Cantenac |
| Chateau d' issan | Cantenac |
| Chateau lagrange | Saint – Julien |
| Chateau langoa Barton | Saint – Julien |
| Chateau Giscours | Labarde |
| Chateau Malescot – Saint Exupery | Margaux |
| Chateau Cantenac – Brown | Cantenac |
| Chateau Palmer | Cantenac |
| Chateau la Lagune | Ludon |
| Chateau Desmirail | Margaux |
| Chateau Calon – Segur | Saint – Estephe |
| Chateau Ferrier | Margaux |
| Chateau Marquis d' alesme – | |
| Beekar | Margaux |
| Chateau Boyd – Cantenac | Cantenac |

**4TH GROWTH**

| | |
|---|---|
| Chateau Saint – Pierre | Saint – Julien |
| Chateau Brannire – Ducru | Saint – Julien |
| Chateau Talbot | Saint – Julien |
| Chateau Duhart – Milon | Pauillac |
| Chateau la Tour – Carnet | Saint – Laurent |
| Chateau Rochet | Saint – Estepha |
| Chateau Beychevelle | Saint – Julien |

| | |
|---|---|
| Chateau le pricure | Cantenac |
| Chateau Marquis – de – terme | Margaux |

**5TH GROWTH**

| | |
|---|---|
| Chateau Pontet – Canet | Pauillac |
| Chateau Batailley | Pauillac |
| Chateau Grand – Puy – Lacoste | Paulliac |
| Chateau Grand – Puy – Ducasse | Pauillac |
| Chateau Lynch – Bages | Pauillac |
| Chateau Lynch – Moussas | Pauillac |
| Chateau Dauzac | Pauillac |
| Chateau Mouton –d' armailhacq | Pauillac |
| Chateau du tertre | Arsac |
| Chateau Haut – Bages – Liberal | Pauillac |
| Chateau Pedesclaur | Pauillac |
| Chateau Beigrave | Saint – Laurent |
| Chateau Camensac | Saint – Laurent |
| Chateau Cos – Labory | Saint – Estephe |
| Chateau Clerc – Milon – Mondon | Pauillac |
| Chateau Croizet – Bages | Pauillac |
| Chateau Cantemerie | Macau |

*Source: Harvey' wine Guide, Bristol (England).*

**SOME CLARET VINTAGE**

It may said that the life of table wines is in direct proportion to the quality given to them by the year in which they were made and to the distinction of the property from which they come.

Thus it is only clarets of the greatest years from the best known Chateaux that still survive today in a drinkable state from as long ago as the nineteenth century, and even wines of the first thirty years of the last century.

It is proposed therefore only to give notes on those years which may be of practical interest at the present time.

1928 A great year which produced very big, 'hard' wines. They were very slow to develop but many of them are now ready to drink.

1929 Also of great distinction, but its wines were better balanced and more attractive than the 1928's. both these years were among greatest of the 20th century to date.

1934 These wines also were slow in maturing and though good were not as uniformly excellent as the 1928s and 1929s they have a high tannin content.

1937 The wines of this year took a long time to reach maturity. They had a high tannin content and most were drunk before they were ready.

1942. 1943, 1944

these war-time years, though not in the first rank produced wines which became well known in Great Britain in the post-war period when wine was scacre.

1945 One of the really great years of the century. It produced small quantities of wines which are developing slowly and are likely to prove exceptional.

1947 This was a great vintage whose wines in general developed faster than those of 1945. Many of those which remain are of real excellence, but should be chosen with care.

1948. A year in which some fine full - bodied wines were made. In their early youth they were less attractive than the 1947s and 1949s but they have developed well in bottle and most of the finer wines should last for many years.

1949. A very good year in which light attractive wines were made: many are delicious to drink now. They are unlikely to be particularly long-lived.

1950. This year also produced charming soft wines. They were among the least explosive of post-war wines available in Great Britain, have developed well, and should now be drunk. Those from the pomerol district and outstanding.

1952. A very good vintage, particularly in the districts of St. Emilion and Pomerol. The wines are firm bodied and are now approaching their best.

1953. A very good year, which produced charming soft wines with lots of fruit. They are now at their best.

1954. A rather indifferent vintage in which a few good wines were made by the most skilful growers.

1955. This year produced wines of medium body with much finese and elegance. They are developing early. Some of the wines from the lesser districts are very fine, and have helped to create a new interest in good, sound bourgeois growth wines.

1957. Good wines with plenty of fruit were made. They are maturing rather slowly and whereas the cheaper wines will be drinkable soon, the finer require several more years in bottle.

1959. Unusually hot weather at vintage time tried the skill of the wine growers, but some good wines were made. They are on the light side, but have an attractive fruitiness the vintage promises to mature early.

## WHITE BORDEAUX

White wines of great varieties are produced throughout the Bordeaux area, but the districts which are known particularly for their white wines lie on either side of the river Garonne from the outskirts of Bordeaux itself southwards to Langon. The districts are as follows:

### Graves

This district, whose name is derived form the gravelly nature of its soil, produces some of the most famous dry white wines in the world. The best of them come from the communes of Pessac (almost in the city of Boreaux), Villenave'd Ornon Leogn ___ Martillac and are usually sold under the names of their respective Chateaux, but the district as a whole produces a great quantity of dry white wine sold simply as 'Graves' or 'Graves Superieures' according to its alcoholic strength.

### Cerons

Immediately to the south of the Graves district lies Gerons, whose wines are fuller and sweeter than those of the Graves. They have been described as" the true connecting link between the best wines of the Graves and the great rich wines of Sauternes".

### Sauternes and Barsac

This small district, which is frequently described merely as the Sauternes country, produces perhaps the best sweet wines in the world. It actually comprises five communes: Bommes, Fargues, Barsac, Preignac and 'Sauternes' but a great quantity of the wine is sold as 'Sauternes' or 'Barsac' and as such is famous the world over.

The wines are full and sweet, and sometimes possess a quite remarkable sugar content. This is achieved by allowing the grapes to remain on the vines until they are overripe and have been attacked by the Pourriture noble or 'noble rottenness' a grey mould known technically as

Botrytis Cinerca. The mould extracts water from the grapes, concentrating the sugar content of the juice. As the grapes are partially dried before being pressed the quantity of wine produced is small it is consequently expensive.

In addition to the classification of the Medoc, some the leading wines of this district were also classified in 1835.

Details of these follow, and it will be seen that chateau d' Yquem, whose name is probably the best - known of all wine-producing estates, was placed in a class by itself as the Grand Premier Cru. This position it has maintained virtually unchallenged throughout the century that has followed.

**Sainte Croix Du Mont and Loupiac**

These two rather less well-known communes lie on the right bank of the river Garonne opposite Barsac and produce high quality wines of medium richness. Although in really good years some of them may attain extremely high sugar content.

**Premieres Cotes De Bordeaux**

This is an elongated strip of land on the right bank of the Garonne stretching north-westwards from Loupiac and including the villages of Cadillac, Langoiran, Rions and Camblanes. Wines of great variety are produced but mainly of medium sweetness.

**Entre Deux Mers**

A district between the rivers Garonne and Dordogne composed of a great many communes which produce mainly light medium-sweet wines of average quality. The emphasis has changed in recent years to drier wines in response to popular demand.

**Red Burgundy**

The heart of the burgundy country is the cote d' Or. Whose name may well have been derived from the rich and splendid colour of the vine leaves in the autumn on the sloping hillside. The cote d' Or produces the greatest wines of Burgundy It is situated between Dijon in the north and Chagny in the south and consists of a low range of hills whose slopes face south and east. There are two main divisions in this region, the Cote de Nuits and the Cote de Beaune. Each of them producing wines of a different style. The wines of the Cote de Nuits are generous and tend to keep well. They are firmer more robust and full bodied than those of the cote de Beaune. The latter are more soft and supple and are inclined to develop more quickly.

The principal communes are given below, together with a description of the style of their wines:

**Cote De Nuits**

***Gevery Chambertin***

This communes takes part of its name from the famous vineyard of La Chambertin. The wines are firm, well constituted and have a rich flavour and elegance. Clos de Beze and Clos de Lambrays are other well-known vineyards.

***Morey***

Wines of distinction; noted amongst them is the famous Clos de Tart.

***Chambolle Musigny***

These wines have a superb bouquet coupled with great delicacy and finesse. It is said that if chambertin in the King of wines of Burgandy, then Masigny is there Queen. Bonnes mares vineyard lies within this commune.

***Vougeot***

The wine of clos de vougeot is soft, supple and elegant. A noted Burgundian has described its bouquet as a subtle blend of the aromas of truffles, violets and wild mint. More than 50 proprietors share this vineyard which, like many other famous European vineyards owes its origins to the church.

***Flagey Echezeaux***

These are not big wines but they have exceptional finesse, combining body with strength.

***Vosne Romanee***

Collectively this commune is perhaps the greatest of the Cute d' Or. Here are grouped some of the finest vineyards, La Romanee Conti, Romanee St. Vivant Richebourg, La tache and Malconsorts.

**white burgundy**

Some of the most famous white wines in the world come from burgundy. Unlike the white wines of Bordeaux these are without exception dry wines. If the Cote de Nuits produces the finest red wines, then the cote de beaune certainly produces the best white wines. Also famous for White Burgundy is Chablis, a small town of the Yonne department, about ninety miles north-west of Dijon.

White Burgundies are best drunk when young and fresh, as in general they do not greatly improve with bottle age.

**Aloxe Corton**

This village, which is at the north end of the Cote de Beaune, not only produces the Splendid red wine of be corton, one of the finest of all in burgundy, but it also has the corton Charlemagne which derives its name from the Emperor Charlemagne who made a gift of the Clos Charlemagne to the college of saulieu in A.D. 775. It is a white wine with great attraction, rich in alcohol, with a strong nutty taste.

**Meursault**

A kingdom of white wines which are so well known that one is apt to forget that quite good red wines are also made here. The white meursults have a lovely green -

golden colour. They are rich in alcohol and are at the same time both dry and mellow, with a delicate and perfumed bouquet.

**Puligny montrachet and chassagne montrachet**

These two commune share the glory of the name Montrachet, the greatest of all white burgundies. Alexandre Dumas wrote that one should drink Montrachet "on one s Knees with ones head bared" Batard Montrachet and Chevalier Montrachet these two communes produce a whole range of fine, mellow and particularly fruity flavour.

**Chablis**

Clean, dry fresh wines which normally should he drunk young. The wines produced from the vineyards of chatils have made the name famous throughout the world.

**Rhone Wines**

The wine-growing districts of the Rhone stretch from just south of Lyons nearly to Avignon, and this widely spread area produces wines of great variety. The hermitage wines come from Tain I'hermitage in the central district and are big, robust and full of character. Further to the north, the wines of the Cote Rotie are lighter and softer. In both these districts, the vineyards are planted in exceedingly steep and stony hillsides, so that even in very wet summers, the excess of water runs away and the warm sun is retained by the well-drained soil.

The wines of Chateauneuf de Pape come from the vineyards around the town of the name, eight miles north of Avignon. 'They are big, full - bodied wines with deep colour and attractive bouquet. They develop quickly in bottle. From Travel, on the opposite (west) side of the Rhone to, Chateauneuf, come some of the best rose wines of France.

**The Wines of the Loire**

From the extensive vineyards on the banks of the river Loire in the Provinces of Anjou and Touraine come wines of many different characters. A quantity of sparkling wine is produced and is mainly found in this country under proprietary labels.

In Touraine the most important wine-producing district is centred around Vouvray. The white Vouvray is the better known, being sweet, full of fruit and green - gold in colour. The district is also noted for its sparkling wines.

From the vineyards of the commune of Pouilly-sur-Loire, which is much further upstream, come other well-known white wines. These have a very pronounced bouquet and a known as Pouilly-Fume or 'smoky' Pouilly.

**Alsatian Wines**

Alsace is the most easterly of the great wine-producing districts of France and produces white wines similar in style to those of Germany, although on the whole lighter and alcoholic strength. They are unusual in that they are known by the grape from which they come.

The principal grapes in use in this area are the sylvaner, Riesling, and Traminer. The sylvaner prodices light, medium wines, the Riesling good quality, crisp dry wines and the Traminer (and Gewurztraminer) makes the spicier, but more elegant and distinctive wines.

Vintage in Alsace correspond on the whole with those of the White Burgundies and not the German wines, 1953 was a very good year and was followed by the rather less good 1955 vintage. Some pleasant wines were made in 1957. While 1959 produced some of the finest wines.

**Hock and Moselle**

The great wine areas of Germany have been under cultivation for over two thousand years, and owe much of their greatness to the interest taken in them by the Church during the middle ages. In particular, such famous vineyards as the Steinberg at Kloster Eberbach and Schloss Hohannisberg in the Rheingau owe their origin to monastic vintners. In Rheinhessia, the church of the Liebfrauenstift at Worms has given its name to liebrfaumilch, which no longer signifies anything more than a pleasant medium German wine.

The vineyards have been destroyed or damaged in war and in recent years have suffered serious visitations by frost.

Even before the Hanseatic league brought German wines to England knowledge of them had been introduced by St. Boniface. In the early years of the ninth century, he spent a considerable time at Hochheim, and was in all probability the first exporter of German wine to England.

The name 'Hock' is almost certainly a corruption of 'Hochheimer' - the wine from Hochheim, which was known as 'Hockamore' in England during the 17th and 18th centuries.

The principal districts which produce wines of high quality are the Bheingau, Bheinhessia and the Palatinate, and the valleys of the nahe, the Moselle, the Ruwer and the Saar.

Good wines are also produced in franconia around the old city of Wurzburg, and these are becoming increasingly popular in this country.

**Hock**

The greatest wines come from the Riesling grape, although the Sylvaner and Traminer are also used, especially in the Palatinate.

**Rheingau**

The wines from this area take longest to mature and are renowned for their elegance. The range from the light and dry to the full and rich and the most famous vineyards are at Hochheim Eltyille, Rauenthal, Marinsthal, Kiedrich, Erbach, Hallgarten, Hallgarten, Hattencheim, Oestrich, Winkel, Johannisberg, Gaisenheim and Rudesheim (rheingau).

**Nahe**

The wines from this area show a close affinity to those of the Moselle. They are steely and clean in flavour with a distinctive Slatyness. The finest dry Hocks come from this area and the most famous growth are those of Schloss Bockelheim, Rudesheim, (Nahe) Niederhausen and Bad Kreuznach.

**Rheinhesuia**

This district produces a great variety of wines from light -weight table wines to the most exquistie dessert qualities. On the whole they are softer than those of the Rheingau and the Nahe, while less rich than those of the Palatinate. The finest vineyards lie along the banks of the rhine at Nierstein, Oppenheim and Nackenheim.

**Palatinate**

The wines from this area are mild and mellow, with less acidity then those from the other districts. Some are of great sweetness. The Palatinate produces a large quantity of ordinary medium quality table wines and some very fine dessert wines which come particularly form the great vineyards of Forst and Deidesheim

Other important vineyards centres are Neustadt, Duerkheini and Wachenheirn

**Moselle**

The description 'Moselle' covers the wines from the main valley of the river and also its tributaries, the Saar and the Ruwer. This area is predominantly planted with the Riesling grape and the wines have a Clean, fresh flavour, and often show a natural effervescene. When this occurs they are described as 'Spritzig'. They have a low alcoholic strength and are generally dry with a fine bouquet and a pleasant refreshing acidity

The finest quality wines come from the Vineyards of the Middle Moselle at Wehlem, Zeltingen, Berncastel, Braunebergh Erden, Uerzig, Grasch and Piesport.

## Franconia

The principal vineyards in the old German Province of Fronconia are stretched long the banks of the river Main around the town of Wurzbugh, which is about 75 miles east of Mainz, where the Main joins the Rhine. The wines are often called 'Steinwein' and are bottled in a distinctively shaped flask known. as 'Bocksbeutel'. They have a fruity flavour of their own, and are most attractive, clean wines. They have recently gained considerable popularity in UK.

## Labelling of German Wines

From the label of a Hock or Moselle bottle one can learn the village where the wine was produced, the particular vineyard from which it came, the date of the vintage, the type of grape and sometimes the time of harvesting the grapes and the name of the proprietor.

For instance, in the case of, say Oppenheimer, Krotenbrunnen Spatlese, one would know that the wine came from the vineyard of Krotenbrunnen, near the village of oppenheim, and that the grapes were gathered late in the season. If it was Estate Bottled, it would bear the words 'Original' and the name of the proprietor.

The meaning of terms are as follows:-

**Spatlese**: Grapes gathered later than the date officially fixed for the normal vintage. The grapes should be riper with a higher sugar. Auslese: Made from bunches of late gathered grapes specially selected for their ripeness.

**Beeren Auslese**: Made from selected single grapes, chosen from best bunches.

**Trockenbeeren Auslese**: Made from over-ripe, half dried grapes only. Those which are raisin- like and affected by the 'edelfaule' or 'noblerot' (as in Sauterns) may be used. It is only possible to make such wines in good years and they are always rare and expensive. The word 'Cabinet' originally meant the finest wines selected for the private cellar of the proprietor but it has been corrupted by use and now has little or no significance. The original Cabinet cellar is in the old Monastery of Kloster Eberbach.

**CHAMPAGNE**

When one realises that the juice of most grapes is white and colour only comes from the skins it is easy to understand that champagne can be made from a blend of the juice of white and black grapes. And' that is how it is made.

The black grapes are grown on the slopes of the Montagne de Reims - a hill to the south-west of Reims with its southern point at Epernay. There are also extensive vineyards in the valley of the River Maine downstream of Epenay.

The grapes are pressed three of four times, lightly the first time to produce the best wines, each successive pressing producing more tannin and colour from the skins.

The various vineyards take their names from the villages round which they cluster and each has a character of its own. The shippers have their own vineyards and also buy from the local growers the red and white grapes in the proportion which ensures that the habitual style of their wine is maintained. The juice ferments in glass lined vats and is then transferred to casks and taken to the cellars of the shippers.

In March the "Cuvee" is made. This is the blend of the wines from the various black and white grapes in the proportions which will produce the correct balance of quality and style; the skill in blending this Cuvee is the secret of the success of the great brands of Champagne.

As soon as the cuvee is blended it is bottled and corked with a temporary clamp on the cork, instead of the final wire.

A few weeks later a second fermentation takes place in the bottle and it is this which produces the sparkle in the Champagne the wine now stacked and left to mature for several years until the time comes to put in the final cork and prepare the wine for shipment.

In the process of maturing a sediment is thrown and to get rid of this the bottles are placed at an acute angle, cork downwards in special racks, known as 'Pupitres'.

Periodically they are shaken and each time replaced at a more acute angle until eventually the sediment is resting in the neck of the bottle on the cork. This is a very skilful operation, carried out by the highly-trained 'Remeur'.

The bottles are then taken, still cork downwards, to the bottling and corking department, where the clamp and temporary cork are removed and the sediment ejected by one of two methods in the process known as degorgement. The bottles may be placed with their necks in a freezing solutions so that when the clamp is released a small 'block' of frozen wine containing the sediment flies out, or this same process may be carried out with the wine unfrozen. In either case the bottle is raised immediately so that only a small quantity of forth and wine escapes.

The bottles are then placed in a machine which automatically fills them and at the same time a small quantity of liqueur (i.e. sugar and wine) is added, the quantity being varied to suit the taste of the country to which it is to be exported. This is known as the 'dosage'.

The cork is driven in, the wire put on, and the bottle is now ready from the gold foil and labels.

## WINES FROM OTHER COUNTRIES

Besides the great table wines of France and Germany and the fortified wines of Spain and Portugal many others are produced throughout the world.

Some of these wines are produced along the same lines as their more famous 'European counterparts and If one should encounter, say, a South African Claret one can - assume that it is a wine similar in character to a red wine of Bordeaux but produced in South Afiica Many of these wines are of considerable quality and work is continually being done to improve them, but however good they may be in themselves they can never hope to rival the wines on which they are modelled.

However, from Italy, India; the Balkans and from Spain and Portugal come various table wines each of their own individual character. Chateau Indaz and sula are fine Indian varieties.

## ITALIAN TABLE WINES

Chianti is the best known of the Italian wines. It is produced from the vineyards of three villages in the province of Siena and Tuscany. The red wine is fairly light in body and has a refresing slight acidity. It is suitable for drinking with highly spiced foods. A lesser quantity of a dry white wine is also produced under the same name.

Asti is a white wine from the Piedmont district. Asti Spumante is a sparkling wine produced in the same area.

Lacrima Christi is a sweet white wine of considerable richness from the neighbourhood of Mount Vesuvius.

Orvieto is a white wine, with sweet and dry varieties, produced in Umbria in England, it is usually found in rush-covered flasks and is often confused with the white Chianti.

## SPANISH TABLE WINES

The Rioja district in ragon produces the best known Spanish table wines. More red wine is produced than white, and it has wide reputation as vin ordinaire. It could be compared with the red wines of Boredeaux but has rather more body and alcoholic strength.

Tarragona and Malaga are sweet wines coming from the provinces of Ctalonia and eastern Anadalusia respectively. As found in this country they are often fortified. Their popularity has waned considerably since the introduction of Empire and other 'Port Type' wines. Malaga is a blend of new and old wines and although dark in colour is produced from white grapes.

## COGANAC

The name cognac is protected by French law and can only be applied to brandy which is distilled from the wine of a few specified white grapes grown in strictly de - limited areas around the town of Cognac. There are five, such districts; Grande Champagne, Petite Champagne, Borderies, Fines Bois and Boris Bois. The finest brandies come from the Grande and Petite Chamagne. Fine Champagne' is a blend of brandies from Grande and Petite Cahampagne and must contain at least 50% of the former.

Cognac is usually sold under labels which are indications of age and consequently of quality. Three stars denote a brandy that has spent at least five years in wood before being bottled. V.O. is from tenth twelve year old, V.S.O.P. from 12 to 17-years old and extra is over 40 years old. V.S.O.P. stands for Very Superior Old Pale XO means extraordinary Pale.

It must be understood that the law requires Cognac so designated to be a minimum age of four years and that the different shipping houses are at liberty to interpret the ages given above in accordance with their own tradition and practice.

Most of the great Cognac Shippers use their stocks of old brandy for their well-known branded marks, but it is still possible to obtain very fine Vintage Brandies, which are usually unblended and come from the Grande or Petite Champagne districts. Such Cognacs are expensive since they need many years in wood and this causes considerable evaporation.

A fine Cognac should be pale in colour and has a distinctive bouquet which is derived from the long years it has spent in casks of Limousin oak.

## ARMAGNAC

It has been said that a good Armagnac is better than a poor Cognac, although Armagnac never reaches the heights of a well matured Grande or Petite Champagne

Cognac. The area which produces it lies to the south of Bordeaux and is divided into three districts - Bas Armagnac, Tenareze and Haut Armagnac.

The finest Armagnacs come from Bas Armagnac and are darker in colour than Cognac and fuller in flavour. They derive their distinctive character from the local black oak, which is rich in tannin.

## THE SERVING OF WINES

The question of what wines are the best to serve with different dishes may be answered very generally. Suggesting white wines with lighter foods, such as Fishes, Poultry and Egg dishes, and red wines with meat and game. It is very different to draw a hard and fast line in this matter and the individual preference of your guests is the most important factor. However, the experience of gastronomes through the centuries have found that certain wines and food go best together. Some suggestions, based on these findings, are given below:

As an aperitif: Dry Sherry, Dry Madeira or Champagne.

| | | |
|---|---|---|
| Hors d'Oeuvre | — | Sherry or Dry white wine. |
| Oysters | — | White burgundy, graves, champagne or moselle. |
| Soup | — | Dry Sherry or Dry Madeira |
| Fish | — | White Burgundy, Greaves, Champagne, Hock, Moselle or Alsatian |
| Game and meat | — | Claret, Red Burgundy, Red Rhone, Wines or firm bodied Hock |
| Sweets | — | Sauternes, Barsac, Champagne or a rich Hock |
| Cheese | — | Port, Rich Sherry, Burgundy or Hock |
| Dessert | — | Port, Rich Sherry or Madeira |
| Coffee | — | Brandy or Liqueurs |

Rose wines, which in character can be said to be midway between red and white wines, can be drunk throughout informal meals. Champagne goes with all food and also can be drunk throughout a meal. With vinegary dressed salads and highly-spiced foods it is best to avoid serving fine wines of either colour as the flavour of the food will smother the attributes of the wine.

It is important that the temperatures of the wine should be correct at the time of serving. But any adjustment to it should he made gradually; no wine should be chilled or heated suddenly.

White wine, including Sherry and Champagne, should be served at cellar temperatures or slightly chilled. If it is served too cold some of the flavour and bouquet, will be lost cooling should be achieved by placing the wine in an ice-bucket or a refrigerator for a short period.

Red wine should be served at the temperatures of a comfortable warm room and this is best attained by leting it stand for a time in the room in which it is to be drunk. Under no circumstances should the bottle be immersed in hot water or placed in front of a fire. Sudden changes of temperatures are most detrimental to any wine and it is often better to explain matters to your guests to hold up the food in order that the food and wine be served together to their best mutual advantages.

## DECANTING

All red wine which has been in bottle for a considerable time will throw a deposit which should under no circumstances be allowed to become mixed with the wine before it is served.

Careful decanting, is therefore, always necessary in the case of vintage port and sometimes with vintage Clarets, Burgundies and other red wines.

This should be done at the bin in which the wine has been lying in order that the crust or sediment may not be disturbed before pouring into the decanter. The bottle should be raised carefully in the same position as that in which it has been lying, and poured slowly with its neck shown up against a candle flame or other light, in order that pouring may cease immediately the sediment moves towards the opening.

Normally wines may be decanted an hour or so before use but very old wine deteriorates shortly after exposure to the air, so that decanting should be delayed until just before it is required for drinking.

## THE STORAGE OF WINES

Ideally a cellar should be underground, with a well-drained concrete floor. In any case, it should always be clean and well-ventilated dark and free from any vibrations and at a cool and even temperatures away from any form of artificial heating.

An even temperatures is most important and this should be maintained at about 58°F throughout the year. White wine usually prefer a lower temperatures to red and this can often be achieved by storing the white wines nearest to the floor where it is likely to be cooler.

It is absolutely essential that the cellar should be free of draughts and strong smells. While it is in bottle, the wine is 'breathing' through the cork and can there be contaminated by outside influences. Great care, therefore, should be taken to avoid the presence of spilt wine, mouldy straw and broken bottles in the cellar.

All wine bottles should be stored on their side with the wine touching the cork and so keeping it damp and swollen to fit the neck or the bottle tightly. It is best that they should to fit the neck or the bottle tightly. It is best that they should be stored in well constructed bins with plenty of room for the air to circulate around the bottles. All straw wrappings should be removed-before binning to minimize the activities of the cork weevil, and the capsules or seals or the corks should be examined from time to time. If the wine is to remain in the bins for a considerable time, it is advisable to leave the tissue paper wrappers on the bottle in order to protect the labels.

Wines stored for long periods, especially vintage Ports, throw a crust on the undersides of the bottle. Care should be taken to see that such wines are always stored in the same position.

Labelled wines should be stored with the label uppermost and Vintage port with the white painted blaze likewise, in order to ensure that, if and when the wine is moved, the Crust will always re-form in the same position.

Sprit bottles should be stored in an upright position as their contents may adversely affect the corks.

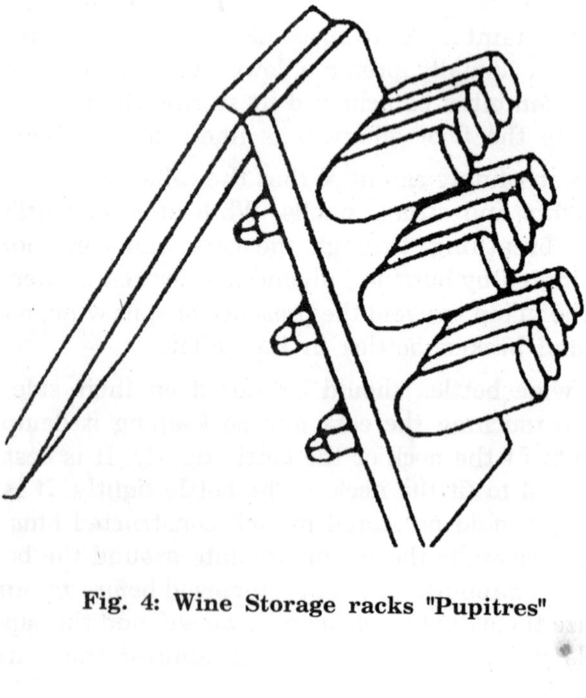

**Fig. 4: Wine Storage racks "Pupitres"**

## CHAPTER 16

# NON-ALCOHOLIC BAR PROVISION

In order to manage and run bars the operators must stock several provisions other than alcoholic beverages. These provisions are in general indicated as under.

### WATER AND MINERAL WATER

Water is an important provision necessary in Bar. Thus, good arrangement for sufficient supply of Potable water is necessary for mixing and uses.

It is now-a-style to have mineral waters or branded bottle water like Bisleri/Aquafine/Swats and many other brands. These are mostly packed drinking water only disinfected by U-V ray and ozonized and not mineral water.

TRUE natural spring or mineral water are normally not available for sale in India. All natural mineral water which are intended for human consumption must be obtained from ground through a spring, well or bore hole.

In Europe, USA natural spring waters are available for sale in Bars and there are customers who demand them for health reasons and can also afford it.

### AERATED WATER AND MIXTURES

Manufactured aerated water (often termed as mineral water) is plain or contain flavouring for example, Ice cream soda, cola leamode, orangeade, ginger beer and many more brands available in the Indian market. All these are best served chilled specially during summer time they are often taken as such or may be mixed with spirits e.g. Rum and Pepsi, Vanila favoured coke for whisky.

Mixers are some manufactured aerated waters and they are drunk as such or mixing with drinks.

## MOST COMMON MIXERS INTERNATIONALLY USED IN BARS

| | |
|---|---|
| Bitter lemon | Contain lemon and quinine |
| Ginger ale. | Contains Ginger |
| Ruachian | Peech flavored rose colored |
| Soda Water | Colorless and carbonated |
| Tonic water | Contains quinine and is colorless. |

### Ice

Ice is the most prominent and useful provision and ingredient for any bar. For bar, ice is made in ice machine in various sizes and shapes.

Ice must be made out of clean and safe water. Bar must have good stock and supply. For shaken and stirred cocktails and mixed drinks small cubes are also suitable for regular bar drinks. Crushed ice and ice granules are made in ice crushing machine. These are also used for making drinks and serving cola, fruit juice etc. Ice should be placed in an insulated container. A splash of soda over the ice cube, will prevent the cubes of ice sticking together.

## JUICES, SYRUPS AND CORDIALS

### Fruit Juices

All these are also essential provisions needed in the Bar. Most bars use tinned or tetra packed fruit juice for convenience.

The most popular fruit juice are orange, lemon, grapefruit, grape juice, pine apple water melon and mixed fruit juice etc. Bar should keep castor sugar stress paper napkin coaster etc. handy for serving fruit juices.

**Syrups**

Syrups can also be useful and essential provision for bars.

The syrups may be of plain sugar or flavored with other ingredient. These are mostly used for preparing cocktails the following syrups are in common use.

**Cassis**

Black currant flavour and purple colour.

Mango syrup, Lichi syrup, Rose syrup, Khus khus syrup. Kokam is manufactured in India (Goa).

Citra is Lemon flavour syrup yellowish.

Orgeat is almond flavoured and colourless.

Gamboise is pomegranate flavoured red colour syrup.

**Cordials**

This word is derived from Latin word meaning heart is invigorates drink made of fruit etc. Lime cordials is far the best know cordial and was very popular in England. There are many other flavoured cordials marketed in England in particular. There are green, white pepper mint, grenadine cordials available in good bars.

Gin and Lime cordial was introduced in Indian Bars by the Britishers in their colonial days are popular in most Bars.

**Diet Coke**

In America and Europe, the diet coke has become one of the major products to be sold among customers along with nonalcoholic beer. Diet coke first appeared in Britain almost 20 years ago. In fact according to an estimate diet coke has beaten the sales of Coca cola by more than 15 million in 2003.

The silver can carrying coke's famous red typography is now a regular fixture in any drinks dispensing desk/ bar.

Some nutritionist voice strong concerns about its caffeine and additive contents and its effect on bone density (when consumed in large quantities).

Another British nutritionist and associate of Dietetic Associatpui Ms. Amenda Ursele said that phosphoric acid in the drink which is used to enhance the taste had been proven to raise blood acidity and lower bone density in the body. Its stingiest properties raised heart rates. Diet coke was introduced in USA in the year 1982 had variation in the original coke formula devised by a pharmacist in Atlanta, Georgia, 96 years ago. 'Vanilla Coke' has now been introduced in India.

## TEA, COFFEE, BUTTER MILK AND LASSI ETC.

Normally, the above non alcoholic beverage are served away from Bar counter which specifically severs alcoholic drinks. As a matter of house policy, these are dispensed from the bar. In some places there are Tea-lounge and separate coffee bar for the purpose. Generally, bar operation is restricted for serving alcoholic beverages only and the arrangement and facility planning is done accordingly for the purpose.

## EATABLE PROVISIONS IN THE BAR

Many people is in the habit of taking titbits or simple eatables while drinking. These are usually salted nuts, wafers etc. Other namkins and provisions can be kept to provide these eatables as and when asked for. These are provided from kitchen and placed before the guests. Billing is usually done separately for the eatables consumed in the bar.

In places where arrangement is there for Bar-cum-restaurant, drinks and eatables/foods etc. are served and a final bill compounding bar bill and kitchen bill are raised for receiving payments

## TOBACCO

Cigars and Cigarettes etc. are very favoured items with the customers in Bar. Although world wide campaign is going against smoking, still it is in demand from large number of customers.

Sufficient stock should be kept in any Bar for these items to be sold as demanded with extra prices for revenue.

Cigarettes of popular varieties like India King, Classic, Gold Flake etc. be kept in 10s and 20s pack.

Foreign brands are available in 20 pack only like Dunhill, 555, Benson and Hedges, Malborough, John player, Silk-cut etc. No smoking regulation has to be followed.

There are different varieties now a days with low tar content known as mild, ultra mild etc. and a bar man must be conversant with the brand and their prices and other things. Full packet may be sold with special match box with house (Bar) Logo on it as a tool for sales promotion. If asked for, packet should be served opened on a plate. All bar waiter must keep lighter with him to help customer light his cigarettes or cigars. A good knowledge of cigar is essential for bar staff in case he/she encounters foreign guests or guest looking for cigars.

Cigars are made in many parts of the world such as Havana, Java, India, Myanmar (Burma). Manila Mexico etc. Holland and Switzerland also produce some good cigars. Wrappers of cigars are tobacco leaf mostly imported from Sumatra, Borneo, America, Havana etc.

The imported cigars available in many countries mostly come from Havana. To check the authorities of Havana cigars, one should see the Green Label affixed to every box as the certified Govt. warranty. Some famous brands are:

Churchills, Lonsdale, Corona, Petit Corona, Half-a-corona, Mergaritas etc.

| | |
|---|---|
| Brands from Havana | La Corona |
| | Monte Cristo |
| | Romeo and Juliate |
| | Punch |
| Brands of Jamaica | La Invieta |

| | |
|---|---|
| | El Salvador |
| Brands of India | Baby Corona |
| | Corna |
| | Prince |
| | Golden Corona |
| Brands of Manila | Manila Gold |
| | Manila Price |
| Brands of Myanmar | Burma special |
| | Burmese Wonder |

Following terms indicate quantity of cigars

| | |
|---|---|
| (ccc) Claro | Light variety |
| (cc) Colardo claro | A little darker |
| (c) Colorado | More dark than above |
| Colorado Maduro | Medium Dark |
| Maduro | Rich and very dark |

A good cigar depends first and foremost on reputation which indicates the quality of filler and wrapper tobacco. Its correct maturing, grading, rolling, storing and packing.

Cigar boxes should be stored properly away from any other smelly substances and at suitable temperature so that the quality remains unaffected. Many Cigars are individual packed in metal tubes. These are very good for bar which are situated on sea side, as salty air has detrimental effect on a cigar.

Cigars are usually offered at the end of the meal with coffee. If there is liqueur trolley, the cigars should be shown to the guest who will chose the cigar he requires. Now-a-days smokers are seated in 'Smoking Zone', as WHO is rigorously campaigning against smoking.

CHAPTER 17

# STAFF ORGANIZATION IN THE BAR

Through the bar has special set up with bar stools and counter and bar tenders behind the bar – to serve and take payments – but in most of the bars (drinking places) have medium to large space where sofas, tables, etc. are laid out for guests to enjoy their drinks in more comfortable style (Indian) attitude.

However, in order to run bar services methodically, a good number of staff is necessary. Following is a typical requirement and their organization them:

**EXAMPLE I**

General manager

↓

Food a beverage manager

↓

Restaurant/Bar manager

↓ ↓

Dispense Bar Staff | Bar tenders

**EXAMPLE II**

Head waiter
- → Cashier
- → Wine waiter
  - → Commis
    - → Trainees

**EXAMPLE III**

Bar Manager
- → Maitre D' hotel
  - → Chef De rang
- → Hostes

**EXAMPLE IV**

F & B Manager

↓

Maitre D' Hotel/Chef de Rang

↓

Commis De Rang

↓

Apprentices

In foreign countries bar tender's wine waiters are mostly female. They add grace and mood to the guests who assemble in the bar. This practice is not yet introduced or seen in Indian bar or restaurants. The major manpower or human resources come from various catering institutes who are more or less trained and aware of their duties or responsibilities. They are also knowledgeable to some extent about materials and material handling in Bars. Further training and teaching the trade practices are easier because of their Institutional background.

But in many small and disorganized sectors, ordinary low paid people are hired for running the show and doing the business. It becomes difficult for the management to train them and retain them for best satisfaction of the employer and guests both.

Following are typical job descriptions of the key staff in the Bar/Bar-cum-restaurant.

## JOB DESCRIPTION

| | |
|---|---|
| JOB TITLE | **Food and Beverage Manager** |
| RESPONSIBLE TO | General Manager/Resident Manager |

### Scope and Purpose

To achieve marketing, sales, profitability and quality service goals for the Food and Beverage Department by developing and executing marketing strategies, preparing and executing the budget, providing quality service to the guests and employing leadership and managerial skills effectively.

### Duties and Responsibilities

- Attains fond and beverage sales goals and targets by executing marketing strategies and controlling costs:
  - — Prepares market plan by developing strategies to increase market share. Analyses sales, reviews competitive surveys and deve1ops new plan.
  - — Executes market plan by implementing agreed upon strategies, evaluates results and adjust Strategies as required.

— Ensures that menu engineering supports marketing goals by selecting menu items and recommending prices based on competition and market trends.

— Maintains marketing and merchandising standards of operation by following the laid down service standards.

- Achieves profitability goals for entire department while providing the guest with quality service:

  — Develops the Food and Beverage budget by reviewing the outlet head's recommendations and trends, preparing a budget package and presenting the complete budget to the General Manager for approval.

  — Implements the approved budget. Monitors revenues and costs on a daily basis and takes corrective action where necessary.

  — Controls cost by adhering to standards of operations for forecasting, budgeting scheduling, overtime control, and other Cost Control measures

- Ensure that each department is run in accordance with the Food and Beverage standards of operations.

  — Maintains control of food, beverage and supply costs and inventory by adhering to standards for purchasing and inventory control.

  — Assists Chef in setting up specifications and standards on food material (raw, canned, and any other) and beverage items for the Purchasing Manager being a PFA nominee. Testing, guarding and approving of new products in the market.

  — Does surprise shacking of raw materials to conform to standards and specifications as stipulated.

- Utilizes leadership skills and motivation techniques in order to maximize employee productivity and satisfaction.
  - — Helps in selection of qualified employees and provide orientation and training.
  - — Conducts employee meetings and counselling sessions in order to maximize employee morale and productivity.
  - — Determines and communicates standards of performance to employees. Evaluates employee performance on a regular basis.
  - — Develops employees to maximize potential, and prepare them for future promotional opportunities through career development schemes.
- Ensures that departmental training goals are executed on an ongoing basis:
  - — Ensures that all new employees receive departmental orientation and go through on-the-job training programs.
  - — Ensures that management employee's utilize 'Train the Trainer Skills' while conducting training programmers.
- Achieves banqueting goals by ensuring that marketing and sales strategies are executed in order to maximize sales and that guest service standards are adhered to:
  - — Maximizes banquet sales by ensuring that banquet sales personnel utilize sales promotion guidelines like direct selling verbal merchandising and upsetting techniques.
- Keeps immediate superior promptly and fully informed of all problems or unusual matters of significance coming to his/her attention so that prompt corrective action can be taken when appropriate.

- Performs all unties in a timely and efficient manner in accordance with established company policies to achieve the overall objectives of this position.
- Maintains a favourable working relationship with all other company employees to foster and promote a cooperative and harmonious working climate, which will be conducive to maximum employee morals, productivity, and efficiency/ effectiveness.
- At all times, projects a favourable image of Ashok Group to promote its aims and objective; foster and enhance public recognition and acceptance of all of its areas of endeavour:
- Ensures all licences related to his department are processed timely.
- Performs other duties as requested.

**Authorities**

- To ensure availability of all officers under his control.
- To recommend rewards for the outstanding performances and disciplinary action against defaulting employees within the department as per standing orders.
- To recommend purchase and condemnation of articles and indent material
- To cancel/amend Guests bills after giving full justification.
- To entertain CIP's with Food and Beverage to be ratified by GM.
- To extend courtesies to CIP's and VIP's within the hotel such as Cakes/Bouquets/Hampers etc.
- To send give away like Cakes/Fruit Baskets. Hampers to CIP's /VIP's on special occasions or otherwise, to be ratified by GM.

- To recommend refurbishing/replacements of interiors, equipment's etc.
- To recommend Advertising / promotional plans to GM.

**Authority**

1. To make the duty roster for the staff.
2. To sanction all types of leaves for the staff under control.
3. To authorize deployment of staff after the normal duty hours.
4. To recommend reward for outstanding performance, disciplinary action against defaulting employees under his control as per the standing orders.
5. To recommend purchase and condemnation of articles and indent material.
6. To cancel/amend the guest bills after giving full justification.
7. To entertain commercially important guests with food and beverages to be ratified by the F & B Manager/Gen. Manager.
8. To recommend refurbishment/replacement of all interiors.
9. To extend courtesies to CIPs/VIPs with the restaurant, such as Cakes, Bouquets, Hampers, give away etc.
10. To send give aways/cakes/fruit baskets/hampers etc. to CIPs/VIPs on special occasions or otherwise to be ratified by Food and Beverage Manager.
11. To recommend advertisement plans to F & B manager.

**JOB DESCRIPTION**

JOB TITLE : **Maitre d' Hotel**
RESPONSIBLE TO : Outlet manager

PURPOSE and SCOPE : To ensures quality service as per standards.
To ensures smooth operations of his area

**Duties and Responsibilities**

Overall responsible for his area and to ensure high standards for product quality:

1. To ensure upkeep, maintenance and cleanliness of the entire Restaurant.
2. To ensure that all registers, forms to be filled in are maintained in the specified manner.
3. Handling all guest complaints with regard to quality of service and staff discipline.
4. Ensure that all records of the outlet are maintained.
5. To implement control measures.
6. To ensure staff discipline and grooming.
7. Maintaining liaison and cordial relations with other departments.
8. To accord personalized attention, service to all VIPs/ CPIs.
9. To maintain good and cordial relations with guests.
10. Briefing to be taken daily with the service staff.
11. To assist the manager in his work and to look after his jobs in his absence.
12. Any other jobs assigned from time to time
13. To possess thorough knowledge of the menu/bar card, style and standard of service and all operational procedures and policies
14. To assist the planning and execution of special event.

**Empowerment**

1. To recommend disciplinary action to the manager
2. Deployment of staff after normal duty hours as per requirement.

3. To recommend cancellation, amendment and/or replacement of order and bills to the Manager
4. To present cakes, fruit baskets, welcome drinks to guests.

**JOB DESCRIPTION**

JOB TITLE : **Hostess**

RESPONSIBLE TO : Maitre D' Hotel/Outlet Manager

PURPOSE and SCOPE : To maintain guest relations

**DUTIES and RESPONSIBILITIES**

1. To receive and welcome guest and escort guest to the table
2. To present menus/Bar card to guest after they are seated
3. Paying attention to all guests. Specially to children and VIPs
4. Seeing off all guests and to present bouquets, flowers baskets and souvenirs to guest
5. To possess thorough knowledge of the menus, restaurant and the hotel.
6. To obtain opinion on guest comments cards.
7. Assisting in banding awkward situations
8. To maintain the following forms and registers:
   (a) Table reservations
   (b) Log Book
   (c) Guest History Cards
   (d) Record of events
   (e) Guest comment cards
9. To send Birthday/Wedding anniversary cards to regular guests.
10. To perform any other tasks as assigned.

## JOB DESCRIPTION

| | | |
|---|---|---|
| JOB TITLE | : | **Chef de Rang** |
| RESPONSIBLE TO | : | Maitre d' Hotel |
| PURPOSE and SCOPE | : | To provide quality service, preparation of restaurant |

### Duties and responsibilities

1. To perform organize and check mise-en-place and mise-en-scene.
2. Attending to the guest, once the hostess /maitre d' Hotel has seated them.
3. Presenting menu, taking order and executing them as per the standards specified
4. Presenting the bills as per bill presentation standards and completing transactions
5. Receiving/Escorting the guest in and escorting the guest out
6. All Housekeeping and maintenance needs to be informed to MDH
7. Maintaining inventory and stock taking
8. Maintaining good and cordial relations with the guest
9. Reporting any untoward incident to Maitre d' Hotel/ manager
10. Coordination with Comes de Rang and doing actual food service /clearance to ensure prompt, timely and efficient service to each guest
11. To assist maitre d' Hotel in special dishes.
12. Any other job as assigned:

## JOB DESCRIPTION

| | | |
|---|---|---|
| Job Title | : | **Commis de Rang** |
| Responsible To | : | Chef de Rang |

Purpose and Scope : Perform Mis-en-place
To provide quality service to the guests

**Duties and Responsibilities**

1. Responsible for the proper set up of all tables in his station
2. To ensure linen, silver, china glassware and all other table items and his area is clean and in proper condition before use.
3. Receives order from the guest or through chef de Rang for food and beverages and places them in the kitchen /bar
4. He should promote sales through suggestive selling.
5. Must be able to describe all dishes on menu to the guest
6. He should know daily special/items not available, table reservation before the start of the service.
7. To pick up orders for station in kitchen bar according to sequence and serve them to guests.
8. To refer complaints on food beverage items or service to his Superior
9. Prompt clearance of dirties from the tables/station to dish washing and getting them cleaned.
10. To exchange dirty linen for linen fresh linen from linen room and to store in the appropriate airy place
11. To draw service ware consumable from stores as and when requisitioned
12. To accept payment for orders served, remits cash or signed restaurant check to cashier and if cash transaction returns full change to guest
13. To show due courtesy and respect to the guest
14. To perform any other task as assigned

**Briefing of the Employees**

As a routine the briefing of the people is essential for getting boot out of them. Depending upon the policy the briefing resign may be everyday before start of work at the and of the work also feed back should be ascertained. The following are important check points for briefing:

1. *Punctuality* - preferably half an hour before the bar opens.
2. Take attendance and find out reuses for absentees.
3. All at job responsibility
4. See that waiters are carrying the following items
   a. Wets clothe.
   b. Ball pen with small pad
   c. Bottle openers
   d. Handkerchief
   e. Name plate Identity card
   f. Match box/lighter
5. Discussion institutions
   a. Recap on previous days operation/then over/ sheet feed back
   b. Important functions
   c. Graph/party handling
   d. VIP guest impact of any
   e. Update management policy/instructions
   f. Mine/bar card/menu
   g. Not available items /day special
6. Questioning
   a. Ask quotation regarding promise menu the new cocktails to on once that staff are in fall knowledge.
7. He briefing time to enhance job knowledge

8. Ask for problems faced by staff on their job
9. Guide staff to ensure that they follow laid cut standard and directions
10. Motivate the staff from time to time
11. Listen and ask for suggestion to increase efficiency /sales
12. Inspect and check premises/tables stock etc. personally
13. Briefly emphasis on sales promotion through suggestion selling, sales gimmicks

**Grooming of Bar Staff**

Strict supervision is essential for grooming and personal and oral hygiene in particular. No bad or foul smell from mouth or bad body odour be allowed from the service staff This is very critical in bar.

***Lady employee***

| | |
|---|---|
| Shoes | : flat well polished a closed heeled |
| Hair | : properly tied and well groomed |
| Nails | : well manicured too highly polished |
| Perfume | : No strong perfume be used |
| Excessive jewellery | : should be avoided |
| Makeup | : only light |
| Uniform | : should wear decently and in immaculate manner |

***Male employee***

| | |
|---|---|
| Hair | : close cut and clean shaved |
| Uniform | : clean to iron complete all respects to socks/name badge proper fit polished |

| | |
|---|---|
| Nails | : manicured |
| Shave | : close shave and beard properly trimmed |
| Hygiene | : No body likes down to bed breath |
| Physical optima | : should not be sloppy or over weight. Must look smart and alert. |

**Bar Service Standards**

1. Bar will open punctually at scheduled times, as per local excise rules.
2. All guests will be greeted at the door within 10 seconds by Hostess/Maitre/Chef de Rang Assistant manager.
3. All guests will be escorted to the table by the person receiving them.
4. All guests will be addressed by their names, wherever means of identification exists.

   **Note**: The bar staff should make an effort to remember the names of their guests.
5. No guest will ever be seated at a table which is not clean.
6. The guest will be seated by Barman Commis person escorting them chairs will be pulled back for the eldest lady first and the gesture will continue till the last guest is seated.
7. Bar card will be presented within two minutes of the guest being seated presentation of the bar card will be done as follows.
   a. Present bar card with a polite word "May I have your order Sir, Madam?" From the right hand side of the guest.
   b. Present individual bar card to each guest.
   c. Order will be taken and suggestion offered to

upset by recommending in a respect of cocktails and premium brands of spirits. Order will be taken on a BOT.

8. The drinks will be served within 5 minutes of taking the order in appropriate glasses and at the right temperature. Ask for ice it required.
9. The snacks menu will be offered after the drinks order has been taken it asked to come back menu will be presented only after the drinks have been served.
10. On receiving a verbal or non-verbal indication from the guest the snacks order will be taken as per standards specified.
11. When about to serve the order to the guest is reading a magazine or has his hands on the table courteously say "Excuse me Sir".
12. All drinks will be served from the right hand side and cleared from the right hand.
13. All snacks will be served in the appropriate manner.
14. Presentation of snacks on the plate would conform to the standards laid down by the Chef.
15. All complimentary snacks will be placed on table
16. Barman Commis de Rang would be watchful of the guests needs. Next order will be taken, when the drinks in the glass is about to finish.
17. The service of all drinks will be presented when asked for.
18. The bill will be presented when asked for.
19. The bill will be charged correctly and checked before presentation by the Barman it will be presented in a folder along with the ball pen within 3 minutes of the guest asking for the bill.
20. The money paid for will be discreetly checked and receipted by the cashier and returned to the guest within 5 minutes.

**Order taking and service in the bar**

- Presenting bar menu/wine line
- Explaining the wine/spirits /cocktails
- Assisting the sheets to make
- Writing wine order

**The staff in-charge should have the ability to**

- Tender wine list
- Suggest wine suitable for meal at tables when it is so needed and required

**The staff should have knowledge of**

- Wine terminology
- Wine available in the bar
- Vintage years
- Name of various wine and major origin
- Prices
- Relevant legislation
- Various wine in relation to food
- Quality and characteristics of various types of wines.
- Establishments marketing policy

**Attitudes**

- Salesmanship
- Tact
- Accuracy

**Technique of serving beer**

1. Take the order
2. Obtain the beer bottle
3. Present it to the guest and open the bottle with the opener

Romer
green stem for mosel
Hock Mosel
amber for hock
Champagne
Saucer
Cocktail
Brandy
Elgin
Copita
Sherry

**Fig. 5**

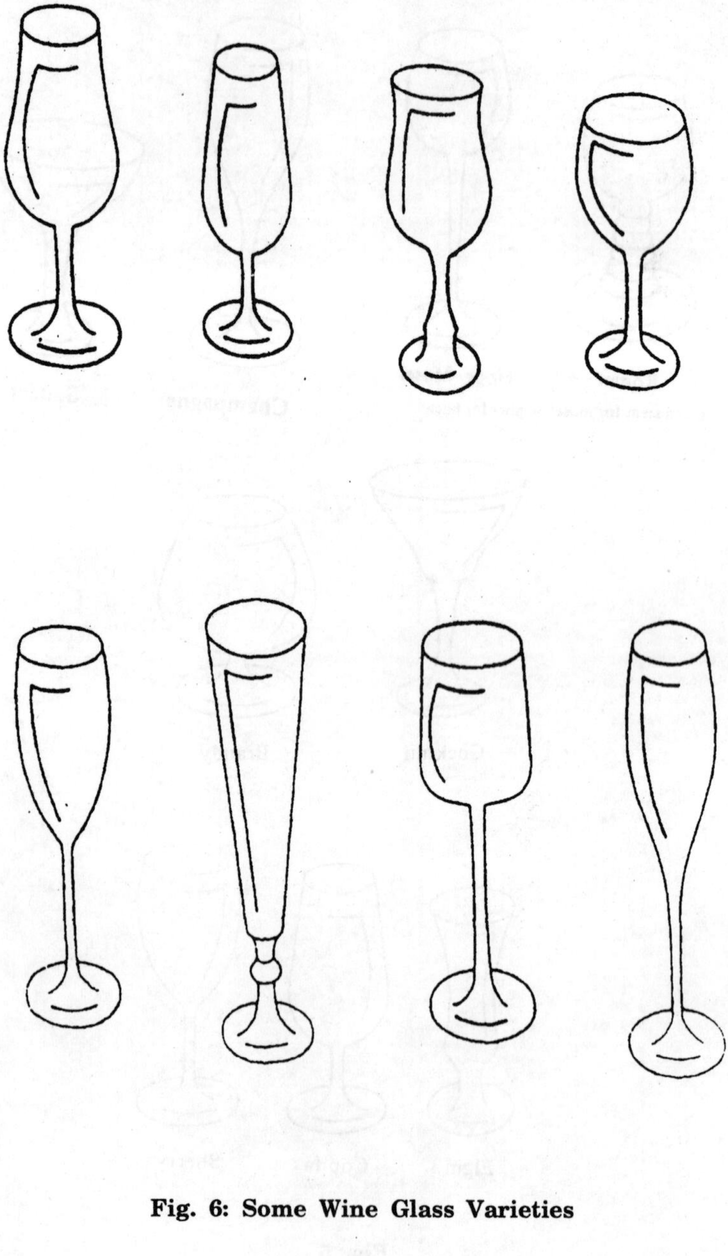

**Fig. 6: Some Wine Glass Varieties**

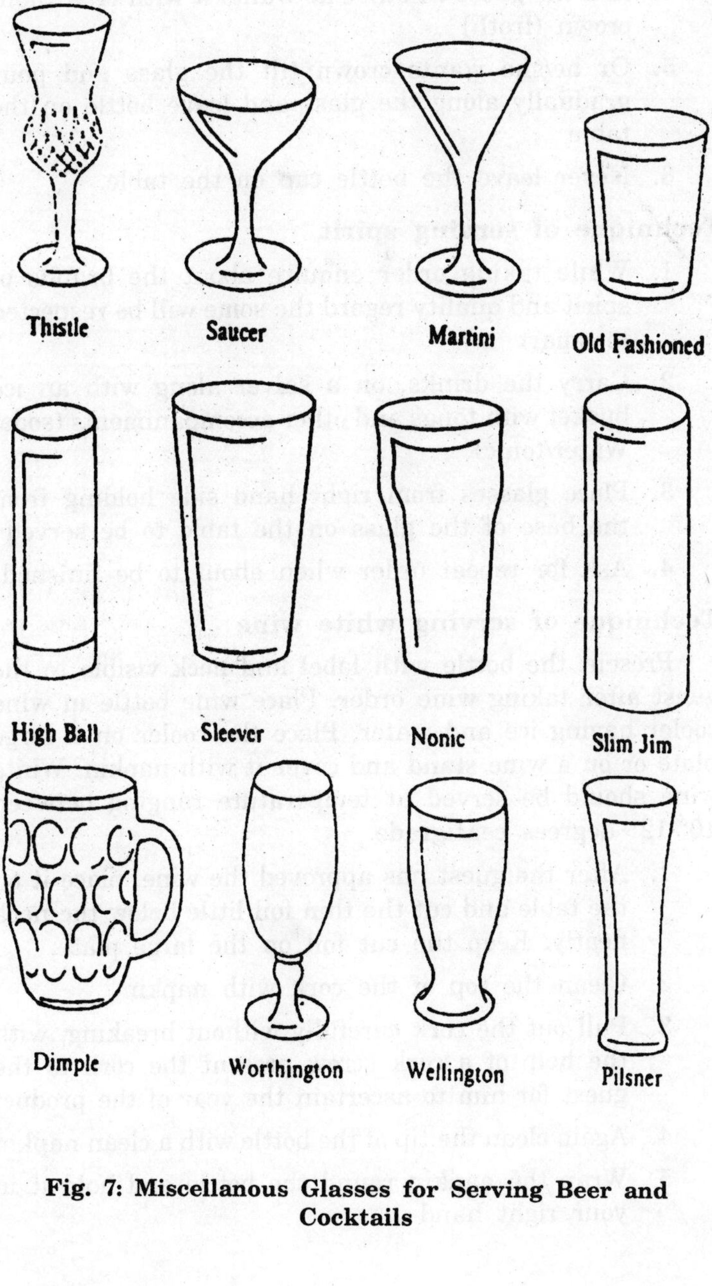


**Fig. 7: Miscellanous Glasses for Serving Beer and Cocktails**

4. Ask the guest whether he wants it with or without crown (froth)
5. Or he/she wants crown tilt the glass and pour gradually along the glass and leave bottle on the table
6. Never leave the bottle cap on the table.

**Technique of serving spirit.**

1. While taking order enquire about the brands of spirit and quality regard the some will be respected to smart
2. Carry the drinks, on a salver along with an ice bucket with tongs and other accompaniments (soda/ Water/tonic)
3. Place glasses from right hand side holding from the base of the glass on the table to be served
4. Ask for repeat order when about to be finished.

**Technique of serving white wine**

Present the bottle with label and neck visible to the guest after taking wine order. Place wine bottle in wine cooler having ice and water. Place the cooler on a large plate or on a wine stand and cover it with napkin. White wine should be served at temperature ranging between 10°-12° degrees centigrade.

1. After the guest has approved the wine, place it on the table and cut the thin foil little below the neck neatly. Keep the cut foil on the large plate.
2. Clean the top of the cork with napkin
3. Pull out the cork carefully without breaking, with the help of a cork screw present the cork to the guest for him to ascertain the year of the product
4. Again clean the tip of the bottle with a clean napkin
5. Wrap the napkin round the bottle and hold it in your right hand

6. Pour a little wine for the 'Host' to taste to check whether it is at right temperature and approve.
7. First some all guest and the lost at the and never fill the glass folly not only 2/3rd of it.
8. After this keep the bottle in the wine cooler. If, however, the guest says that the wine is very cold, it can be kept on the table with a coaster/cloth napkin underneath till it attains the right temperature.
9. When the bottle is finished asked the guest whether he would like to have another bottle of wine.

**Serving Technique of Red Wine**

1. Red wine Is served at cool room Temperature i.e. 180°-20°C.
2. Present the bottle to guest as usual
3. Cut the foil as In white wine
4. Clean tip of the cork with napkin
5. Pull out the cork with the cork screw
6. Present the cork to the guest for him to ascertain the year of the product
7. Clear the tip of the bottle with a clear napkin
8. Pour a little wine to the host for tasting and approval
9. Serve to all other guests s in case of white wines and then to the host.

Red wines which have sediment are brought in a wine cradle to avoid any disturbance. This wine is decanted in a carafe (or decanter) and used from the decanter.

**Serving Technique of Champagne**

1. Present the bottle of Champagne in wine cooler at 5°-7°C
2. Present it to the guest as in white wine

3. Keep it in the table remove the foil
4. Loosen the wire around the cork and remove it
5. Keep your left hand thumb on the cork while loosening the cork
6. Arrange all the champagne glasses in a straight line on the table, touching each other.
7. Release the cork slowly
8. When the cork is pulled some wine will ooze out so keep the bottle on top of glasses so that such over flow should go only into the glasses
9. After this present the cork to the guest for him to ascertain the year of the product
10. Pour a glass of champagne to the host for tasting and removes other as used so in the care of white wine.

## TECHNIQUE OF HANDLING FAULTS IN WINE

### Corky wine

Corky wine compliant comes from the guest because of smell of cork in the wine.

The wine waiter or sommelier should apologize to the customer, remove the wine check it himself and if it is out of condition he should replace the bottle with another of the same type. If the wine is in the correct condition, It is prudent to offer a replacement wine of another type rather than having an argument about it. If the sommelier has detected this cockiness before serving the wine he should replace It with another bottle of the same type without offering the defective one to the customer.

In busy bar in western countries wines are sold as per glass basis instead of the full bottle. Thus, there is no difficulties or problem with any bottle which is opened but returned by the customer based on his assessment even it the condition of the wine is ok.

## Broken cork

If a cork breaks and part falls in to the bottle of wine, it should be removed with a cork extractor decant the contents of the bottle. These works should be done away from the table.

## Effervescent wine

If the wine is seen to be fizzy or slightly effervescent an it should discarded. This condition will make the wine small yeasty. Attention should be given so that replacement bottle should not have the same defect.

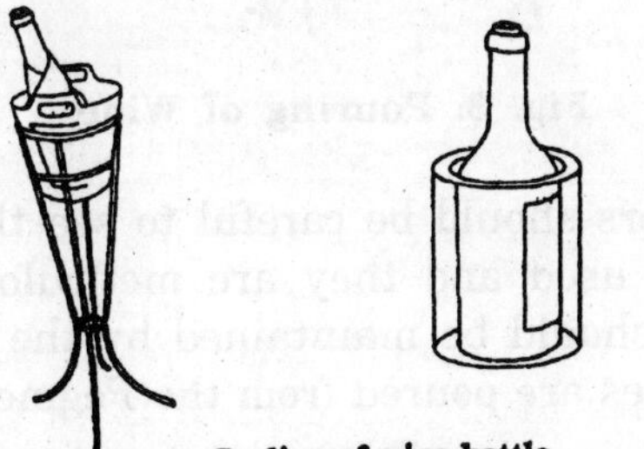

**Cooling of wine bottle**

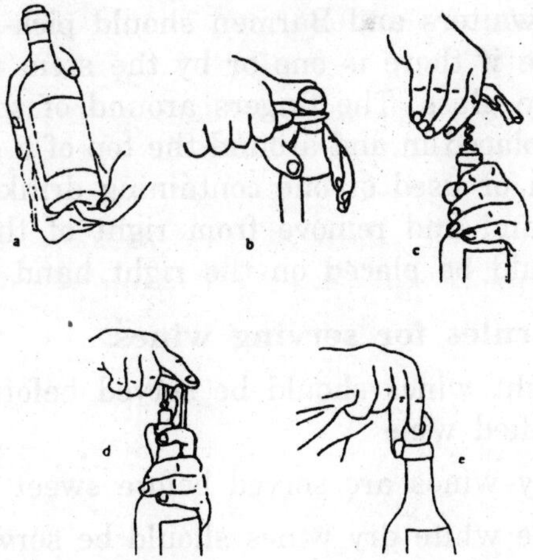

**Fig. 8: (a) Presenting of Wine Bottle and (b), (c), (d), and (e) Opening of Wine Bottle**

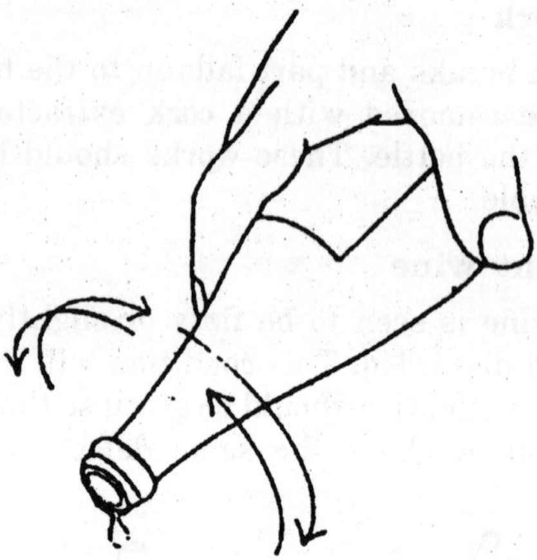

**Fig. 9: Pouring of Wine**

Wine waiters should be careful to see that right type of glasses are used and they are meticulously clean. A careful cheek should be maintained by the waiter to see correct measures are poured from the Pegmeasure or from other devices

Wine waiters and Barmen should pick-up glasses by the handle if there is one or by the stem or the bottom half of the glass. The fingers around of the hand must never be placed in and around the top of a glass whether it is clean or used or one containing drinks. The waiter should stand and remove from right of the guests and glass should be placed on the right hand side.

**General rules for serving wines:**

- Light wines should be served before rich or full bodied wine
- Dry wines are served before sweet wines.
- The white dry wines should be served before the red wine
- Do not advise dry wine with sweet foods or any foods that have sweet taste.

## SERVING TECHNIQUE OF COCKTAILS

Cocktails are combinations of alcoholic drinks and other ingredients which are mixed according to set standards (recipes). They should taste without any one ingredients predominating.

Cocktails are offered as short drinks which are suitable to be drunk as aperitif stimulating the gastric juices for the meal to come. Others are suitable as after dinner drinks, such as Brandy Alexander. The many large drinks which are popular are also known as mixed drinks.

## COCKTAILS COME UNDER TWO BASIC CATEGORIES

1. The one, prepared by shaking the ingredients together with ice in a cocktail shaker then straining the drink into a glass.
2. The other one prepared by stirring the ingredients together through ice in a mixing glass then serving the drink mw glass:

There are cocktails which are made up of just two ingredients the vast majority comprise three as well sometimes more than three as well.

The major three parts consist of

1. A Base : usually a spirit
2. A Sweetening : either syrup sugar or liqueur
3. A Souring : bitters fruit juice or other similar ingredients.

**Examples as follow**

White lady contains lemon juice Gin and cointreau. Bronx contains vermouth Gin and orange juice. Old nick has Drambuie and rye whisky and lemon juice.

Both alcoholic and non alcoholic cocktails may be prepared by shaking or stirring. Other mixed drinks are prepared by combining various ingredients together.

In Mumbai, Goa, Kolkota, Kerala etc. coconut water, Kokam mixed with Gin and Vodka is very popular. Lassi can be made alcoholic drink when mixed with vodka, gin or cointreau.

In fact these are some Internationally well established combination. Some of which are listed below but because of individual choice and availability of serving ingredients many spot Cocktails can be prepared for service.

## EXAMPLES OF SOME COCKTAILS

| | | |
|---|---|---|
| Angelface | : | 1/3 dry Gin |
| | | ¼ apricot brandy |
| | | ¼ apple brandy |
| | | shake and remove in cocktail glass |
| Angel kiss | : | Mixture of cocao, brandy and cream |
| Alexander | : | ½ Cognac |
| | | ¼ cream de cocao |
| | | shake and remove in cocktail glass |
| Bloody Merry | : | 1 part Vodka, lemon |
| | | 4 part and tomato juice. |

A does of Worchester sauce and lemon juice some people like a dash of Tabasco sauce in the mixture.

Which is served in small brandy balloon or in a high

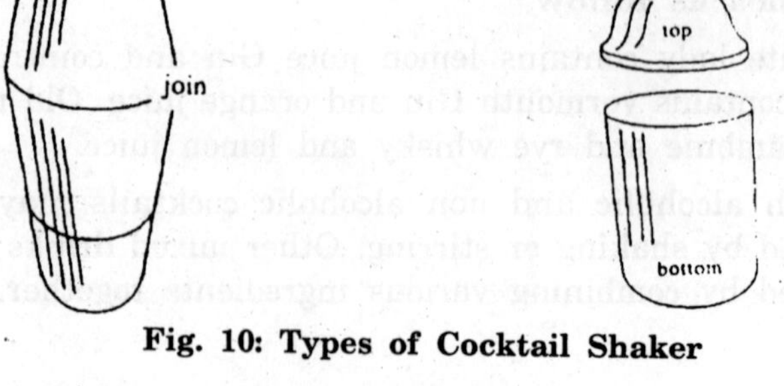


**Fig. 10: Types of Cocktail Shaker**

ball glass

**Bamboo**

Equal portions of sherry and vermouth same with a twist of lemon in a martini glass

**Black Russian**

Mixture of coffee liqueur and vodka

**Brandy Paunch**

Mixture of orange, lemon, juice, sugar, brandy, soda, water, and Ice.

**Rum flip**

Mixture of egg, sugar and rum.

**Champagne Cocktail**

The sugar cube is placed in a Champagne glass soaked with Angosturabitter Cold. Champagne is a added and topped with Cognac Finish with half a slice of orange or cherry pierced in a cocktail stick.

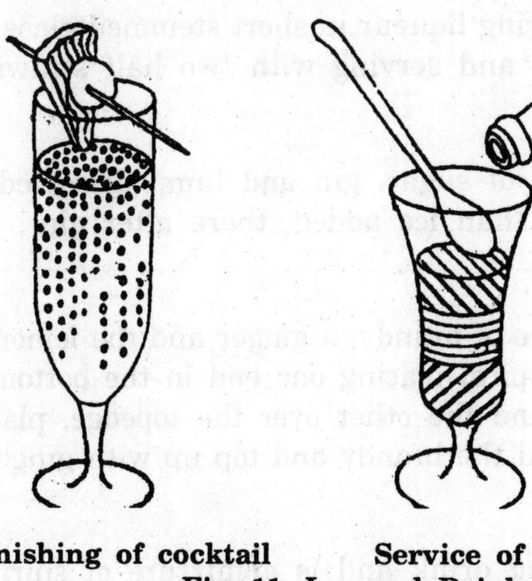

**Garnishing of cocktail** **Service of Layered drinks**

**Fig. 11: Layered Drinks**

**Cuba Libre**

It is a mixture of white Rum, cola and juice of lemon (half).

It is made by adding rum and limejuice in a light ball glass half filled with ice and topping up with cola.

**Rum Cooler**

It is a mixture sugar syrup, lime, juice, rum and soda water.

**John or Tom Collins**

1 Part London dry gin juice of medium sized lemon, tea spoon Gomme syrup, and soda water. The glass is half filled with ice then Gin is added with syrup over it Soda is added and stirred decorated with a slice of lemon and straws.

**Dry Manhattan**

It is a mixture of (½)rye whisky and 3/4 dry vermouth.

**Fizz and Frappe.**

Fizzes are similar to collins except that all the ingredients except the soda water are shaken. Frappes are made by pouring liqueur in short stemmed glass filled with crushed ice and serving with two half straws.

**Gin sling**

It is mixture of sugar, gin and lump dissolved in a little water and than ice added, there after gin.

**Horse's neck**

It is a mixture of brandy, a ginger and the lemon skin peeled in along spiral placing one end in the bottom of a high ball glass and the other over the topedge, place ice into the glass add the brandy and top up with ginger ale.

**High Balls**

This is a long drink and is a mixture of spirit and

some effervescent like soda water, lemonade, ice cream soda etc. They are all served in high ball glasses.

**Harvey Wall banger**

1 par vodka, and small bottle of orange juice and little galliano.

**Kir Royal**

It in mixture of half a measure of Creme de cassis topped up with Champagne and served in Champagne glass

**Manhattan**

There are three types of Manhattan Sweet, Medium and Dry.

**Sweet Manhattan**

1½ measures rye whiskey 3/4 measure sweet Vermouth, dash of angostura bitter. Stir and strain before service.

**Medium Manhattan**

1½ measure of rye whisky 3/8 measure of sweet Vermouth 3/8 measure of Dry Vermouth. Stir and Strain before service with garnish of cherry or lemon slice.

**Dry Manhattan**

½ measure of rye whisky ¾ measures of dry Vermouth service as of other Manhattan.

**Martini cocktails**

Martini cocktails are three types: Sweet Medium and Dry.

**Sweet Martini**

½ measure of gin

¾ measure of sweet Vermouth Service style is same as Manhattan and garnish with cherry.

**Dry Martini**

Half (½) measure of gin, ¾ measure of dry vermouth. Stir and strain in a cocktail glass before service with a twist of lemon. A dryer version is known as "American Dry Martini". This is mixed with five parts of Gin one part of Vermouth.

**Old fashioned**

It is a mixture of one large measure of whisky, angostura bitter, castor sugar and little water

A small cube of sugar is placed in to on Old Fashioned glass saturated with Angostare bitter. Some water is added to dissolve the sugar. Then the glass is half filled with ice then over which whiskey is added. The drink is garnished with cherry and orange slice and a cocktail stick is provided for stirring.

**Pink lady**

It is a cocktail of 1 large measure of gin, ½ measure of Grenadine, 1 egg white. All the ingredients are shaken and strained into a small cocktail glass

**Pink Gin**

It is a Gin based cocktail. The original Pink Gin was made with Play month Gin and this is still recognized as the right base. The Gin is served with little bitter pouring iced water on top.

**Pina colada**

It is a cocktail of white Rum, pineapple juice and coconut cream.

**Pausue Café**

These drinks are made by layering syrups, liqueurs and spirit on top of each other in a narrow glass, to give multiple coloured layers appearance. The order in which the liqueurs are added, depends on the specific gravity (sp. gr) of each layered syrups, the heaviest settle at the bottom over It liqueurs and on top the spirit being lightest. Pouring should be done carefully without disturbing the layers.

Many colourful combinations, tri-colour National flag for surprise welcome drinks can be served in this style.

**Screw Driver**

It is mixture of vodka and orange juice

**Side car**

It is mixture of scotch whiskey, Cointreau and Lemon juice

**Tequila Sunrise**

It is a cocktail of tequila, orange juice and little Grenadine.

**White lady**

It is a mixture of Gin, Cointreu and fresh lemon juice.

**Whisky sour**

It is a mixture of 1½ scotch whisky, I lemon juice, ½ measure Gomme and ½ white of egg.

Non alcoholic cocktails are also served from bar on request. From orange juices with lemonade is very popular. The best known non-alcoholic cocktail is "Pusy Cat" - is a mixture of orange, lime and lemon juice with a dash of Greandine and egg yolk.

For ladies who do not prefer alcohol in cocktail in India, "Widow Marry" has taken over the place of "Bloody many" without the vodka.

Many guests venture drinks in company of ladies or families to order mixed drinks of their choice. This can be attended to. New cocktails or "cocktails of choice" can be made on the spot in the Bars.

However, it is the duty of the Bar man to guide and help the guests for their best satisfactions whims, and ego.

Some guests behave on whims during drinking beverages other than cocktails. There is a saying in India that "Beer before whisky, no fear, Whisky after beer can be-risky". A Bar man should discourage tactfully the possible risky situations in his bar.

The bar staff should be well conversant about mixing the cocktails as per recipe and proper garnish and serving style. Nothing, however, prevents him for adding his own artistic flare while garnishing mixed drinks. He/she must ensure that the bar has at least the following ingredients in adequate quantities.

a) Lemon, lime, mint, cherry, oranges, olives, stuffed olives (both black and green varieties). Juices and Syrups of different varieties should be in stock.
b) Castor and Cube Sugar.
c) Cream
d) Pen and Pickled onion
e) Eggs
f) Green chilies (for vodka in India)
g) Salt and Pepper
h) Tabasco and Worchester Sauce
i) Cucumber, Tomato, Tomato juice
j) Pine apple and Pine apple juice
k) Plain nuts and salted nuts.
l) Cheese cubes
m) Chips, Wafers, Papad, Namkin, Bhujia
n) Ham, Pork, Salami, Sauges etc. Whenever there is a demand otherwise arrangement for freshly fried pakoras, Baby corn fries etc.
o) Soaked lentils, grams or green bengal gram (in season) are very popular in Indian Bars.

In India, bars have limited capacity at the counter like many other countries. Hence, in most of the places remaining floor area where bar is located, tables and chairs are placed with formal setting of tables as in restaurants. Sometimes, sofas are also placed for relaxation while drinking. Hence, no of waiters are needed more and some service time has to be allowed for carrying out orders.

In India many bars and restaurants had developed new cocktails and their garnish which are well accepted even among foreigners who visit the country. All these, are added to the satisfaction of guests and creativity among the bar men.

New concoctions with Classics Daiquiri and Margarita have also been developed recently.

Renedezvous (with cherry brandy, campari and cheries), Prince Edward Martini (with Drambuie, lemon and honey), Mango, mint Daiquiri, Frozen Daiquiri are some of the latest twists in the classics. Flambe' cocktails are also interesting and magical in Bars for parties.

## CHAPTER 18

# BAR STAFF AND CUSTOMER CARE

People who are involved in the service of food and drink must be acceptable with customer. They should have good personal hygiene, appearance, petitness and skill etc. Good health is an essential requirement for a bar person as the jobs demand long hours of working and standing. Body odour, bad breath are both unacceptable and can be unpleasant for a customer to be served by somebody having such health problem. Staff should be daily advised to wash regularly and take daily bath. Should also be advised to use antiperspirant.

The staff should be advised not to touch mouth, nose etc. and the handle glasses without washing hands. They should be taught not to cough, spit, sneer, over drinks. They should be prevented from smoking while on duty. Attention should be given for proper bandaging of cuts, burns etc. if any and to keep clean all service cloths etc.

In general, staff should keep good health standards and habits.

Bar staff should be positive in their attitude and be happy. They must not be clumsy and should not lean on a table or bar counter or side board rather they should look smart and alert during duties. They should speak properly in low voice but audible as the bar is noisy place.

Customer should not be annoyed or impatient while communicating with the bar staff.

The bar staff should be able to welcome customer properly with smile. They should also be tactful and diplomatic communicating things particularly. When a customer has problem or complaint cheerfulness and good spirit creates happy atmosphere which is very essential in bar and it also helps to diffuse difficult situations.

The customer is entitled to be treated nicely and pleasantly. The bar staff punctuality and reliability is very important their absence will disturb the show which even GM etc. can not compensate. It is unlike office Job'- in the bar, show must go on.

Self-confidence comes with knowledge, and experience Bar staff must believe in his/her own ability and he/she must be able to project this to the customer.

A lack of confidence on the part of a bar man or sommelier may lead to a loss in sales and may be cause of accidents as well.

At times a customer can be very difficult to serve. He may create problems unwarranted and may appear to be objection able to the bar staff. The bar staff must always keep his cool and be polite, usually the customer will then calm down. If the situation can not be handled by the staff concerned he/she should ask a superior to deal with people. For this one should know how others think and react to certain situations.

**Team work and communication**

The whole establishment as well as the food and beverage services section must work as a team. This is essential to cooperate with other departments and to give them information which may be useful to them. For example, a bar man may notice that a party of 20 customer arrived when he/she knows that the place is expecting only 15. This information should be passed immediately to concerned authority so that whole team can serve tc the satisfaction of the customers.

For a pleasant and efficient working, staff should work together and help each other. This is achieved without doing anything extra at all.

A pleasant and efficient working atmosphere will only be achieved by people thinking of other rather than just themselves. Staff should be polite and respectful to supervisors and should follow their instructions. Staff who can accept criticism and act upon will become better at their job and get more job satisfaction.

If staff are to do good job, they must be motivated. In order to motivate one has to be firm at the same time friendly. The staff need to feel that superiors are really interested in them and that they are trying to help them. It is important to offer praise when they deserve It or things are well done. It is advised to give credit where credit is due rather than snatch the credit for oneself when other have earned it. Staff should be offered advice and encouragement when it is so needed to help the staff to perform and finish his task to perform and finish his task properly. This can be done with smile and friendly way so that the staff feels at ease. Instructions should be such that they are clear and unambiguous and that the staff to whom they are given understands them.

From the above paragraph, it is seen how important the staff is and his attitude for providing services to the customer and to look after them.

We know that good service is difficult to define or measure as it is a subjective matter because

- Service even in the same country can be looked into differently by people with different education, culture and background.
- Depending on mood and needs the service can be perceived differently.
- People have different standards of quality.

However, it may be noted that when guest "expectation" is "realized" in a situation it is termed as "good service".

If it is not, then it is "bad or substandard service".

When guest's "realization" is more than his "expectation" - then it is "excellent services"

There are three parties involved in customer care

1. Establishment
2. Customer
3. Staff

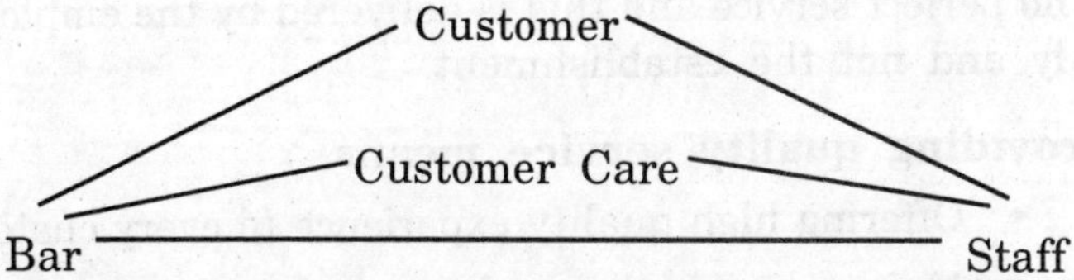


The benefit of good and effective customer care is felt and shared by all the three parties in establishment, customer and employee.

These benefits may be outlined as follows:

For the establishments (Bar or Hotel)

- Satisfied guests
- Goodwill
- Increased sales and profit
- Good "word of mouth" publicity
- Staying above competition
- Job satisfaction of the employee
- Repeat business

**For the staff**

- Good relation with guests
- The satisfaction to see guest happy
- Satisfaction of doing good job
- More happiness and less stress

**For the customer**

- Happy experiences

- Happy and satisfactory surroundings
- Helpful and interested staff
- Being cared for and treated as an individual
- Respect and recognition

**Providing quality service**

Perfect service does not mean perfect product. Hence, even a perfect product may not satisfy a guests if there is no perfect service and this is delivered by the employees only and not the establishment.

**Providing quality service means**

- Offering high quality experience to every customer
- Maintaining high standards and repeat them every time
- Developing good system and making them work nicely
- Developing practices for task to be performed so that good habit develops and mistakes totally avoided.

Even when things go wrong, you can still offer the customer a quality service by sorting out the problem properly, quickly and correctly.

Staff must be conversant with the special needs of the guests in order to satisfy them properly. Some customer's priority is punctuality, privacy etc. where as some look for value of money, relaxation friendly service. It is the job of the waiter to identify the needs as far as possible to ensure that service matches if not exceeds the guest's expectations.

The elderly person, foreigners, physically challenged guests require understanding and sensitive handling.

Waiter should Judge whether elderly persons need special help and they should be treated with respect and patience.

## Telephone Practice

Handling telephone calls skilfully is very important. The first priority is to answer all calls properly, it may so happen that you may loose booking in your establishment.

- Always answer with greeting, good morning etc.
- Always identify your establishment this is 'Chandni Bar' etc.
- Always Identify yourself: this is Mohan from Chandni Bar
- Question the caller's need : What can I do for you Sir/ Madam? How I may be of any help?

By following the sequences the staff has achieved a number of things. He has greeted a potential customer in a polite manner. He/She has ensured the caller that he/ she has come through the right place by identifying it. The receiver also identified himself thereby giving the caller a reference and the necessary information. This practice project the image of the bar and thus it is a professional and efficient practice.

The following points are useful while answering telephone calls:

Be polite and helpful

Speak clearly and slowly

Do not use technical or unfamiliar words

Carefully listen

Try to ascertain caller's name for use

Make notes if necessary

Inform notes of necessary

Take section you have promised to the caller you should have all the necessary references materials and information close at hand for answering calls.

## Transferring calls

In case of the staff decides that he is waiter to provide the required information on caller's request, sometimes it is necessary to transfer the call. The staff concerned must be aware of the duties and responsibilities of various employees. Always match the caller's need to the person responsible and put them in contact with one another.

While transferring the call the staff should

- Advise the caller regarding transfer.
- Provide the caller information as to whom he is going to talk
- Brief the staff regards the caller and his need
- Then make connection and transfer

It should be ensured that the now person would answer the queries of the caller. Call should not be transferred just to avoid any problem. It is frustrating for a caller to be transferred from a person to another for number of times. This can lead to anger and angry clients will not buy service on offer no matter how good it is.

Normally, a caller should not be "put on hold". In case it is absolutely necessary, then one should advise the caller that he/ she is put on hold and in between it is ensured whether the caller wish to remain in line.

## Taking Message

Sometimes in the absence of contact persons it is necessary to take messages and transmit them to the person concerned on their availability. The staff should

- Note the date and time.
- Note the name of the person and his/her contact number.
- Note the name of the person to be contacted for the caller.
- See that the message is passed to the right individual and see that action on the message has

been carried out whenever possible and within jurisdiction of the message taken.

All the employees should be trained and directed proper use and cleanliness of telephone equipments in particularly faults should be immediately reported for rectification. Disinfection is also recommended for telephone sets.

**Handling guest complaints**

from guests if any are very important and must be recorded in the complaints book. All complaints should be reported to the management who should speak directly to the guest concerned. Action should be taken to see that some problem or issue does not occur again.

**Compliments**

Compliments offered by guests should be received with courtesy and the guests thanked for it.

**Handling drunken customer**

In the bar waiter often find same customer under the influence of alcohol. Law clearly states that such customers should not be served any move alcohol. But often the situation becomes unpleasant for the other guests. In such case, management should be called for to handle the situation. Tactfully the drunken person should be taken away from the bar for dialogues or for sending him home firmly but without causing him any physical injury.

**Handling customer's illness or accident**

Every effort should be made to prevent accidents because or floor, from metal sticks, from broken furniture etc. In case major problems bar manager must be informed, to handle the issue with compensation for his belongings. When a customer with special he/she may be provided with special attention in a quiet and comfortable place away from the bar and should be provided with glass of water. If first is necessary this should be arranged properly. If necessary doctor may be called. Whichever of these situation occurs, the details must be carefully recorded with time, date etc.

### Handling loss of customer's property

It is usually notified by way of display that management not responsible for any loss or theft of any properly belonging is handed over to any authorized bar staff, he/she is duty bound to return it. In case of loss or theft is reported by a customer the same to be notified to the management for action with police where it is warranted.

### Welcoming and Departure of customers

When a customer arrives in he must be greeted and welcomed and should not be left standing or ignored. Depending upon the relationship between customer and the staff if any because of = earlier regular visits he/she should be politely addressed in the normal forms in. Good evening, Sir, Good morning, Sir/madam etc. or Good evening ladies and gentlemen. When there is a group of customers. VIPs should be addressed with extra care and with special formality wherever the situation so demands. Formal addressing of dignitaries have been available in the reference book "Debrette's correct form".

When customer leaves the bar, the staff should say "Good night" Sir, madam (for ladies), and hope to see you again, or hope, you have enjoyed the evening, ensure that they have not left any personal belonging or the table or empty chairs when they were seated.

Peg counting disputes: This should be avoided and customers should not feel that he/she was cheated on quantity or quality. Copies of bill at the time of services are sometimes recommended for the guests so that he/she himself keep note of his/her drinks.

## CHAPTER 19

# SALES PROMOTION IN THE BAR

The objective is to gain customer confidence, achieving satisfaction and achieving and maximizing sales.

For achieving the above objectives the bar staff must be well trained and motivated. They must be trained on the techniques of pleasing the customer with their services and style of entertaining with a bet of personal touch. The bar staff should be well aware of the various products in the bar and they should have special knowledge of the wine varieties and other liquids etc. so that they are able to suggest and push sales to the customers.

Many customers are attracted to a bar for the showmanship of the bar staff and their care for the customers. Customers like to be treated as individuals and to feel that they are valued and welcomed by the bar. Cleanliness, tidiness must be maintained from opening till closing and for days together to attain the good will to draw customers from far and near.

Every thing in the bar should be maintained on high standard to attract customers. The Bar menu must be attractive and explicit in terms description, price and other details. Composition of cocktails there explanation etc. if any must be properly projected for sales promotion. Wine list etc. should be attractively printed so that customers may like to venture new products with confidence. Names of International wine varieties are difficult to pronounce by Indians, hence suitable aid in the wine list may be provided to help guests to pronounce it properly, so that he/she can place order confidently. The pronunciation can be simplified if translated version is also printed in local languages.

"Tent cards" recommending particular drinks may be placed on the tables in the bar. This is a proper sales aid and this displays the products that is to be prompted.

The display shelves should not be used for storage of glasses etc. This waste valuable display space to product promotion. Attractive posters and sales promotion literatures may also be suitably displayed.

Some bar provides some times namkins, peanuts etc. free of cost with bottle of beer etc. this is also a method of sales promotion.

## ONE COMPLIMENTARY FOR ONE ORDERED

In association with the manufacturer of alcoholic drinks, many bar now-a-days promoting their bar sales offering complimentary drinks.

### "Happy hour"

This is a new concept in India. During the less crowded time or beyond "pick hours" of the bars discount on drinks offered. This helps the establishment to run with greater capacity during so called empty hours.

Company sponsored cocktail parties and other festive occasion help bar to promote sales in their establishment. A proper control is necessary for managing such events.

In fact the beverage sales staff should be smart enough and should have the ability to judge the spending mood and power of their guests and accordingly he should be able to push the sales.

The bar man/service staff should properly offer/suggest guests to select their drinks/cocktails from the very start of the dinner/ lunch where guests comes for food as well as for drinks. Bar staff should be alert to judge guests well in advance for repeat drinks instead of waiting for the guest's call for order. They should also promote finishing drinks at the end of a meal where ever possible.

In a big bar or in restaurant where drinks are served, "liqueur trolley" helps sales. The arrangement and supply are visible and attractive for the guests - and they sometimes invariably order for liqueur/Brandy etc. and the customer also appreciates seeing full measure being poured out in front of him. In fact, either from the trolley or out of salves, the service should be in front of the customer to see for himself. A positive approach in order taking and service will surely increase sales. Customer may be always encouraged into ordering by a positive approach when they might otherwise not have bothered.

Properly introduced bonus schemes can be an incentive to staff to promote sales.

Bar management sometimes consider providing additional attraction in the bar like dance, music cabaret, disco etc. These are very much related to sales promotion. Over all policy should be to provide relaxation and entertainment. Some customer gets high after couple of drinks and sometimes misbehaves with ladies. Such situation should be strictly avoided and customer must not have any unpleasant experience. Any disputes with drunken customers should not be allowed at any cost and avoided tactfully.

# CHAPTER 20

# BAR CONTROL

In general the control principles are more or less same as that of food cost control. Hotels/Bars etc. have Bar licences - one for sale of liquor in bar and second for service in rooms or other outlets.

The place for storage of bottles as well as the vending has to be separate for both the licences. All State Excise laws must be adhered to. All liquor, soft drinks and tobacco be maintained in the bar stock register and maintained by the bar man. The proforma of a bar-stock register is given over leaf.

### Bar spoilage

Any flat bear or spoiled drink is written off by F and B manager/F and B controller or is returned to the supplier for replacement whenever possible. Those broken or spoiled in store/celler and can not be replaced by supplier are destroyed by a committee comprising of F & B controller and/or chief accounts officer and manager (M.M.& D.) and written off. Sales of the shift of each bar is recorded bill wise in a wine pricking sheet (WPS) (see sample format).

### Bar billing procedure

All BWS, spirits cigar and cigarettes can only be picked up from the bar against a Bill/Bar order picked (BOP).

**Control means**

- You adhere to your predetermined standards while you exercise restraint or direction over the price you pay to buy, prepare and sell drinks.
- You know your market as your bar calls to a specific market. Standard vary for different markets. You set standards appropriate to your market before you buy, prepare and sell.
- You prepare cost control procedure for controlling all your costs you need records which give you information you must have in order to make sensible and wise decision to control and improve your bar service and functions.

**Salient Features of the Beverage Control**

- Cost control saves money for the establishment..
- Boost profit.
- Cost accounting cuts unnecessary spending.
- Avoiding pitfall in purchasing.
- Boosts quality service and control.
- Professionalism in management and service.

**Control cycle**

The four major steps are involved in beverage control as under.

- Establish standard
- Check actual performance
- Identify deviation from predetermined standards
- Take corrective actions

## SCOPE OF CONTROLS

**Control before the event (Pre-control)**

- Setting target
- Budget

- Budgetary control

**Control during the event (concurrent control)**

- Purchasing
- Receiving
- Storing and Issuing
- Service and cash

**Control after the (corrective control)**

- Setting up control system
- Calculation of product cost and preparation of cost reports
- Analysing reports and advising management for correction action.

**The beverage operation cycle**

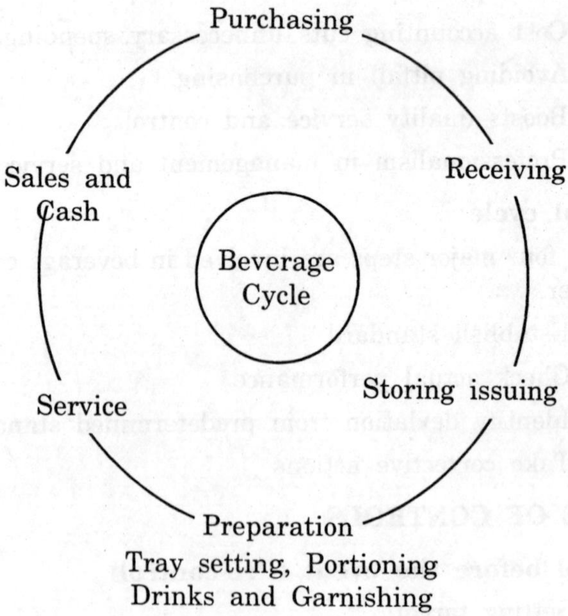


Each of these six stages constitute a highly critical area of food and beverage cost control.

## Organisation and duties of control staff

In large organization F and B controller post can be kept but in small establishment one control assistant should be made responsible for control and report to his superior in assistant F and B manager onto similar designated authority.

In elite and classic category of ITDC hotels as examples following organisation is in effect.

### A. Elite category hotels

Dy. Manager/Asst. Manager (F & B Control)

↓

Supervisor

↓

Control Assistant

### B. Comfort category hotels

Assistant Manager (F & B)

↓

Control assistant

Their duties and responsibilities are described as follows:

### Job description

| | |
|---|---|
| Title | : **Food and beverage controller** |
| Response to | : General Manager |
| Purpose and scope | : Implement procedures, control food and beverages cost and advise the management on cost control measure |

### Duties and Responsibiuties

- Make ongoing profit and loss studies of all the food and beverages cost centres.
- Recommend changes to reach profit potentials.

- Submit the monthly food and beverages cost report.
- Make food tests with chef to help purchased items as per specification. Keep result on record.
- Make standard recipes, check portion and maintain butcher yield tests in consultation with the chef.
- Check competitor items, portions and prices on regular basis.
- Take periodical food and beverage inventories and non-scheduled bar inventories.
- Spot check receiving, storage and issuing of food and beverage items to be sure of proper turnover of supplies.
- Review of employees and complimentary meals and report those not in line with the procedures.
- Spot check the banquet functions for the actual numbers and the billed numbers.
- Check random records of stores and correct short coming. Give instructions and suggestions.
- Report any deviation or violation in respect to the KOT/BOT checks.
- Directly supervise the food and beverages control system (Sales analysis, inventory control and standard specification etc.).
- Analyse banquet menus to establish cost spot checks to head count at the banquet/parties.
- Spot check, receiving and issuing of food p - material.
- Take inventories of all food and beverage items (in Kitchen, Restaurants, Room service, Bar and Stores) on the last day of each month and calculate food and beverage cost for the month.
- Calculate on monthly basis cost of officers and employees meals.

- Personally check the main bar and room service bar register every month.
- Tally the bar stocks with the ledger stocks. Also to verify the monthly assessment fees before it is counter checks by the excise officer, where applicable.
- To ensure the renewal of all the bar licences and to obtain special bar licences for Private Parties/ Special Occasion etc. in states require under the guidance of F & B Manager.
- To arrange all the necessary excise permits or road permits for transfer or liquor from the distributor/ inter unit.
- To ensure the stamping of all the peg measures and weighing scales/machines from the department of weigh and measures every year as per state bye laws.
- Should ensure that all wines are stored at proper temperatures and that all liquor and beer bottles are stacked/kept properly on the storage racks.
- Should periodically check the cold stores and deep freezers etc. and to inform chef regarding rotten or spoiled food item.
- All imported food items should be stored properly at the right temperatures both in general stores and the production areas.

**Authority**

He is authorised to check, control all inventories, stock, cash, records, register etc. in respect of food and beverages service and production and associated stores thereof.

**Job Description**

Job title : **Control Assistant**

Responsible to : F & B Controller

Purpose and scope : Perform various control functions like taking inventories, KOT analysis making cost report, spot checking of receiving, storing, and sales outlets.

**Duties and Responsibilities**

- To make daily BOT allocations and analysis and report irregularities.
- To check bills are made for all BOTs and report irregularities. To make dish popularly chart.
- To take daily/surprise bar inventory and inform variance to F & B controller.
- Costing of indents and requisitions.
- Accounting and review of employees meal and executive entitlement.
- To spot check receiving, storage, issuing and sales of food items.
- Make food and beverage cost report.
- Calculation on monthly basis officers and employees meal.
- Check main bar and room service bar register every month to tally stock with ledger stock. Also to verify the monthly assessment fee before it is counter checked by the excise officers where applicable.
- To assist in the renewal of all bar licences.
- To obtain special bar licences for private parties and special occasion etc.

## CELLER CONTROL

A system of celler control (wine stores) and proper costing must be introduced. The system, however, varies from establishment to establishment. In general following books of records are necessary for the control system:

- Order book
- Goods inward book

- Celler cards
- Bin cards
- Goods return book
- Stock book
- Departmental requisition book
- Daily consumption sheets

The celler is the focal point for the storage of alcoholic and non-alcoholic beverages. All service points such as bars, dispense bar, lounge bar, cocktail bar, saloon bar and other places draw the stock on a daily or weekly basis from the celler (stores). Adequate space is to be provided depending upon the establishment and their sales.

All the bars shall keep a separate stock of liquor which is sufficient for a period of one day or week. At the end of this period of time they requisition for the amount consumed for that day or week, thus bringing their total stock up to the set stock, that is keeping the stock upto a particular level to be determined by the requirement in view of turnover.

In the celler where bin cards are used then every time wine received or issued, it will be entered on the appropriate bin cards to indicate remaining total balance. Thus, bin cards provides information at any given time the total amount of each particular wine held in stock. This will alert the celler man to arrange further stock on ordering from the supplies.

## BIN CARDS FORMAT

In the dispense bar, as all drinks are checked for before issue, a daily consumption sheet is completed each day alter the service by writing down the sales shown on the top copy of wine checks. The consumption sheet will record the complete stock hold in the dispose bar.

Bin cards may also be completed for checking the liquor. At the end of the week the consumption sheets may be totalled up, thereby showing the total sales for that period.

These totals may than be transferred on to a bar stock book for costing purpose. Where liquor consumed is not checked for any way then either a daily or weekly stock is taken so that the amount to be requisitioned from the celler may be noted. This then brings the bar stock book up to its required level, which is the 'par' stock. The daily or weekly consumption (sales) would then be costed and the cash total to the daily or weekly income. That is cash in the 'till'.

| Name of liquor/wine | | Bin No. | |
|---|---|---|---|
| Date | Received | Balanced | Issue |
| | | | |

The format as under can be introduced to record daily consumption. A store book format for alcoholic drinks should also be introduced.

**Format of Daily consumption Chart**

| Name of the drink | Bin No. | M | T | W | TH | F | St | Sum | Total |
|---|---|---|---|---|---|---|---|---|---|
| | | | | | | | | | |

**Format of Stock Book**

| Name of the drink | Bin No. | Opening | Receipt | Total | Closing stock | Con-sumption | Principal unit | Total |
|---|---|---|---|---|---|---|---|---|
| | | | | | | | | |

Those are several formats of some ITDC group of hotels. (Elite/Classic and comfort) are also shown as example in the following pages.

**Wine Card Mix**

| Imported | Elite 5 and Maximsum | Classic 4 Minimum | Classic 3 and Maximum | Comfort Minimum |
|---|---|---|---|---|
| Red | 4 | 2 | 2 | 1 |
| White | 4 | 2 | 2 | 1 |
| Champagne | 3 | 1 | 1 | 1 |
| Indian | | | | |
| Red | 4 | 2 | 2 | 1 |
| White | 4 | 2 | 2 | 1 |
| Champange | | | | |
| Sparkling Wine | 1 | 1 | 1 | 1 |

अशाक ग्रुप **THE ASHOK GROUP**

Shift ________

Sale Point ______

दिन और दिनांक
Day & Date ______________

बारमेन का नाम
Name of Barman ____________

## वाइन पिकिंग शीट
## WINE PICKING SHEET

| | आयातित मादक पेय Imported Beverages | | | | | | | | | इन्डजिनियस पेय Indigenous Beverages | | | | | | | | | हल्के पेय Soft Drinks | | | | | | | सिगरेट और सिगार Cigarettes & Cigars | | | | | | | |
|---|---|---|---|---|---|---|---|---|---|---|---|---|---|---|---|---|---|---|---|---|---|---|---|---|---|---|---|---|---|---|---|---|---|
| | वाइन्स Wines | | एपरेटिफस Aperitifs | | | सपिरिटस Spirits | | | | वाइन्स Wines | | सपिरिटस Spirits | | | | | | | | | | | | | | | | | | | | | |
| वाउचर सं. Voucher No. | शपेन Champage | आर.डब्लू. वाइन्स R.W. Wines | शेरी Sherry | वरमाउथ Vermouth | कम्पनी Campan | डीलक्स व्हिस्की Dix. Scotch | रेगुलर स्कॉच Reg. Scotch | कॉनियक Conagac | मादक पेय Liqueurs | आर.डब्लू वाइन्स R.W. Wines | स्पेशल व्हिस्की Spl. Whisky | रेगुली. व्हिस्की Reg. Whisky | ब्रांडी Brandy | रम Rum | जिन Gin | वोदका Vodka | बियर Bear | केन बियर Cane Bear | शरबत Squash | डिब्बा बंद जूस Tinned Juice | बातल जूस Bottle Juice | सोडा Soda | कैम्पा कोला Campa Cola | मिनिरल वॉटर Mineral Water | फ्रेश लाईम Fresh Lime | इंडिया किंग India King | गोल्ड फ्लेक 20 सि. Gold Flake 20's | गोल्ड फ्लेक 10 सि. Gold Flake 10's | विल्ज किंग साईज 20 सि. Wills K.S. 20's | विल्ज किंग साईज 10 सि. Wills K.S. 10's | विल्ज नेविकट Wills Navy Cut | क्लासिक Classic | रोथ मैन Rothman |
| | | | | | | | | | | | | | | | | | | | | | | | | | | | | | | | | | |
| | | | | | | | | | | | | | | | | | | | | | | | | | | | | | | | | | |
| | | | | | | | | | | | | | | | | | | | | | | | | | | | | | | | | | |
| | | | | | | | | | | | | | | | | | | | | | | | | | | | | | | | | | |
| | | | | | | | | | | | | | | | | | | | | | | | | | | | | | | | | | |
| | | | | | | | | | | | | | | | | | | | | | | | | | | | | | | | | | |
| | | | | | | | | | | | | | | | | | | | | | | | | | | | | | | | | | |
| | | | | | | | | | | | | | | | | | | | | | | | | | | | | | | | | | |
| Total | | | | | | | | | | | | | | | | | | | | | | | | | | | | | | | | | |

Prepared by:

Checked by:

# HOTEL ABC
## BAR CONSUMPTION REGISTER

Date __________

| Shift | I | | | | | II | | | | III | | | |
|---|---|---|---|---|---|---|---|---|---|---|---|---|---|
| | O/B | Rece | Total | Sale | Bal. | Rec | Tot. | Sale | Bal. | R | T | S | C/B |
| Imported | | | | | | | | | | | | | |
| Chivas Regal | | | | | | | | | | | | | |
| Scotch Pre. | | | | | | | | | | | | | |
| Scotch Reg. | | | | | | | | | | | | | |
| Cognac | | | | | | | | | | | | | |
| Liqueurs | | | | | | | | | | | | | |
| Sherry | | | | | | | | | | | | | |
| Port | | | | | | | | | | | | | |
| Vermouth | | | | | | | | | | | | | |
| Campari | | | | | | | | | | | | | |
| Champagne | | | | | | | | | | | | | |
| Table Wine | | | | | | | | | | | | | |
| Indigenous | | | | | | | | | | | | | |
| Spl. Whisky | | | | | | | | | | | | | |
| Reg. Whisky | | | | | | | | | | | | | |
| Brandy | | | | | | | | | | | | | |
| Rum | | | | | | | | | | | | | |
| Gin | | | | | | | | | | | | | |
| Vodka | | | | | | | | | | | | | |
| Liqueurs | | | | | | | | | | | | | |
| Table Wine | | | | | | | | | | | | | |
| Beer Spl. | | | | | | | | | | | | | |
| Beer Reg. | | | | | | | | | | | | | |
| Soft Drinks | | | | | | | | | | | | | |
| Mineral Water | | | | | | | | | | | | | |
| Squash | | | | | | | | | | | | | |
| Tinned Juices | | | | | | | | | | | | | |
| Apple Juice | | | | | | | | | | | | | |
| Soda | | | | | | | | | | | | | |
| Lmnd./Ale/Tonic | | | | | | | | | | | | | |
| Cola/Lime | | | | | | | | | | | | | |
| Cigarettes/Cigar | | | | | | | | | | | | | |
| India King | | | | | | | | | | | | | |
| Classic | | | | | | | | | | | | | |
| Gold Flake 20's | | | | | | | | | | | | | |
| Will's K's 20's | | | | | | | | | | | | | |
| Will's K's 10's | | | | | | | | | | | | | |
| Will's Med | | | | | | | | | | | | | |
| Cigars | | | | | | | | | | | | | |

**Standard Complimentary Snacks to served with BWS in the BAR**

| S.No. | Snacks | Elite 5/Classic4 | Classic3/Comfort |
|---|---|---|---|
| 1. | Vacuum packed such as wafers, Cheeseballs etc. | 3 | 3 |
| 2. | Roasted peanuts | 3 | 3 |
| 3. | Mixture | | |
| 4. | Cashewnuts/Almonds | 3 (Discretionary) | 3 VIP's only |
| 5. | Tikkas/Kebabs | 3 (Discretionary) | 3 VIP's only |
| 6. | Olives/Canapes | 3 (Discretionary) | 3 VIP's only |

**P.S.:**

- For vacuum packed products, well known such as 'Uncle Chipps', 'Lehar Pepsi', 'Haldi Ram's' etc. should be used.
- High quality local products can be used in non-metro hotels.
- Appropriate temperature for all snacks to be maintained during service.
- Non-metro city hotels, should take into account local factors, guest choice should not too limited.

**Bar Card**

| | Elite 5 and Maximum | Classic 4 Minimum | Classic 3 and Maximum | Comfort Minimum |
|---|---|---|---|---|
| Long Drinks | 8 | 4 | 6 | 3 |
| Cocktails | 8 | 4 | 6 | 3 |
| Aperitifs (Compari/ Sherry/Port/Vermouth) | 4 | 3 | 2 | 1 |
| Imported Spirits | | | | |
| Delus (J.W. Blue label/ Royal Salute) | 2 | 1 | - | - |
| Scotch premium (Chivas/ J.W.B./Black dog/ Glenfiddich) | 4 | 2 | 2 | 1 |

| | | | | |
|---|---|---|---|---|
| Regular (J.W.R./L./White/ Horse/J and B/Cutty Sarc/ Grants) | 5 | 3 | 3 | 2 |

| | Elite 5 and Maximum | Classic 4 Minimum | Classic 3 and Maximum | Comfort Minimum |
|---|---|---|---|---|
| Napleon Camus | 1 | - | - | - |
| Cognac VSCOP (Remy Martin/Martell/Hennessy Campus) | 3 | 2 | 2 | 1 |
| Indian Spirits | | | | |
| Delux (Antiquity/single malt) | 2 | 1 | - | - |
| Whisky premium (Peter Scot/Royal Challenge/ Mcdowell/Vintage | 4 | 2 | 3 | 2 |
| Whisky Regular (Mcdowell No.1 Red knight/Diplomat/ Bagpiper | 3 | 2 | 2 | 1 |
| Rum (Old Monk/ No.1 Mcdowell/Old adventurer | 3 | 2 | 2 | 1 |
| Gin (Aristocrat/Blue Riband/Boths) | 3 | 2 | 2 | 1 |
| Vodka (Red Czar/ Aristocrat/Romanov | 3 | 2 | 2 | 1 |
| Brandy (honey bee) | 2 | 1 | 2 | 1 |
| Beer | | | | |
| Premium | 3 | 2 | 2 | 1 |
| Regular | 4 | 2 | 2 | 1 |
| Soft Drinks | | | | |
| Aerated water | 8 | 6 | 6 | 4 |
| Tinned juices | 5 | 3 | 3 | 1 |
| IMPORTED LIQUEURES | | | | |
| Creme de menthe/ Cointreau/drambuie Curaco/Coffee Liqueur/Benedictine/ Grand Marnier/Malibu/Cherry Brandy/Bailey's Irish Cream | 10 | 6 | 6 | 1 |

**Check procedure for high coat and loss**

In the following areas of control are not imposed result high cost and loss:

**Purchasing**

- Purchasing at high price
- Pilferage/leakage
- Too much open market purchases
- No standard purchase specification
- Not availing and book discounts
- Not sensitive to market fluctuation
- Unwise purchase
- Failure in right purchase method
- Not buying right quantity at right time
- Same person purchasing as well as receiving

**Receiving**

- Faulty receiving without referring purchase
- Accepting substandard quality!
- Overlooking defects in the supply
- Time gap in receiving and storing
- Absence of senior people during receiving
- Lack of knowledge in the part of receiving person.

**Storing and Issuing**

- Improper storage
- Spoilage, pilferage and breakage in stores
- Stock register not up to date
- Issuing without proper requisition
- Not following F/FO procedure
- Not keeping records of slow moving and dead items.

**Property of products**

- Not following proper recipe
- Not following measures
- Indenting not according to need
- Unskilled staff
- Faulty equipment
- Over measure or short
- Lack of co-ordination among staff
- Lack of inventory control in caller
- Pilferage and waste
- Lack of sale forecast
- Using expensive items where cheaper substitute can be used
- No record of transfer, entertainment
- Not following FIFD
- Not using right procedure and equipment.

**Service**

- Lack of sales promotion
- Lack of salesmanship in staff
- Pilferage
- Not reporting and returning unused items
- Defective BOT control
- Misuse of costly ingredients
- Unskilled order taken
- Accidents etc.

**Cash**

- Under charges
- Cheating
- Money collected without preparing bill

- Accepting invalid and expired credit card
- Accepting counterfeit currency notes
- Bad debts
- Discounted sales
- No proper audit
- No study of sales summary,

**Control department:**

- Not making BOT/KOT will bill
- Not analysing BOT/KOT
- No periodical check on cost and inventories
- Not comparing market position for fixing sales cost

CHAPTER 21

# BAR LEGISLATION & LEGAL PROVISIONS

Running of bar comes under business activity. Thus, for any other business all legal, Municipal, State and control rules and regulations have to be followed.

Firstly for any business - a firm or company has to be floated. It may be a private company, public Ltd. company. One can start business on his/her own by registering with Shop and Establishment Act. Some places are responsible only for operation only or as franchisee.

In whatever circumstances, the company or establishment is to duly register the firm then the proprietor or partners have to ask for various licences:

**Municipal licences**

1) For the premises (commercial use)
2) Trade licence
3) Health licence
4) NOC from Pollution Control Deptt.

**Police licence**

These come from police authorities

1) NOC from traffic deptt. under police.
2) NOC from local P.S.
3) Milk and milk products licence from police.

4) Water licence
5) Coffee selling licence
6) Waste disposal licence
7) Weights and measure approval.
8) Excise permits.

There are many other statutory requirements which are required to be complied with in order to obtain licence from various authorities.

Hotels, restaurants and bars in particular employ persons for working and as such there are statutory obligations for their benefits and working conditions of the workers. In general, these are looked after by various Govt. Deptt. Under various departmental orders and Acts.

- Payments of Wages Act
- Engagement of Child Labour Act
- Minimum Wages Act
- Payments of Bonus Act
- Payment of Gratuity and Pension Act
- Apprenticeship Act
- Subsistence Allowance Act
- Terminal Benefits Act
- Employees Provident Fund Act
- Fatal Accident Act
- Employees State Insurance Act
- Workmen Disputes Act
- Trade Unions Act
- Leave and Leave salary Act

In addition to the above brief list employees leave, leave travel concession (if any) overtime, holidays, weakly off are regulated and guided by set of norms based on relevant rules, laws and acts under which the establishment and the business fall.

Bar and the establishment are also required to keep profit and loss accounts and other statutory books of accounts required by excise, sales tax, income tax authorities for their annual verification etc. Disputes can be settled through appropriate tax tribunal/court of law.

Bar mainly deals with alcoholic products obtained locally or from foreign countries through authorized agents. The alcohol being an excise commodity thus, its purchase, store and sale etc. are strictly regulated by excise regulations and acts.

No one is allowed to trade with alcoholic commodities in any—from without obtaining proper 'Bar licence and details of excise rules and regulations varies from state to state in India and in every other counties.

Bars do require strict compliance or Excise Department's directives and maintenance of all purchase and sales records. For violence, strict penalties along with the suspension or cancellation of licence may result.

## SALIENT FEATURES OF EXCISE PROVISIONS

### Credential of the licence

Detailed examination background, police verification, family business details are sought before selecting person for offering licence. Licence should be granted to a particular person by name. After his death the licence may vest only to his next kin/wife only and not to any other person nor the licensee can be sold to anybody.

### Location

It is easier now in many states to apply for bar licence in the existing premises of hotels/restaurants. For opening a new bar many formalities, including NOCs from various authorities are need which includes local P.S., social bodies, local MLA, local MP, *jiladhipati*, religious orgnisations etc. to name a few. In fact in some states like West Bengal it is difficult to obtain even a "off licence". This approach is determinental to the development of hotel catering and entertainment industry in the present days where social drinking is on rise. Separate licences are needed if music, dance, cabaret etc. are introduced in bars. It is illegal to harbar prostitution or other such elements from bar.

**Issuance of licence**

This is regulated by Licensing Act and Law of the land for the particular matter. There are two types of licences:

a) *Off-licence*: This licence is required for sale of liquor for consumption off or away from the premises where it is being sold. Let may be for sale of all types of liquor or for sale of beer, cigar and wine etc.

b) *Full on licence/Public home licence (Bar)*: This licence is required for the sales of liquor for consumption on or off the premises to any person permitted by law to purchase alcoholic beverages.

c) In U.K. and U.S.A. many other types of licences such as restaurant licence, residential licence. weekly or seasonal licences are issued.

d) *Occasional licence*: This licence allows for alcoholic drinks to be served in special parties, garden parties, steamer parties which places are not licensed. It can hold a full on licence applicable for occasion.

e) *Occasional permit:* This may be obtained by a person who does not holds a full on-licence and who can be an ordinary member of the public. On behalf of organization such as HRAEI, IHM's reunion parties, food festival etc. This permit is intended for individual events. In U.K. only four occasional permissions may be obtained by any organization in a year.

**Government official's entry**

The Customs, Police, Excise officials have right of entry to licensed premises except registered clubs. In U.K. and in many other countries timing and hours of official's visit for duty are also specified. The authority may also enter the premises under occasional licence for the purpose of his duty and it is the obligation of the licensee to allow him to do his duty whenever necessary.

In fact, bar licensee should keep good rapport with local P.S. in particular to keep peace and law order under control in bars. It is very common to have occasional brawal and disturbances for which police intervention is necessary.

Licensee can also apply for small arms such as pistol, revolver for their personal safety and safe running of business which are promptly sanctioned and licence granted for the liquor licensee.

## Permitted laws

Licence specifies about the time of doing business. This must be strictly adhered to. There is also a weekly "Dry day" for licences should mean on dry day no business should be transacted. Bar licence must be very up to date as regards to frequent amendments and subsequent circular notifications etc. in matter of permitted hours, special closure days and similar other matter.

In most of the places in India, the business community dealing with alcohol has their own association or national bodies which take up licences, taxing and other issues pertaining to bar, hotel and restaurant business on behalf of members.

## General regulations

In U.K., employers and employees on licensed premises must abide by Weighs and Measures Act, Hygiene Regulations, Food Regulations, Sex discrimination, Race Regulations/Act etc. In India various Sales Acts are to be abided by as and when executed or those that are already in existence.

From the off shop only sealed bottle or canned alcoholic beverages are sold. Those containers have different measure marked officially on them. Accepted measure of a full bottle is 750 ml or one litre = 1000 ml.

In India beers are mostly sold from bottle and not from beer dispensing machine. Where such machine is installed this is required to be certified by Weighs and Measures authority.

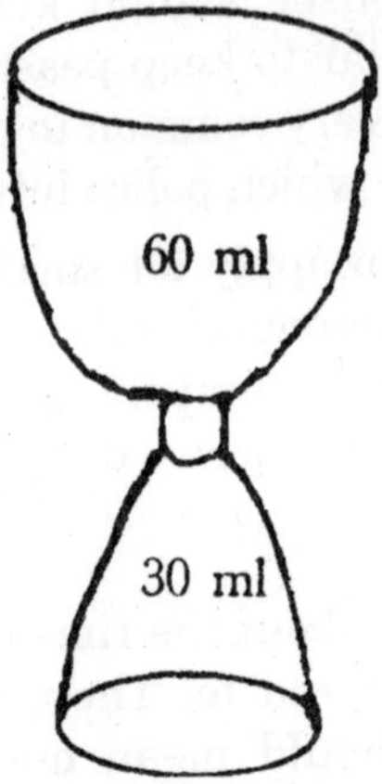


**Fig. 12: Peg Measure**

In bar Gin, Whisky, Rum and Vodka etc. may only be served either in full "peg" or as half peg. A full peg measures 60 ml whereas half peg is 30 ml (see Fig. 12). The peg measure is required to be stamped and certified by Weights and Measures Authority and Excise Deptt. as well.

## Service and dispensing

It is an offence under licensing act to serve drink to a person who is drunk. It is also an offence for licensee to allow drunkenness, violent or disorderly conduct in bars.

It is an offence under the act to serve drinks in incorrect measures. It is also an offence to dilute or mix products and sale to the customers without customer's specific request and without informing customers.

Employer or employees of a licensed premises must not to serve any customer beyond permitted hours or beyond any extension period officially granted. A time period of 15-20 minutes is allowed to consumer to drink after the last order within the permitted hours.

**Age restrictions**

Children under the age of 18 years (minor) are not allowed to enter bar. In U.K. young people over 14 years, may be allowed to enter bar, but they can only buy non-alcoholic beverages. Person between the age 16 to 18 years may only buy cideror beer in bar and above the 18 years of age he may buy any drinks from the bar. It is also the responsibility of the licensee to see that any sick or otherwise unfit persons are discouraged to consume alcohol in the premises to avoid any untoward situations or litigations. A couple of formats (police licence, fire licence are shown in the appendices).

# APPENDICES

*APPENDIX I*

# THE CHAMPAGNE REGIONS

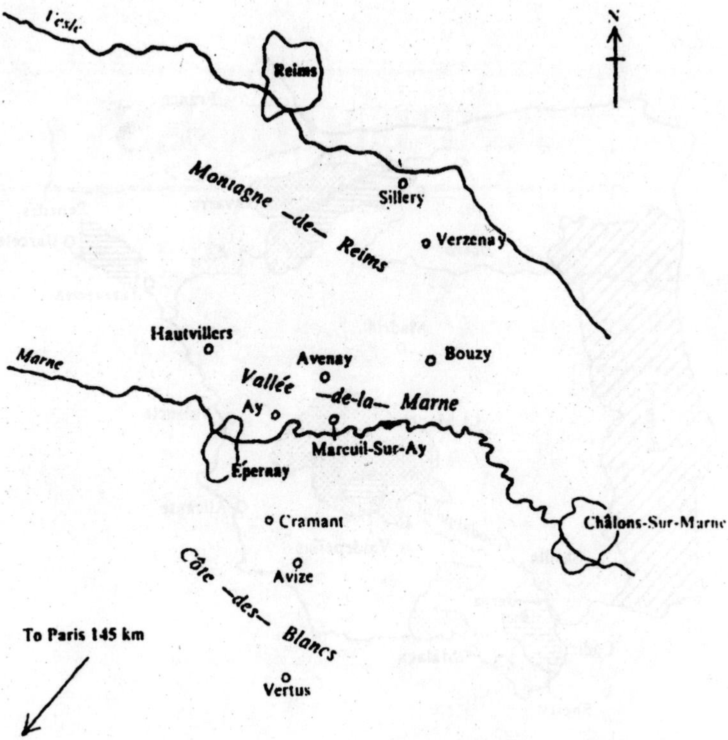

*APPENDIX II*

# WINE GROWING AREAS OF SPAIN

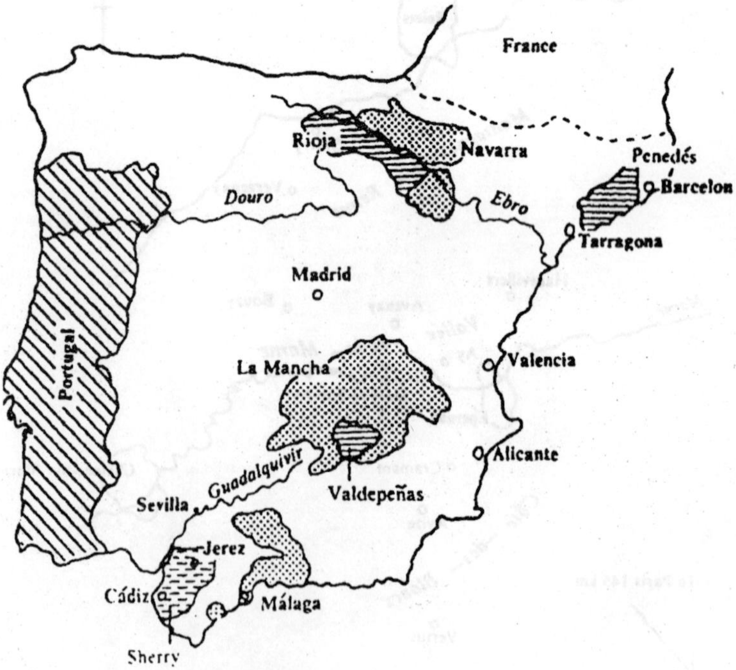

*APPENDIX II*

# WINE GROWING REGIONS OF ITALY

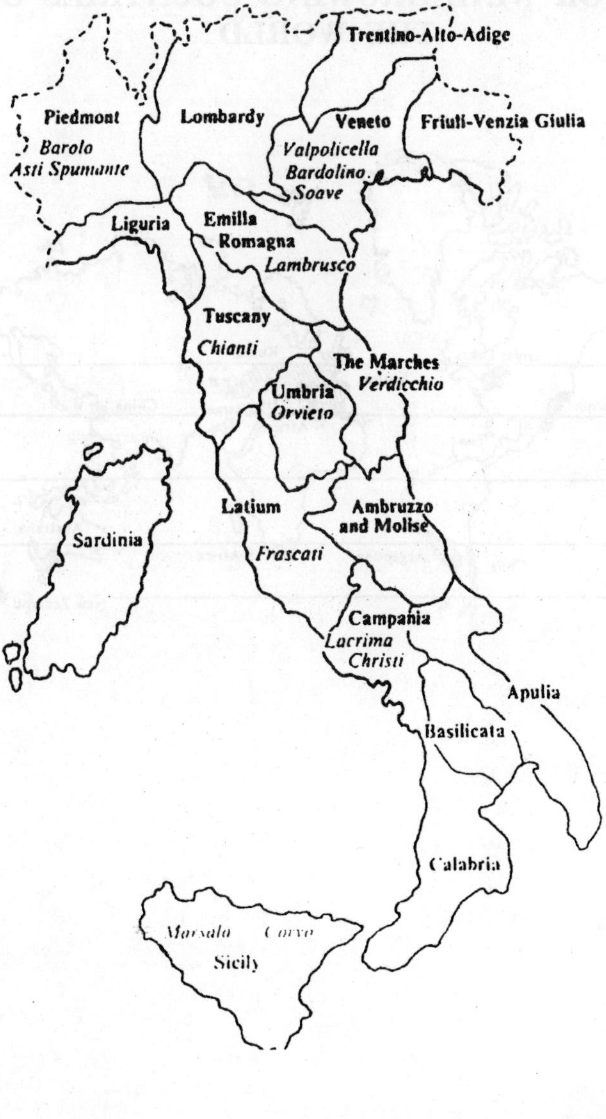

*APPENDIX IV*

# MAJOR WINE GROWING COUNTRIES OF THE WORLD

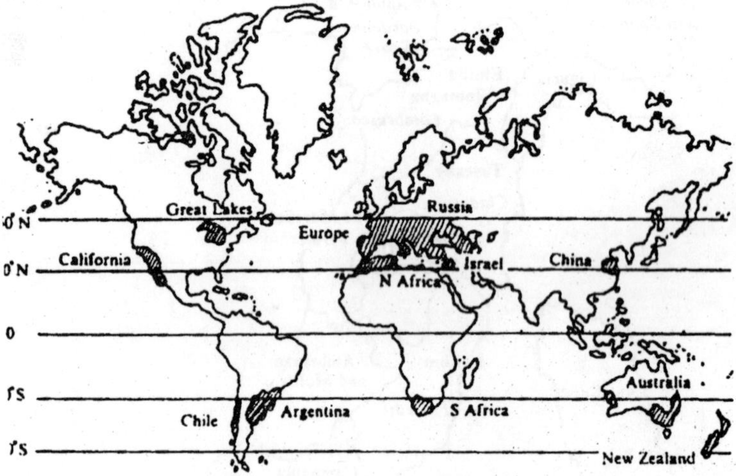

*APPENDIX V*

# FRENCH WINE GROWING REGIONS

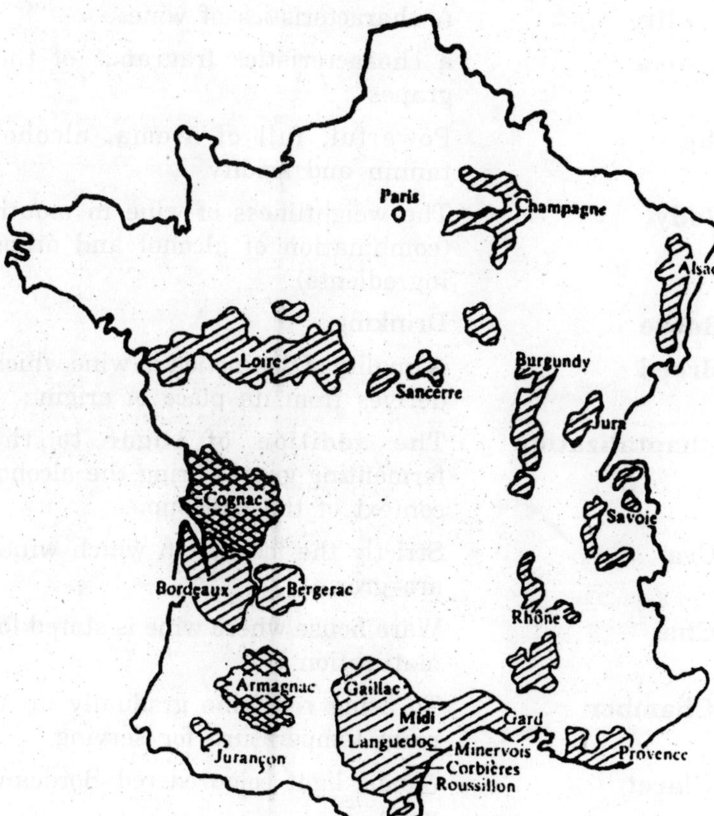

*APPENDIX VI*

# WINE DRINKER'S GLOSSARY

| | |
|---|---|
| **Alcohol** | Means the potable alcohol. |
| **Acidity** | A characteristics of wine. |
| **Aroma** | a characteristics fragrance of the grapes |
| **Big** | Powerful, full of aroma, alcohol tannin and acidity |
| **Body** | The weightliness of wine in mouth (combination of alcohol and other ingredients). |
| **Booze** | Drinking |
| **Breed** | A quality of distinction in wine which derives from its place of origin |
| **Chaptalization** | The addition of sugar to the fermenting grapes bring the alcohol context of the wine up. - |
| **Cra** | Strictly the locality in which wines are grown |
| **Chai** | Ware house where wine is stored for maturation |
| **Chamber** | To bring red wine gradually up to room temperature for serving |
| **Claret** | Means light coloured red Bordeaux wine |
| **Cabinet** | Wine of Bordeaux (France) |
| **Fragrance** | The attractive natural meant of the grapes |

| | |
|---|---|
| **Fruity** | Means distinctive taste and source usually in young wine |
| **Madeirised** | A process of oxidation in wine which imparts deep colour and special flavour reading 'Madeira". |
| **Noble rot** | A fungus which attacks white grapes and improves their quality |
| **Oenology** | Science of making wine |
| **Pinot Noir** | Red wine of Burgundy (France) |
| **Piquancy** | A sharpeners of flavour in wine induced by high acidity |
| **Tannin** | A chemical constituent of red and some pink wine, derived from pips and skin of the grapes. |
| **Tafelwein** | Table wine |
| **Vinification** | Technical process of fermenting wine |
| **Vinosity** | Alcohol character of wine |
| **Viticulture** | Cultivation of wine |

*APPENDIX VII*

# MAJOR WINE PRODUCING COUNTRIES OF THE WORLD

| Countries | Average Production in Hecto litres (Rounded up) |
|---|---|
| Italy | 75,000,000 |
| France | 72,000,000 |
| Spain | 35,000,000 |
| Argentina | 25,000,000 |
| USA | 15,00,000 |
| Portugal | 10,000,000 |
| Germany | 10,000,000 |
| Romania | 8,000,000 |
| Algeria | 7,000,000 |
| South Africa | 5,500,000 |
| Greece | 6,000,000 |
| Chile | 5,200,000 |
| Australia | 3,000,000 |
| Brazil | 2,200,000 |
| Switzerland | 1,100,000 |
| Uruguay | 200,00 |
| Canada | 600,000 |
| Turkey | 400,000 |
| Israel | 400,000 |
| New Zealand | 250,000 |

*Source:* Office International De Vin

*APPENDIX VIII*

## POLICE LICENCE FORM AND CONDITIONS

File No. PS/

West Bengal Form No. 4562

Fee Rupees

### FORM B

### OFFICE OF THE COMMISSIONER OF POLICE, CALCUTTA

### LICENCE GRANTED UNDER THE PROVISIONS OF SECTION 22 OF BENGAL ACT II OF 1866 AND SECTION 39 OF BENGAL ACT IV OF 1866

WHEREAS by section 22/39 of Bengal Act II/IV of 1866 read with section 2 of Bengal Act V of 1909 and Section 3 of Act VII of 1912, it is enacted that "the Commissioner of Police may, at his direction, from time to time, grant licence to the keepers of such houses or places of public resort and entertainment as aforesaid for which no such licence as is specified in the said Act V of 1909 is required upon such conditions, to be inserted in every such licence, as he with the sanction of the said governor in council from time to time shall order, for securing the good behaviour of the keepers of the said houses or places of the public resort or entertainment and the prevention of drunkenness and disorder among the persons frequenting or using the same and the said licence may be granted by the said Commissioner for any time not exceeding one year.

And whereas, has made application for a licence under the provisions of the said Bengal Act II/V of 1866, and

I, the Commissioner of Police, am willing to grant the licence applied for under and subject to the conditions hereinafter mentioned.

Now know all the whom these presents shall come, that I, Dy. Commissioner of Police, HQ do by the presents, grant these licence up to the said applicant to have and keep a certain No. of streets in the Town/Suburbs of Calcutta, from the date here of the 31st day of March 20 and no longer, subject nevertheless to the conditions (on next page) mentioned on the reverse (which have received the section of the said Governor in Council) or any other conditions that may be ordered hereafter.

Section Town/Suburbs
Calcutta
The Entd.

Deputy Commissioner
of Police

License Inspector HQ.

## CONDITIONS FOR OBTAINING BAR LICENCE

This licence is granted subject to the following conditions:

1st That the licence shall not permit gambling, drunkenness or other species of debauchery whatever or any kind or sort of riot, after or disorder within his premises.

2nd That on any riot, affray or disorder or apprehension of a breach of the peace in or in the immediate neighbourhood of the premises coming to his knowledge, the licence shall give instant information thereof to the officers of police in the nearest section house or to the police officer, Lalbazar.

3rd That the licence shall, as soon as he possibly can, give separates and special notice to the Commissioner of Police or any person resorting or coming to his premises whom he may have reasonable cause suspect to be a deserts or person charged with any crime or against whom any warrant of apprehension has issued from any criminal court or police office in respect of any offence whatever.

4th That any member or members of the Calcutta police shall be instant and unrestrained access on demand by day or by night to any or every part of the premises and that the licence shall afford all possible aid to him or them in the discharge of his or them in the discharge of his or their duties.

5th That the licensee shall not at time during the currency of the licence subject, hire out or transfer his business to any other person or persons without the written sanction of the commissioner police.

6th That the licence shall not wilfully harbour any person known to be charged with may crime or any person against whom any warrant of apprehension shall have issued. To his knowledge or behalf from any criminal court or police officer for any offence whatever and shall be in force and shall not knowingly permit prostitutes or persons notoriously of bad character to frequent or remain in the said premises. That no spirituous or fermented liquors of any description shall be sold or consumed within the premises, (the word "consumed" does not apply to ordinary boarding houses).

7th That no music vocal or instrumental, and no dancing or other entertainment shall be permitted on the premises without special permission from the commissioner of police (does not apply to ordinary boarding houses), that the licence shall keep a register of person admitted into the premises showing Name, Country, Address (Village, Police Station and District). Date of arrival, Date of departure and Place or destination and that he shall submit the same officer (applies only to ordinary lodging houses).

8th That the licence shall keep a register of seaman admitted into his premises showing their names, last ship, date of licensee and date of departure and if shipped, the name of ship for which they have engaged, and that have will submit monthly return of the same to the officer of the commissioner of police.

9th That the licensee shall give immediate information to the Shipping Master in every case in which a seaman who has left the premises in engagement returns to it before the completion of the terms of his engagement (applies to only Seaman Boarding houses).

10th That the licensee shall not keep or lodge at any one time more than persons and shall keep the premises and order and clean to the satisfaction of any person appointed by the Commissioner of Police to inspect the said premises (apply only to Seaman's Boarding Houses and ordinary Lodging Houses).

Shipping office on or before the 5th every month (applies to Seaman's Boarding Houses).

11th That the premises shall be closed at 1 a. m. and not opened before 5 a.m. (does not apply to pilgrims Houses and ordinary and Boarding and Lodging Houses).

12th That the licensee shall not knowingly receive or harbour in the said premises any deserter from the Military service of the Union of India ships belonging to India Navy, or from any merchant vessel; that he shall not receive or horbour any person reasonably supposed to be a soldier or seafaring man without in the case of the latter asking of his discharge certificate and shall appear to the Magistrate before whom any case may be heard, to have been all that was required to satisfy himself that the person so seeking to be received or harboured, was not a deserter (applies only to Boarding House, Lodging Houses for Pilgrims, Ordinary Lodging Houses and Seamen Boarding Houses)

15th That licensee shall not at times to, perform, keep and observe the classes and provisions of the said Bengal Act II/VI of 1866 in this behalf.

(G.O. No., 1688 p., dated 7-2-1917)

**Note:** If the holder of the licence shall commit any breach of any of the are foregoing conditions he shall be liable, for conviction before a Magistrate, to a penalty not exceeding one hundred rupees for such offence and he is further liable at the direction of the commissioner of police subject to the general direction and control of the said governor in council to the forfeiter of this licence in addition to any other penalty or punishment that shall be imposed on him.

*APPENDIX IX*

# TRADE LICENCE FORMAT
## (Kolkata Municipal Corporation)

**Terms and Conditions Applicable under all Sections**

1. This certificate is granted without any prejudice to the nights of the Kolkata Municipal Corporation to processed for any penalty already incurred or for arrear dues and does not cover liabilities under any other section of the Calcutta Municipal Corporation Act 1980. Payment of such fees shall not absolve the holder of certified/licence/permission of any liability to take out any licence or permission under the act bid of any other law for the time being in force.
2. Written permission of the Municipal commissioner shall be obtained annually on payments of the prescribed fees in advance, where applicable.
3. Any person to whom written permission/1icense/ certificate is granted under the Act bid small indemnity and keep the corporation indemnified against all claims, damages, actions, suits or any other legal proceeding which the corporation may incur or be liable to in this behalf.
4. Any person committing beach of any one of the provisions of the Act. Bid or any other law for the time being in force or falls to comply with any requisition lawfully made upon him shall be liable to be punished with such fines of imprisonment as are provided in the act, bid or any other law for the time being in force.

5. That the premises shall not causes or be maintained in a manner which is likely to cause injury/danger to life, health or property, nuisance, annoyance or offence to the sense of sight, smell or hearing of persons residing in the neighbourhood, and that smell or not cause or be maintained in a manner so as to cause any danger to life or injury to health of persons employed in business or residing in the neighbourhood or injury to property or in any other cause to be maintained in manner so as to cause any inconvenience or any injury to the public and shall always be kept and maintenance in a secure, neat and tidy condition.
6. That the licence is not transferable, in respect of place or person.
7. That it only relates to the premises of part of the premises and purposes for which it is granted and not otherwise.
8. That no addition, alteration be made in the area of the land or m the building to which the licence relates.
9. That a board shall be kept affixed in a conspicuous part of the premises covered by licence/permission/ certified upon which shall be legibly written the. name, premises no. purpose, years etc.
10. In case of failure to obtain licence under W.B.F.S. Act 1950/ any other law/rules regulations/ by - laws order for the time being in force where applicable, permission/licence granted provisionally would be liable to be revoked/ cancelled/suspended.
11. The licence shall at all time, during the continuance of the licence/permission be responsible for the due fulfilment and observance of all conditions of the licence, permission and provisions of the Calcutta Municipal Corporation Act. And by - laws, rules, regulations made there under so far as they relate

to his business, and if violated the licence/ permission shall be liable to be cancelled and shall be subject to other panel action under the provisions of the CMC Act. 1980 and other laws for the time being in force.

12. The holder of the licence/ permission/ certificate shall give access to the premises to any officer/ employer of the Kolkata Municipal Corporation for the inspection etc. all reasonable hours.
13. All registered dog shall wear and collar to which shall be attached a metal token issued by Municipal Corporation /LO.

*APPENDIX X*

**Specimen Form No. 8**

# LICENCE FOR THE RETAIL VENDING OF FOREIGN LIQUOR IN A HOTEL TO BE DRUNK IN THE PREMISES

**District.............................................**

**Note:** Counterfoil of this licence will be signed by the licensee and filed in the Collector's office.

No of licence in Register No . . . . . . . . . . . . . . .

Name of vendor . . . . . . . . . . . . . . . . . . . . . . . .

Locality of vend . . . . . . . . . . . . . . . . . . . . . . . .

Be it known that. . . . . . . . . . . . . . . . . . . . . . . resident of. . . . . . . . . . . . . . . . . . . . . . . . . is hereby authorised by the undersigned Collector of to sell POTABLE FOREIGN LIQUOR from the date of this licence to the 31st March in a Hotel situated at called or styled the. . . . . . . . . . . . . . . . . . . . . . . . . Hotel.

It is required of the holder of this licence, as a condition of this licence remaining in force, that he duly and faithfully perform and abide by the following articles and the general conditions applicable to all Excise licences hereto annexed.

I. That he pays to Government an annual fee of Rs.. . . . . . . . . in the following:- One quarter's fee at the time of engaging to take this licence, and the remaining after on the 1st day of every succeeding quarter until the whole of the fees due on this licence shall have been paid.

That he pays the same into the Treasury / Sub - Treasury at

II. That he does not, under colour of this licence, sell any country liquor.

III. That he does not alter the nature of the liquor of the label under which he has purchased it.

IV. That he does not sell Whisky, brandy or rum at a lower strength than 25° under London proof of Gin at a strength lower than 35° under London proof.

V. That he does not store any FOREIGN LIQUOR to be sold under this licence in ally PREMISES other than those named herein without previously obtaining the written sanction of the Collector on the reverse of this licence.

VI. That he does not set up and maintain within the said Hotel premises any BAR for the sale or service of Foreign liquor without a separate Bar licence.

VII. That he does not use for the purposes of selling or serving liquor any room in, or any part of, the said Hotel premises which the Collector may at any time decide to be a Bar or Restaurant without a separate Bar or Restaurant licence.

VIII. That all spirits or liquors sold under this licence be served and drunk within the said HOTEL premises.

IX. That he does not sell or deliver any spirit to any person apparently under the age of eighteen years, whether for consumption by on or off the premises.

X. That he confines sales of liquor to bona fide lodgers in the Hotel to their friends and visitors, and to persons taking their meals there.

XI. That he does not employ or permit to be employed in any part of his licensed premises where liquor is consumed, either with or without remuneration, any person under the age of eighteen years, during the hours in which such premises are kept open "business".

XII. That he does not during the hours in which his licensed premises are kept open, employ or permit to be employed in any part of such premises where liquor is consumed by the public, either with or without remuneration any woman otherwise that with the permission previously obtained in writing from the Board and endorsed on this licence.

XIII. That the retail sale of foreign liquor is permitted in the licensed premises from sunrise to 10 PM unless otherwise permitted by a late dosing licence. The violation of any of the above conditions or of the general conditions applicable to Excise and Opium vend licences will render this licence liable to be cancelled and the holder thereof liable to the penalties prescribed by law or rule. No sell shall be affected on the Republic Day (26th January) and on the Independence Day (15th August)

COLLECTORATE OF Collector

**List of Authorized Agents or Salesmen**

| *Name* | *Father's Name* | *Age* | *Native village thana and district* | *Signature of the licence* |
|---|---|---|---|---|
| *1* | *2* | *3* | *4* | *5* |
| | | | | |

*APPENDIX XI*

**Specimen Form No. 52B required in Bar**

# PASS FOR THE IMPORT FROM THE PROVINCE OF FOREIGN LIQUOR MADE IN INDIA OR OF RECTIFIED SPIRIT ON WHICH DUTY HAS BEEN PAID

## PASS

1. Registered No. of Pass: . . . . . . . . . . . . . . . .
2. Date of issue: . . . . . . . . . . . . . . . .
3. Name and address of residence : of importer . . . . . . . . . . . . . . . .
4. Licensed premises of the importer: . . . . . . . . . . . . . . . .
5. This pass authorise the import into Bihar and Orissa of the quantity of Foreign Liquor in 6 below purchased from of in the District of in the province of by or his agent and the subsequent transport of such liquor to the destination noted in above.
6. Description Quantity Strength Equivalent in of foreign in bulk L.P. Gallons liquor gallons . . . . . . . . . . . . . . . .
7. Rate of duty levied: . . . . . . . . . . . . . . . .

   (If duty is to be at a Concession rate, quote Govt. order)
8. Amount of duty Rs . . . . . . . . . . . . . . . Paid by Challan No. Dated

Treasury / Sub-Treasury

9. Route of Transit . . . . . . . . . . . . . . . . .

This pass is current for . . . . . . . . . . . days and is to be return the undersigned with particulars in 14 below and duly filled up by the person to whom this pass . . . . . . . . . . . is issued . . . . . . . . . . .

The Collector of . . . . . . . . . . . 20. . . . . . . . . . . Collector

*APPENDIX XII*

## PER CAPITA BEER CONSUMPTION IN SOME SELECTED COUNTRIES

**(Figures in Litres: 1993 estimate)**

| |  |  |
|---|---|---|
| 1. | Austria | 116 |
| 2. | Australia | 97 |
| 3. | Belgium | 108 |
| 4. | Canada | 68 |
| 5. | Czech Republic | 153 |
| 6. | Denmark | 126 |
| 7. | Finland | 86 |
| 8. | Germany | 138 |
| 9. | Hungary | 77 |
| 10. | Ireland | 123 |
| 11. | New Zealand | 102 |
| 12. | Netherlands | 85 |
| 13. | Portugal | 64 |
| 14. | Slovenia | 100 |
| 15. | Spain | 67 |
| 16. | Sweden | 63 |
| 17. | Switzerland | 65 |
| 18. | UK | 101 |
| 19. | US | 85 |
| 20. | Venezuela | 77 |

*Source* : EBCU.

APPENDIX XIII

# SERVICE STANDARD CHECKLIST

| S.No. | Items | Served in | Presentation | Cover | Accompaniments |
|---|---|---|---|---|---|
| 1. | Hors 'd oeuvres<br>a. Fruit & food cocktails | Cocktail cup | On quarter plate with dolley paper with tea spoon | | Elite (5*/4*) Bread roll-2 Brown bread -2, Bread sticks-2 Melba Toast-2 traditional<br>3* & below plain of brown bread-2, Melba Toast-2, bread sticks-2, if available. |
| | b. General | Half plate | Platter | Small fork a knife | |
| | c. Classical | As per item | As per item | As per item | As per item |
| | a. Soups clear, broth, Thick & Cold | Soup cups/ Soup bowls | Soup saucer | Elite 5*/4* soup spoon 3* & comfort A.P. spoon | Bread and butter as per standard |
| | b. Special Chinese soups | Soup tureen | Soup cup with Soup saucer | Chinese soup spoon | |
| 3. | Fish<br>Deep fried<br>Shallow fried<br>Baked, Grilled<br>Poached, Stewed | Half plate | Platter | 5*/4* Fish knife & fork | Traditional |

| S.No. | Items | Served in | Presentation | Cover | Accompaniments |
|---|---|---|---|---|---|
| 4. | Chicken | Large plate | Platter/Holloware | 5*/4* Large knife & fork 3* & below A.P. Knife & fork | Traditional |
| 5. | Mutton | - do - | - do - | A.P. knife & fork | - do - |
| 6. | Pork | - do - | - do - | - do - | - do - |
| 7. | Beef (Steaks) | - do - | - do - | Steak knife & fork/A.P. knife & fork | - do - |
| 8. | Pasta/Entree | Half plate | - do - | A.P. knife & fork, spoon for pasta | - do - |
| 9. | Vegetarian | Large plate | - do - | A.P. knife & fork | - do - |
| 10. | Indian Chicken | Large plate | Cocotte dish | Large knife fork & desert spoon/A.P. Knife, fork & spoon | Traditional plus Achar, Chutney |
| | Mutton | Large plate | Cocotte dish | - do - | - do - |
| | Fish | Large plate | Cocotte dish | - do - | - do - |
| | Vegetarian | Large plate | Cocotte dish | - do - | - do - |
| 11. | Tandoori Checken | Large plate | Platter | Large knife & fork, A.P. Knife & fork | Lemon, chutney, onion rings |

| S.No. | Items | Served in | Presentation | Cover | Accompaniments |
|---|---|---|---|---|---|
| | Mutton | - do - | - do - | - do - | - do - |
| | Fish | - do - | - do - | - do - | - do - |
| | Vegetables | - do - | - do - | - do - | - do - |
| 12. | Indian Breads | Side Plate | Lined Basket | - | - |
| 13. | Pulao/Biryani/ Plain Rice | Large Plate Large plate | Handl/Platter | A.P. Knife, fork & spoon | Achar, Ralta, Papad, Kachumber |
| 14. | Idli/Vada | Half plate | Preplated | - do - | Traditional |
| 15. | Dosa/Uttapam/ Appam | Full plate | Preplated | - do - | - do - |
| 16. | Raita | | Bowl dolley paper | Quarter plate | A.P. spoon |
| 17. | Papad | Side plate | Lined Basket | - | - |
| 18. | Salads | Bowl | Platter/bowl/ quarter plate | | Traditional dressings |
| 19. | Desserts | Half plate | Platter | Dessert spoon & fork | |
| | Elite (5* & 4*) | Half plate | | | |
| | 3* & below | Preplated | | A.P. spoon & fork | |
| | a. Ice Cream | Ice Cream cups | Quarter plates, doiley paper & tea spoon | | |
| 20. | Cheese | Half plate | Cheese board | Cheese knife/ A.P. knife & fork | |
| 21. | Coffee | Demi-Tasse | Coffee saucer, quarater plate, coffee spoon | | |

*APPENDIX XIV*

# LIST OF SERVICEWARES

| S.No. | Items | Elite 5* & Classic 4* | | Classic 3* and comfort | |
|---|---|---|---|---|---|
| | | In Circulation | In Store | In Circulation | In Store |
| | Cutlery | | | | |
| 01. | Soup Spoon | 1.5 rotation of covers | 0.5 rotation of covers | - | - |
| 02. | Dessert Spoon | 1.5 rotation of covers | 0.5 rotation of covers | 2.0 rotation of covers | 0.5 rotation of covers |
| 03. | Dessert Knife | 2.0 rotation of covers | 1.0 rotation of covers | 2.0 rotation of covers | 0.5 rotation of covers |
| 04. | Dessert Fork | 1.5 rotation of covers | 0.5 rotataon of covers | 2.0 rotation of covers | 0.5 rotation of covers |
| 05. | Fish Knife | 1.5 rotation of covers | 0.5 rotation of covers | - | - |
| 06. | Fish fork | 1.5 rotation of covers | 0.5 rotation of covers | - | - |
| 07. | Large Knife | 1.5 rotation of covers | 0.5 rotation of covers | - | - |
| 08. | Large Fork | 1.5 rotation of covers | 0.5 rotation of covers | - | - |
| 09. | Service Spoon | 1.0 rotation of Tables | 1.0 rotation of Tables | 1.0 rotation of Tables | 0.5 rotation of Tables |
| 10. | Service Fork | 1.0 rotation of Tables | 1.0 rotation of Tables | 1.0 rotation of Tables | 0.5 rotation of Tables |
| 11. | Sugar Tongs | 1.5 rotation of Tables | 0.5 rotation of Tables | - | - |
| 12. | Cheese Knife | 0.2 rotation of Tables | 0.1 rotation of Tables | - | - |
| 13. | Butter Knife | 1.5 rotation of Tables | 0.5 rotation of Tables | 1.0 rotation of Tables | 0.5 rotation of Tables |
| | Holloware/Flatware | | | | |
| 01. | Butter Dish | 1.5 Rotation of tables | 0.5 Rotation of tables | 1.5 Rotation of tables | 1.5 Rotation of tables |
| 02. | Water Jugs | 12 Nos. | 6 Nos. | 12 Nos. | 6 Nos. |
| 03. | Tea Stainers | 24 Nos. | 6 Nos. | 8 Nos. | 4 Nos. |
| 04. | Straw Holders | 12 Nos. | 6 Nos. | 8 Nos. | 4 Nos. |
| 05. | Tooth Pick Holders | 12 Nos. | 6 Nos. | 8 Nos. | 4 Nos. |

| S.No. | Items | Elite 5* & Classic 4* | | Classic 3* and comfort | |
|---|---|---|---|---|---|
| | | In Circulation | In Store | In Circulation | In Store |
| 06. | Round Salvers | 15 Novs. | 3 Nos. | 8 Nos. | 4 Nos. |
| 07. | Finger Bowls | 50 Nos. | 25 Nos. | 36 Nos. | 12 Nos. |
| 08. | Cruet Sets | 1 Rotation per table | 0.2 Rotation per table | 1 Rotation per table | 0.2 Rotation per table |
| 09. | Bread Baskets | 1.5 Rotation per table | 0.5 Rotation per table | 1.5 Rotation per table | 0.5 Rotation per table |
| 10. | Candle Stand | 1 Rotation per table | 0.1 Rotation per table | 1 Rotation per table | 0.1 Rotation per table |
| 11. | Hollow Dish (1 portion) | 3 Rotation per table | 1 Rotation per table | 3 Rotation per table | 1 Rotation per table |
| 12. | Hollow Dish (2 portions) | 3 Rotation per table | 1 Rotation per table | 3 Rotation per table | 1 Rotation per table |
| 13. | Hollow Dish (4 portions) | 0.5 Rotation per table | 0.25 Rotation per table | 0.5 Rotation per table | 0.25 Rotation per table |
| 14. | Flat Dish (1 portion) | 2 Rotation per table | 1 Rotation per table | 1 Rotation per table | 1 Rotation per table |
| 15. | Flat Dish (2 portions) | 2 Rotation per table | 1 Rotation per table | 1 Rotation per table | 1 Rotation per table |
| 16. | Flat Dish (4 portions) | 0.5 Rotation per table | 0.25 Rotation per table | 0.5 Rotation per table | 0.25 Rotation per table |
| 17. | Tea pots | | | | |
| | 2 cc | 18 Nos. | 6 Nos | 12 Nos | 3 Nos |
| | 4 cc | 9 Nos | 3 Nos | 6 Nos | 2 Nos |
| | 10 cc | 3 Nos | 1 No | 3 Nos | 1 No |
| 18. | Coffee pots | | | | |
| | 2 cc | 18 Nos. | 6 Nos | 12 Nos | 3 Nos |
| | 4 cc | 9 Nos | 3 Nos | 6 Nos | 2 Nos |
| | 10 cc | 3 Nos | 1 No | 3 Nos | 1 No |

| S.No. | Items | Elite 5* & Classic 4* | | Classic 3* and comfort | |
|---|---|---|---|---|---|
| | | In Circulation | In Store | In Circulation | In Store |
| 19. | Milk pots | | | | |
| | 2 cc | 24 Nos. | 6 Nos | 18 Nos | 6 Nos |
| | 4 cc | 12 Nos | 3 Nos | 9 Nos | 3 Nos |
| | 10 cc | 6 Nos | 2 No | 4 Nos | 2 No |
| 20. | Sugar Pots | 24 Nos | 6 Nos | 18 Nos | 6 Nos |
| 21. | Sauce Boats | 1 Rotation per table | 0.5 Rotation per table | 1 Rotation per table | 0.5 Rotation per table |
| 22. | Chaffing Dishes | 10 Nos | 2 Nos | 8 Nos | 2 Nos |

# APPENDIX XV

## LIST OF CROCKERIES, STATIONERY & MISCELLANEOUS AND MISCELLANEOUS ITEMS

| S.No. | Items | Elite 5* & Classic 4* | | Classic 3* and comfort | |
|---|---|---|---|---|---|
| | | In Circulation | In Store | In Circulation | In Store |
| **CROCKERIES** | | | | | |
| 01. | Tea Cups | 2.0 rotation of covers | 2.0 rotation of covers | 2.0 rotation of covers | 2.0 rotation of covers |
| 02. | Tea Saucers | 2.0 rotation of covers | 2.0 rotation of covers | 2.0 rotation of covers | 2.0 rotation of covers |
| 03. | Quarter Plates | 2.5 rotation of covers | 2.5 rotation of covers | 2.5 rotation of covers | 2.5 rotation of covers |
| 04. | Half Plates | 2.0 rotation of covers | 2.0 rotataon of covers | 2.0 rotation of covers | 2.0 rotation of covers |
| 05. | Full Plates | 2.0 rotation of covers | 2.0 rotation of covers | 2.0 rotation of covers | 2.0 rotation of covers |
| 06. | Flower Vases | 1.0 (per table) | 0.5 (per table) | 1.0 (per table) | 0.5 (per table) |
| 07. | Ash Trays | 1.0 (per table) | 0.5 (per table) | 1.0 (per table) | 0.5 (per table) |
| 08. | Soup Cups | 1.0 (per table) | 2.0 (per table) | 1.0 (per table) | 2.0 (per table) |
| 09. | Soup Saucers | 1.0 (per table) | 1.0 (per table) | 1.0 (per table) | 1.0 (per table) |
| | Glassware | | | | |
| 01. | Water Goblets | 2.5 rotation of covers | 2.5 rotation of covers | - | |
| 02. | High Ball 8 oz. | 1.0 rotation of covers | 0.5 rotation of covers | 2.5 rotation of covers | 2.5 rotation of covers |
| 03. | Juice Glass 5½ oz. | - | - | 2.0 rotation of covers | 1.0 rotation of covers |
| 04. | Collins Glass | 1.0 rotation of covers | 0.5 rotation of covers | 1.0 rotation of covers | 0.5 rotation of covers |
| 05. | White Wine Glass | 1.0 rotation of covers | 0.5 rotation of covers | 0.5 rotation of covers | 0.5 rotation of covers |
| 06. | Red Wine Glass | 1.0 rotation of covers | 0.5 rotation of covers | 0.5 rotation of covers | 0.5 rotation of covers |
| 07. | Champagne Tulip/ Flute | 0.5 rotation of covers | 0.5 rotation of covers | 0.25 rotation of covers | 0.25 rotation of covers |
| 08. | Brandy Baloon | 0.5 rotation of covers | 0.25 rotation of covers | 0.5 rotation of covers | 0.25 rotation of covers |

**STATIONERY & MISCELLANEOUS**

| | | | | | |
|---|---|---|---|---|---|
| 01. | Cloth Napkins | 3.5 Rotation of covers | 3.5 Rotation of covers | 3.0 Rotation of covers | 3.0 Rotation of covers |
| 02. | Table Cloths | 3.5 Rotation of covers | 3.5 Rotation of covers | 3.0 Rotation of covers | 3.0 Rotation of covers |
| 03. | Buffet Sheets | 2.5 Rotation of covers | 2.5 Rotation of covers | 2.0 Rotation of covers | 2.0 Rotation of covers |
| 04. | Waiters Cloth | 3 No. per Waiter | 3 No. per Waiter | 2 No. per Waiter | 2 No. per Waiter |
| 05. | Dusters | 3 No. per Waiter | 3 No. per Waiter | 2 No. per Waiter | 2 No. per Waiter |
| 06. | Doily paper 3½ | Total Turnover × 3 | - | - | - |
| 07. | Doily paper 5 | Total Turnover × 3 | - | - | - |
| 08. | Menu/Bar Card | 10 Nos. per Side Board | | 8 Nos. per Side Board | |
| 09. | K.O.T. | As per consumption | As per consumption | As per consumption | As per consumption |
| 10. | Scribbing pads | As per consumption | As per consumption | As per consumption | As per consumption |
| 11. | Straws | As per consumption | As per consumption | As per consumption | As per consumption |
| 12. | Bill folders | 6 Nos. per Side Board | 6 Nos. per Side Board | 4 Nos. per Side Board | 4 Nos. per Side Board |
| 13. | Match Box | As per consumption | As per consumption | As per consumption | As per consumption |
| 14. | Bottle Opener | 3 Nos. on each Side Board | 3 Nos. on each Side Board | 3 Nos. on each Side Board | 3 Nos. on each Side Board |
| 15. | Paper Napkins | As per consumption | As per consumption | As per consumption | As per consumption |
| 16. | Bradma-4000 Cash Machine/Computer Terminal | 1 No. | - | 1 No. | - |
| 17. | Liquor Trolley | 1 No. | - | - | - |
| 18. | Paging Board | 1 No. | - | 1 No. | - |
| 19. | Cona Coffee Sets | 4 Nos. | 2 Nos. | - | - |
| 20. | Cona Coffee Jars | 8 Nos. | 4 Nos. | - | - |
| 21. | Pot Holders | 3 Rotation of tables | 3 Rotation of tables | 2 Rotation of tables | 2 Rotation of tables |
| 22. | Reservation | As per consumption | As per consumption | As per consumption | As per consumption |
| 23. | Service Tray(S) (As specified) | 1 Rotation of tables | 0.5 Rotation of tables | 1 Rotation of tables | 0.5 Rotation of tables |
| 24. | Service Tray (L) (As specified) | 0.5 Rotation of tables | 0.5 Rotation of tables | 0.5 Rotation of tables | 0.5 Rotation of tables |

# INDEX